Tommy Boyle – Broken Hero

The Story of a Football Legend

by

Mike Smith

Grosvenor House
Publishing Limited

This book is published by
Grosvenor House Publishing Ltd
28-30 High Street, Guildford, Surrey, GU1 3EL.
www.grosvenorhousepublishing.co.uk

A CIP record for this book
is available from the British Library

ISBN 978-1-908105-82-0

Introduction

In September 1911, Thomas William Boyle walked through the doors of Burnley Football Club and a legend was born. Boyle was one of the most outstanding players of his generation, "one of the best centre-halves who ever stepped onto a football field... a gem amongst jewels," was one football manager's assessment of him. He represented England at international level and in 1914 became the first captain to be presented with the FA Cup by the reigning monarch, His Majesty, King George V. The Yorkshireman won all of football's major honours, but once his playing days were over, something inside Tommy Boyle broke.

On leaving school at twelve, the young Tommy Boyle became a miner and his first sporting interest was in athletics where he competed as a sprinter, but it was football where he made his mark. Despite his stature at five-feet seven, his ability as an attacking right-half was spotted by the Barnsley manager Arthur Fairclough, who signed him to professional terms in 1906. Boyle went on to lead Barnsley to their first Cup final in 1910 and was later sold to Burnley. It was at Turf Moor where he made his biggest contribution to the game. Boyle led The Clarets to promotion to Division One, he represented England at full international level and won the FA Cup. When the First World War came he became Bombardier Boyle serving in the Royal Artillery on the Western Front. It was there he was badly wounded and for a while it looked like his playing career was finished. But being the gritty character he was, Tommy Boyle defied the consultants and fought his way back to play again. He crowned his comeback by winning the League championship in style, leading a Burnley side that stayed undefeated for thirty League matches, a record the club held until the Arsenal side of Dennis Bergkamp and Thierry Henry surpassed it in 2004.

There was no mistaking Boyle on the football field. With his jersey tucked in and his shorts pulled up nearly under his armpits, he would make the most noise, barking his instructions to his teammates. "A real captain if ever there was one," said Charles Buchan about Boyle in 1932. He dominated games with sheer enthusiasm, determination and thrived on conflict. Yet despite all of his successes in the game and the enjoyment he brought to thousands, when his playing days were over Tommy Boyle struggled to come to terms with a life without football.

Broken Hero turns the clock back to the beginning of the twentieth century, revealing the events and people who played the game with Boyle at the time. By the early 1900s, football had changed. With the introduction of the Football League and win bonuses equal to a working man's weekly wage, the former gentleman's game was consigned to history. There was nothing gentlemanly in some of the brutal challenges meted out on Saturday afternoons in games that might also feature a punch-up or the continuation of an ongoing vendetta between players. And more often than not, in the thick of it all was Tommy Boyle, who gave as good as he got, all five foot seven of him.

September 2011 sees the 100th anniversary of Tommy Boyle's arrival at Burnley Football Club. *Broken Hero* covers Boyle's formative years; his background, what influenced him and the period of the First World War which devastated the team he played in. Finally the story looks at how after such an illustrious career, Tommy Boyle ended up with nothing, spending the last years of his life in a mental hospital. Drawing on material not previously published, *Tommy Boyle - Broken Hero* tells the remarkable story of a real football hero who in his prime had character, presence and generosity in abundance, but who in later life became a dangerous man, to himself and others.

Mike Smith
Summer 2011

Acknowledgements

A number of people deserve thanks for helping me put together the pieces of the Tommy Boyle jigsaw. Thanks go to David Wood, Arthur Bower and Grenville Firth of Barnsley Football Club who provided information about Tommy's time there; David Coefield at St. Helen's Church in Hoyland and Geraint Parry and Peter Jones who provided me with details of Tommy's season at Wrexham FC. I'd like to thank Rob Cavallini, Ulrich Matheja, Jan Buschbom and Olaf Sievers for information on Tommy's year working in Germany.

In Burnley, thanks go to local historians Roger Frost, Andrew Gill and Mike Townend at Towneley Hall and to Ken Ashton who manages the 'Asylum' website. Thanks to Roger and Sue Haydock for information from the Lancashire Football Association and to Paul Evans at Firepower, The Royal Artillery Museum in Woolwich. Thanks go to Tony Scholes, editor of ClaretsMad, the online website dedicated to Burnley supporters across the globe and to Charlie Wilson who helped me knock the story into shape. Thanks also to Derek Crossland for his advice and to Phil Drinkwater who helped me find the first piece of the Tommy Boyle jigsaw. Many thanks go to Ray Simpson at Burnley Football Club and to the living descendents of the Boyle family who live all over the world: Eileen Varey, John Jarvis, Maureen Sykes, Kevan Boyle and Sonia St. John, for their photographs and stories of 'Uncle Tommy'.

Nearly finished, but they do deserve a special thanks: Burnley Central Library staff put up with me for nearly three years and provided an endless supply of books and documents from libraries all over the country. Thank you for the fantastic service you provide. If I have missed anyone, my sincerest apologies and I really do thank you for your help and support.

Finally, a special thanks go to my family for putting up with what became 'an obsession' and to apologise for all the lost weekends spent in archives, museums and libraries all over the UK living and breathing old football 'stuff'.

About the Author

Mike Smith was born and brought up in Whittlefield in Burnley and one of his earliest recollections was as a five-year-old seeing the Burnley team touring the town in an open-top coach having won the 1960 League Championship. He has supported Burnley Football Club ever since and still lives in the area. Mike has a passion for sport history and has enjoyed an extensive career working in the engineering industry, teaching in further and higher education and he currently works at The University of Manchester and teaches for the Open University. *Broken Hero* is his first published work.

Disclaimer

The events that took place throughout this story were real. The people named in the story were real and the historical dates, events and facts found from official documents and source material provided in the story are all true. However, in drawing the facts together from over a century ago, the book cannot claim to be a totally accurate biographical account. Some elements of the latter part of the story can only be said to be what the author believes to have happened to the central character based on anecdotal evidence. As such the book makes no claim to be complete in every sense and aims to both inform and entertain.

For Julia, Clare, Dorothy and Norman.

List of Figures

Picture Credits

Contents

Part One:

The Boy from Platts Common

Chapter 1: Primrose Bank Infirmary 1932

> *O the thousand images I see*
> *And struggle with and cannot kill...*
> *Millions may have been haunted by these spirits*
> *As I am haunted.*

— Richard Adlington

The black Humber Pullman with its four occupants slowed to a halt on the gravel driveway outside the rear entrance of the Infirmary. The driver left the engine running and the wipers going as heavy morning rain continued to pour down from black-grey skies. It was also blowing a gale outside where, in the rain, stood two men wearing white hospital-issue jackets with matching trousers. Both held on to an umbrella in an attempt to keep dry. They were waiting for him.

In the back of Humber sat a man flanked by two police officers. "Where's the rest of the welcoming committee? Where's the papers and the bloody mayor?" asked the man. The two officers sitting on either side of him glanced at each other but made no reply. There would be no welcoming committee today, no press and no mayoral welcome. No fuss, that's what The Chief had instructed.

The rear doors of the Humber opened and the two officers and their prisoner, handcuffed to one of them, stepped out. At six foot, the two officers towered over the man in their custody by a good six inches. The prisoner looked pale and undernourished. He wore a long shabby gabardine overcoat with no belt, a shirt buttoned at the neck with no tie and trousers that had not seen creases for some months. Unshaven and reeking of last night's booze, he sported a week-old black eye and looked like he'd slept in his clothes for the last month.

Through bloodshot eyes the man looked upwards through the rain and it suddenly clicked where he was. *Bloody hell...back ere'* He grinned to himself. He knew where this place was; he'd been here before, lots of times. They'd fix him up good style so he could play again, no problem. But right now he could do with something to cure the pounding in his head that felt like it was about to split open.

The two officers and their prisoner went inside and were followed by the two white coats. One of them closed and locked the heavy outer door, then locked the inner iron gate behind it with a loud, *clang*. The door secured the five men shook off the rain and climbed the stone staircase to the first floor, their footsteps echoing in the damp hallway. The white coats followed the three visitors up the stairs and whispered to each other. They couldn't believe who it was.

Figure 1. Primrose Bank Infirmary, Burnley

Tommy Boyle arrived on the male mental wing of Primrose Bank Infirmary in Burnley on Wednesday 24 February 1932 for what was officially deemed *'a period of observation'*. It was said he had been 'unwell' for a number of weeks and had arrived at the Infirmary in a police car following a night in the Burnley police station cells. No charges had been made about the incident that took place on the Tuesday evening and no record was kept of it. Tommy Boyle was a well-known character in the town and had been for well over twenty years. He knew the police and the Chief Inspector well enough from his football days and his previous charity work in the town. He knew them also for another reason, the charges they had made against him nine years before. He'd not forgotten that.

In recent weeks he'd been in trouble again. He had allegedly been barred entry from a number of town centre pubs for causing trouble, so the previous evening when the landlord of one pub refused him a drink, he had gone berserk and swiped all the glasses off the bar. That was one story. The police were called and they carted him off to the station. It wasn't the first time and when the Chief Inspector found out it was the last straw.

On the day of his admittance to Primrose Bank, Tommy Boyle was forty-six years old. The booze had added another ten years to his appearance. Only a decade before, he'd had it all: worshiped by his adoring fans, a local celebrity with a glittering career behind him and idolised in the press. Tommy Boyle, leader of the legendary 'Boyle's Brigade', England international, FA Cup winner and League champion. He'd even met the King. With money in his pocket, his own pub in the centre of town, he was the main man, Mr Burnley and drinks all round. Ten years down the road, he was Tommy Boyle of no fixed abode, on the dole and sleeping rough in the local doss-house. The good times were long gone; in fact, everything had gone: the pub, the house, the money and Annie had left him. If the last eighteen months had seen a decline in Tommy's personal and financial affairs, more worrying was his disturbed mental state and his temper, which after the previous night's performance in the pub, had been brought to the full attention of the Burnley authorities.

Primrose Bank Infirmary was located on a ten-acre site on the outskirts of town. Opened in 1876 as the Burnley Union Workhouse, part of it had been converted to an infirmary twenty years later. As a workhouse, it had employed a strict regime in which inmates faced harsh working conditions in repayment for food and lodgings, and even after its conversion, the place still wasn't exactly The Savoy. The Infirmary was large enough to accommodate male and female patients, the chronic sick and elderly patients and sick children. It also had two secure mental wings that could accommodate up to seventy-four male and the same number of female patients. The mental wings were located on the ground floor, which also contained the guardians' boardroom, master's offices and a storeroom for the inmates' clothes. The master's and matron's bedrooms were located on the first floor at the rear along with the resident medical officers' office. Male patients were accommodated in the west wing and females in the east. To enable segregation of the sexes the corridors were barred with locked iron gates. The facilities for mental patients at Primrose Bank supported mainly short-stay patients until more permanent accommodation could be found.

The procedure of having someone committed under the 1930 Mental Health act was a quite straightforward one. A family member – a father, mother, husband or wife – could inform the authorities that their relative had, in their opinion, gone insane. On their say so committal forms would be completed and signed, sanctioning that the person be taken into care initially for a period of observation. The police would usually be called, as Peter Barham describes in this example from *Lunatics of the Great War*:

John H. remembers the day when his father was taken away. He watched the Black Maria arrive with two policemen to take his father away he recalls. His mother signed the form afraid he might do something violent. John recalls his father chopping up all the furniture into little pieces and putting them on the fire until there was nothing left.

Two independent doctors were required to assess the patient and provide separate opinions. If they agreed then a simple form was completed and the person in question would then be taken in by the Infirmary staff. That was all it needed.

The five men reached the first floor landing. "You'll be okay in here, Tommy," said the officer who was handcuffed to him, "they'll feed you up and look after you." Tommy stared at him, thinking, *after all I've done for you an' all.* He made no reply to the officer who he knew and looked down at the stone floor. *There were people waiting in there, in that room, clever people who would fix things so I can go out and play again.*

In his oak-panelled office on the first-floor landing, William Alexander Mair, the resident medical officer at the Infirmary, sat at his desk preparing the admission paperwork. Outside in the small waiting room were Primrose Bank's master, Mr Ray; the matron, Miss Bennett; superintendent of the male mental ward, Robert Kirby; and chairman of the Infirmary Committee Board of Guardians, Hezekiah Proctor JP. Miss Bennett knocked and notified Mair that their patient had arrived and the group went through to Mair's office. One of the officers handed over a folder to Mair who took it and checked its contents. The other officer released Tommy's handcuffs and Mair thanked both men for their service and they were both dismissed. Tommy sat down in a chair in the middle of the floor facing the window, rubbing life back into his hand. The rain continued to bucket down outside. In front of Tommy was a long bench table and behind it five chairs. In the corner of the room the warmth from a coal-fire was welcoming. *Just like home* Tommy thought as he rubbed his hands in the warm glow of the fire.

Across the table from him, the welcoming committee sat down and prepared themselves. Proctor, Kirby, Mair, Ray and Bennett. Laid out in front of them was an array of files, books, forms and folders, notes and ink pens. Behind Tommy, the two white-coats sat quietly on each side of Mair's door. Tommy maintained a fixed gaze at the pattern on Mair's carpet. He coughed, his chest playing up again and holding his forehead asked for something to fix his splitting headache. Mair indicated to one of the white-coats to bring some aspirin and a glass of water, which Tommy thanked them for.

The formal admission procedure began with a welcome from Bill Mair followed by the staff introducing themselves and their roles. Through the blurred fuzz of the headache, Tommy was told why he was here and the reasons behind his admission. *They all look so bloody miserable, not even a smile for the cat*, he thought. He was to stay in Primrose Bank, Mair explained, for a period of up to fourteen days while they assessed his health and his state of mind. Under the Mental Health Act, fourteen days was the maximum period the hospital could detain a patient under a reception order. After that the patient could be released back into the community or an extension order from a court was required. If the patient escaped and was not recaptured within the fourteen-day period, the whole admission process had to begin again. Mair went on to explain that a thorough medical examination would be carried out to assess Tommy's physical condition and over the following days there would be physical and mental tests, meetings with doctors and checks on his health, all to show that that he was getting better and responding to treatment. Only when the medical staff agreed he was fine would he be released.

Tommy shifted in his seat. He wasn't listening though the headache was subsiding. Since his childhood he had hated small rooms, tunnels or being cooped up anywhere. He had to be outside. *Ever since that day, the day that Jimmy died.* The only thing on his mind right now was for this meeting to end and to get out of this place. He could feel the oak-panelled walls of Mair's office closing in, like the walls of the pit and the bars of the tiny cell he'd just spent the night in.

Mair went on, explaining that they wanted to look after him, sort him out and fix him up, - the whole hospital line. Finally, he asked Tommy if he had any questions. The five committee members looked at him and waited for a response but none was forthcoming. Tommy simply shook his head and at that Mair stood up signalling the end to the meeting. Mair wished Tommy an enjoyable stay and confirmed that they all expected him to get well quickly.

The formalities over, Mair handed over to Robert Kirby and the two white-coats walked Tommy downstairs to the bathhouse where the Infirmary barber, Mr Fothergill, would give Tommy a shave, a haircut and a bath. Fothergill was a busy man. He knew all the male mental patients personally as they were not allowed to shave themselves. He certainly knew the man now sat in front of him, having seen him many times over the years, both in the newspapers and in the flesh in a claret and blue jersey at Turf Moor. Fothergill couldn't believe his eyes as he ran the cut-throat razor up and down the leather strop. Tommy was asked his collar size and other measurements and a white-coat went off to the stores to get a set of male issue clothes while Tommy's were sent to the laundry. After a shave, Fothergill ran a hot bath that was taken with a white-coat present. There was little privacy here. Patients were not allowed to visit the bathroom unaccompanied, not for the first forty-eight hours.

Two months prior to Tommy's arrival at Primrose Bank, an occupancy audit of the mental wings was carried out by the Chief Medical Officer D. C Lamont who recorded that, "60 men were occupying 74 of the available beds in the male mental ward, 57 of them being long-stay patients... with 57 women inmates in the female ward." So Tommy was not lonely on the ward that day. He was allocated a bed in the long male dormitory, and then taken down to the canteen for a meal. Peter Barham describes that one of the Infirmary's first objectives was to feed the patient up: "the inmate would be put on a high-protein diet of eggs, milk pudding and beef tea and, depending on the patient, a dose of bromide or paraldehyde." Following his meal Tommy was given a tour of the ward facilities and shown the day room. As with all patients, the days in the Infirmary were a common routine of sleeping and eating meals, with very few social activities. Essential in the daily regimen were the tests to check whether patients were fit enough to be released and could be trusted not to harm themselves, or anyone else.

After only two days in this environment, Tommy was restless. He hated rules, routines, confinement and the bars on the windows drove him mad. *Hospital? More like a bloody prison camp...* He was unhappy and wanted out. There was nothing to do and there was nothing to interest him: no football, no racing, no papers, no beer and no women. *It was the match Saturday... There was nothing wrong with me anyway. Two weeks in here, in a bloody loony bin?* He paced the floor like a caged tiger. He stood out like a sore thumb and the other patients pointed and stared at him. He shouted and swore back at them. *First chance and I'm bloody out of here...* He planned his escape. *What am I doing here anyway with a load of bloody idiots? Bugger-all wrong, and what the hell was in the food?*

He dragged a chair over to the day room window, stepped on it and climbed onto the window-sill where he sat and looked out through the bars. In the distance he could see farms, hills and green fields. *Just like home.* He closed his eyes and his mind wandered back to the game, down the years to the start of a new season.

He breathed in the sweet smell of the football field, the scent of freshly cut grass, the dressing room odours of tobacco smoke, hot sugared tea, sweat and liniment. The anthem of boot studs stamping on the stone dressing-room floor as he picked up the ball bounced it twice and shouted his war cry, "C'maan then," before marching his boys out to do battle one more time. The increasing roar from the crowd as they emerged from the darkness into the light. Boyle, Dawson, Taylor, Bamford, Halley, Watson, Mosscrop, Lindley, Freeman, Hodgson and Nesbitt always at the back. Seeing the faces of the pretty girls waving and blowing kisses from the enclosure and winking at the ones he'd fancied. The huge swaying crowd all around the arena, squeezed tightly together, cheering him and his boys on, their faces as far back as the eye could see.

Then he was back where it all began, the cold winter harshness of Platts Common. Its grey, snow-covered coal heaps under a heavy sky. Saturday afternoon and a sleet-covered pitch at Hoyland. Hitting the opposing centre-forward hard and taking the ball off him. Easy. Away and up field with it. Out to the winger. Carry on running, the cross coming in. Leaping into the air and connecting with the frozen ball with his temple, BANG and watching the missile fly straight through the goalkeeper's outstretched hands. The cheers from the soaking wet handful of spectators as the ball filled the back of the net. Wiping the blood, the mud and the slush from his forehead with the back of his hand. Laughing, soaked to the skin. Home afterwards and a hot bath in front of the fire. He'd loved every second of it. Then there was the time when he'd played against...

He was abruptly wakened from his dream, a hand on his shoulder pulling him down from the window-sill.

"Come on Tommy, time to see the Doc," said the white-coat.

"Piss off, I'm not goin'."

He put his fists up and started swinging. He was being awkward again so one white-coat dragged him down from the window while the other pinned his arms by his side and fastened the waist belt around him, locking his wrists down by his sides. Then they frogmarched him downstairs.

"More bloody stupid questions? I'm saying nothing. There's bugger all wrong with me I tell thi!" he shouted.

The night-time was worst. *Horrible things happened to people in the dark.* In the dim light of the groaning, coughing dormitory, the haunting nightmares returned. The same terrible visions, over and over. He was miles underground in the bowels of the pit, in the dark, his lamp out. The unforgettable sound of splintering timber roof-props, the crushing, rumbling sound as the roof caved in. The smoke and the dust clearing. His best friend, Jimmy Leach, a boy just like him, only his arms and head visible, reaching out, crying for him to help, the rest of his body trapped and crushed beneath huge boulders of stone. "Help me... get me... out Tommy..." the boy gasped. He clawed at the rock with bare hands, his fingers bleeding, but with no shovel or help it was futile. The look on the boys face. He watched, helpless, for perhaps seconds as the roof crushed down harder and harder and Jimmy Leach choked to death on his own blood. He'd tried but there was nothing he could do. Nothing. He'd tried, again. He shouted for help. He heard them coming. But not men. They could smell the blood and the fear. The army of huge pit rats coming for him and Jimmy Leach. They ran over him to get at their prey. Hungry, slithering, gnawing, he kicked at them with his feet...

Another scene: a smashed landscape that had once been a beautiful city. Ypres and its broken buildings, trees that should have been in leaf turned to matchwood. Shells tearing across the night sky and exploding all around. Looking down and seeing his boot oozing blood through the lace holes. His pants in shreds, covered in blood, all his kit gone and the fear of gangrene setting in. They were here again, the scavenging rats, grown fat on the bodies of his dead mates, coming again, a whole army of them, coming for him... The final reel. He was standing in the doorway of a small bedroom lit only by candlelight. A child, his little girl, lifeless and cold. The most beautiful and precious thing in his whole world gone. His heart ripped out.

He was wide awake, sweating and gasping for breath. Throat dry as a bone. Screaming pains in his head again. The bars at the windows. No way out. The horrible visions gone for now, replaced by a rage and a desperate need to get out of this place. He had tried escaping the night before but another inmate had shouted for the white-coats, so after they'd gone he'd gone over and thumped the daft sod. They'd heard his screams and came running back. He'd been returned to bed, restrained, sedated, with a white-coat posted at his bedside until the calming peace from the morphine eventually came.

Tommy Boyle's stay at Primrose Bank wasn't long. Five days after his arrival he was back in front of Bill Mair and the welcoming committee. There was nothing more they could do for him here. The institution wasn't equipped for violent cases, though it did possess its own 'treatment' rooms that had been refitted in late 1931. Mair completed his report and wrote that Tommy had been, "striking other patients and staff". Mair's mind was made up. It was clear to him the patient was not fit to be released and wanted him off the books. He wasn't alone. The Chief Constable also wanted him removed, as far out of town as possible. The press had been sniffing around the past day or two and asking questions.

"We don't have the facilities you need here, Tommy; you need special care. We're transferring you to another unit," said Mair.

Transfer?

Along with Bill Mair and Robert Kirby, there were three new faces in the room that had not been present five days before. Patients who were to be admitted to a mental institution had to be certified as insane by two independent doctors and a Justice of the Peace. James Alfred Sampson JP was present and had already co-signed the order made out by Bill Mair that was addressed to the superintendent of the forwarding institution. Mair was putting the finishing touches to his report.

From across the room, Tommy looked on to see them in their huddle, gathered around Mair's long table. They all looked serious, asking questions, their voices low and difficult to make out. Finally, they nodded in agreement and looked up. Forms and pieces of paper were signed, contracts exchanged.

Looks like a deal.

They said he was being transferred. But to which club?

"Whittingham," was all he'd heard them say.

"Who the soddin' hell are Whittingham and what bloody league do they play in?"

But they were not joking.

And so on Monday 29 February 1932, five days after arriving at Primrose Bank Infirmary, Thomas William Boyle, forty-six and of no fixed abode, Burnley Football Club's most successful captain in its history, made the final transfer of his career. He was bound for Whittingham Mental Hospital, the former Lancashire County Lunatic Asylum, near Preston, where he became patient number 24281, a number he would become for the rest of his life.

Chapter 2: Roots

Pat Boyle, Tommy's father, came from Collon, a small village in County Louth in Ireland, about ten miles from the east coast. Pat was born in 1847 to parents Patrick and Bridget Boyle and came into the world during the period of the Great Famine. Like many Irish Catholics, Pat Boyle chose to emigrate for a better life. He arrived in England in his late teens, in the middle of the 1860s and his younger brother John followed him across the water ten years later.

Following the short crossing by steamship from Drogheda, Pat Boyle arrived at Liverpool docks. On arrival he had a number of options. He could stay in England and make a career here or, if he had the money, for five pounds sail steerage class on the month-long voyage to America. For another ten pounds he could have gone as far as Australia. With the Civil War raging in America from 1861–5, England was probably the safer option. The economy was booming and labour was in short supply. The industrial revolution was in full swing, driving the growth of the British economy which led the expansion of the Empire across the globe. But this expansion was not possible without a driving source: coal, vital in fuelling Britain's growing industrial base. Coal for the railways and the steel foundries. Coal for powering the thousands of factory and mill engines and for fuelling the British navy patrolling the oceans protecting her interests. The abundance of rich coal deposits in the north of England were crucial in sustaining Britain's place in the world. The nation owed much of its status to the men who dug the black gold, who spent their lives underground in cramped, dangerous conditions, putting their lives at risk each time they descended into the darkness. From the mid-nineteenth century the numbers working in the coal industry grew rapidly and the young Pat Boyle was attracted by the wages the mining industry offered, twice as much as he would have earned working the land back in Collon.

Around the same time that Pat Boyle sailed for England, a young lady, Ellen St. John, made the same crossing. A year younger than Pat, Ellen was born in Tulla, a small village in County Clare, one of the counties worst affected by land evictions.

Pat and Ellen met in Wigan where Pat was working as a coalminer and Ellen as a cotton worker in the mill. At the beginning of the nineteenth century, Wigan was booming. There were fifty-four collieries in the town by 1855 and up to 1,000 pit shafts, leading one town councillor to remark "a coal mine in every backyard was not uncommon in Wigan". Pat Boyle would not have struggled to find work, and for Ellen the cotton mills in Wigan would equally have been in need of workers. The couple fell in love, and set the date for their wedding as 19 November 1870, at St. John's Chapel in Wigan. Pat was twenty-three and Ellen, twenty-two.

Four days before the wedding, there was an explosion at Plattbridge, a pit three miles from Wigan. Twenty-seven miners were killed in the blast. That disaster had followed a similar explosion at the nearby Haydock colliery a year before in which fifty-nine men had lost their lives. Pat Boyle soon discovered that compared to working on the land back in Ireland, mining, though it paid more, was a much more dangerous game. Personal safety may have been one concern on his mind just a few months after getting married, but his main reasons for seeking pastures new were probably the higher wages the Yorkshire pit owners offered and the prospect of getting one of the new pit cottages being built around the collieries. This would be a big improvement on the shared accommodation the Boyles had in Lyon Street and it would mean Pat and Ellen could settle down and start a family.

Barnsley

Originally a major centre for the wire- and linen-making industries, by 1871 Barnsley had become the epicentre of the coal-mining industry in South Yorkshire. Coal had been dug in the area since the Middle Ages and both Silkstone and Orgreave are mentioned in the Domesday Book. Six months after Pat and Ellen were married, the 1871 Census showed Pat was lodging at Number 6, Court 1, Sheffield Road, Barnsley – a boarding house. When Pat arrived there were sixty-three pits operating in Barnsley employing thousands of men. He was employed as a colliery labourer so when he moved to Barnsley he had to start again at the bottom of the employment ladder. Of the twenty-six other people named at the same address in Sheffield Road, half were Irishmen working in the pits.

Ellen joined Pat in Barnsley six months later and the Boyles' first child, Elizabeth, was born in Barnsley in April 1873, almost next door to where Pat had lived when he arrived two years before. Elizabeth was followed a year later in 1874 by Mary. The Boyles' first son, John, was born in 1876, and by 1880 a fourth child, Margaret Ellen, was born.

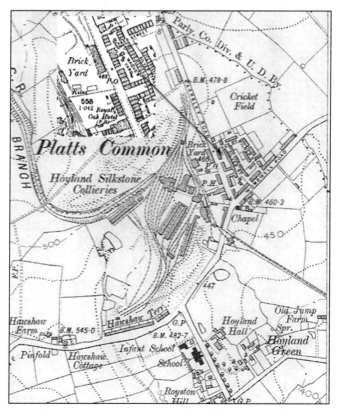

Figure 2. Platts Common 1893 (Ordnance Survey with permission)

Figure 3. Platts Common 1905

Platts Common

By 1881 the Boyle's had moved out of Barnsley to Platts Common, a little village just a few miles south. The village was overshadowed by the recently opened Hoyland Silkstone Colliery bringing hundreds of jobs to the area. The colliery was part of the Rockingham Mining Group owned by Earl Fitzwilliam. Rockingham consisted of four of the biggest pits in the South Yorkshire coalfield: Rockingham, Wharncliffe Silkstone, Skier Springs and Hoyland Silkstone. The village of Platts Common sits at the junction of the Wombwell and Barnsley roads. In the village there was a grocer, a shoemaker, two beer-sellers, a chapel, a cricket ground, a bowling green and a pub, The Royal Oak.

After moving to Platts Common, two more family additions arrived. A fourth daughter, Catherine was born in 1882 and the Boyles' last child arrived on a cold winter's day on Friday 29 January 1886 at Number 5, Hagues Yard. Pat and Ellen named him, Thomas William after Ellen's grandfather.

Hagues Yard was directly across the road from the pit gates. It was a block of twenty-four dwellings that shared a common yard with communal toilets and outdoor wash-house facilities. The houses in Hagues Yard were the oldest in the village. They consisted of two rooms and a pantry that offered little in the way privacy for a couple with six growing children. There was cold running water but no gas or electricity and the heating and cooking facilities were provided by a coal-fuelled, cast-iron range.

The day baby Thomas was born was bitterly cold. The Meteorological Office report for the week ending Monday 1 February 1886 read:

> The weather has continued in an unsettled condition. Cold rain, sleet and snow with lightning and thunderstorms in different parts of the Kingdom. Temperatures between 1 and 4 degrees above freezing. In York the weather never got above 40 degrees Fahrenheit and the previous week has rained six days out of seven.

As the young Thomas arrived in Platts Common, in politics, Lord Salisbury tendered his resignation to Queen Victoria after being summoned to Osborne House, while miners in France were demanding an increase in pay. In football, the *Leeds Mercury* reported that the Leeds Parish Church football team were continuing their northern tour and had played Kendal Hornets the previous day. The game had ended goal-less, the reporter blaming the visitors' tactics, for "repeatedly lying on the ball when it became loose".

A month after he was born, Thomas William was baptised at St. Helen's Church in Hoyland. The Catholic service was conducted in Latin and the baptism register shows his godparents as neighbours John and Sarah Cummins.

The nearest Catholic school for the Boyle children was a long walk away to the nearby village of Stubbin. Erected in 1864, the village school was run by schoolmistress Miss Jennie Nolan and accommodated up to 200 children, so would have had two or more teachers working there. School focused strongly on the three 'R's and Pat Boyle, who could both read and write, was determined to see all his children got an education as his own father had insisted back in Ireland. After the creation of the Hoyland school board in 1873, two new schools were built, one at Hoyland Nether and the other at Hoyland Common. St. Helen's Roman Catholic school was built in 1897 when Tommy was eleven and it's possible he moved here for his final year of schooling as it was much closer to home.

After school, children would play football in the street with a ball made of rags. Street football was a disturbance of the peace, and was one of the principal targets for police prosecutions. But Tommy Boyle wouldn't be caught; he was too quick for them.

In his final year at school at age twelve, Tommy spent half of his day at school and half at work in what was known as the Half-Time system. He would spend his half-days on the pit top sorting coal, possibly working with his elder sisters before eventually going underground with his brother and father once his school days were over. Starting work at the pit would have been a terrifying experience for a twelve-year-old. In appearance, the pit boys resembled miniature versions of their fathers, wearing a jacket, pants, boots and a cap. They would be allocated a job working with the pit ponies as David Tonks describes,

> At twelve a boy became a pony driver, leading a pony as it pulled a set of tubs underground. As he got stronger, at 16 he became a 'putter', and moved to supplying the miners with empty tubs and moving the full ones. Later he would become a hewing putter and at 21 a hewer, working at the face cutting coal with a pick.

The morning shift began at six-thirty a.m. If the men were a minute late they'd be sent away and lose a full day's pay. For a hewer like Pat Boyle, the best-paid job in the pit, he would receive around three shillings and ninepence (eighteen pence) for ten hours labour.

The Conditions

For the first couple of days, Tommy would probably have lost his breakfast as the cage flew down the shaft making his ears pop. At the pit bottom the men would call at the blacksmith's shop to pick up their tools: a wooden pick made of ash or hickory with a steel tip and a short shovel (until the start of World War I, eighty per cent of coal was cut by hand). The men would then make the long journey to the coalface, often taking up to an hour for which they were not paid. On arrival they would strip to the waist to cope with the heat and humidity, then stoop, crouch or lie on their sides for hours on end to rip out the coal from the seam. They would emerge at the shift-end looking like statues, coated in a layer of coal dust that stuck to the pores, got in the eyes, ears and nostrils and attacked the back of the throat. There were no toilets, no drinking water and no prospect of fresh air until the end of the shift. Rats and mice ran in packs and came in various shades from albino to black. The miners said some were as big as cats, with huge, sharp teeth. These creatures were known to steal the men's lunches, if they were not in sealed 'snap' tins.

The job demanded and made physically strong men. The hewer would develop great upper body strength. Alongside the hewer, the putter would shovel and fill the tubs and he needed great strength to get the heavy tubs moving. This involved leaning forwards at an angle with both arms around the tub, head down and pushing forward, often barefooted to give better traction until the tub began to move. Once they had got the load moving, momentum took over until eventually the rope boy with his pony took the coal tubs to the pit bottom. The putter would develop solid upper body and leg muscles – perfect development for an athlete, especially a runner. The putter would regularly catch his back on the low roof, leading to 'shirt buttons' as the skin scraped off along the vertebrae, leaving a blue scar as the open wound mixed with coal dust.

The South Yorkshire coalfield experienced some of the worst disasters in mining history. At the Huskar mine in Silkstone in 1838, twenty-six children, including eleven girls, three of whom were only eight, and fifteen boys drowned during a thunderstorm as they attempted to escape rising flood waters. This incident led to the Royal Commission ending the employment of women and children underground from 1842, though it carried on in some pits. In February 1857 at the Lundhill mine, an explosion killed 189 men and boys, and before Christmas in 1866 an explosion ripped through the Oaks Colliery in Ardsley just to the east of Barnsley, killing 361 men and boys. Only six miners from the entire shift escaped alive. The following day as mine rescuers tried to reach survivors, a secondary explosion killed twenty-seven of them. These events and dozens like them had a massive effect on the local pit village communities, with hundreds of families losing husbands, brothers and sons.

The accident records for the Hoyland Silkstone colliery show some seventy-seven men were seriously hurt or were killed between 1886–1911, the youngest just thirteen years old and the eldest aged sixty-six. An injury to one particular miner at another Barnsley pit was reported in an article in the *Plymouth and Cornish Advertiser* in 1893:

> Yesterday evening Patrick Boyle, a miner from Barnsley was brought home from the New Oaks colliery near Barnsley where

he had been buried six hours and was believed by his friends to be dead. Boyle was working when a large fall of roof buried him and constant falls prevented him from being rescued. His head was bared and his body protected by timber until he was extricated. Strange to say he was only cut about the head and was able to walk when he got home.

It is unclear whether this was Tommy's father as New Oaks was some distance from Platts Common. It is more likely that Pat Boyle was employed just across the road at Hoyland Silkstone, but we can't be certain. Whichever Pat Boyle it was, he had certainly been very lucky to survive his ordeal.

In facing the daily threat of death from roof falls, gas, fire, explosions and floods, miners were and remain a unique band of workers. They face the harsh conditions together with a black sense of humour and a special bond exists among them, a camaraderie unknown in other professions and probably only equalled in the armed forces. Tommy would have experienced this in his formative years. Miners stick together, work together, drink together and when things get tough, fight together. Improvements in working conditions and pay were only won through a hard struggle which continued down the generations, mainly through strikes, which brought great hardship to the men and their families. As a consequence of their actions, they faced lock-outs, scab labour, home evictions, and police and military intervention. Though working conditions improved with the passing of the 1872 Mines Act that gave the miner a ten-hour working day, it was to be another fifteen years before miners enjoyed a half-day off on a Saturday and a working week of fifty-five hours. As their struggle continued, by 1900 the working week for miners was reduced to forty-five hours, by which time the fourteen-year-old Tommy Boyle had been working underground for two years

Figure 4. Hoyland Silkstone Colliery, Platts Common.

Violent times

The Boyle family would have experienced their share of 'the struggle' through a number of disputes, many of them violent ones that took place in Platts Common.

In 1887 Hansard recorded:

> On Monday both excitement and curiosity were caused by the arrival at Hoyland Silkstone of a staff of police from Barnsley, who proceeded to search about 500 of the men and boys employed at the colliery there. It appears that about 9 o'clock in the morning, a girl named Wild, who was picking coal from the rubbish heap of the colliery, found a loaded pistol amongst the dirt which had been thrown out of a corve... The pistol had a screw barrel, and was indifferently loaded with powder and ball, but no wadding or paper had been used for ramming the charge home. Nothing of a suspicious character was found, however inquiries are still being made in order to find out for what purpose the pistol had been taken down the pit. (Hansard, 6 April 1887)

In the summer of 1893, the coal price had collapsed by thirty-five per cent. As a consequence miners faced a twenty-five per cent reduction in wages and were locked out if they refused to accept the cut in pay. Any striking miner was warned he would face eviction from his home if he joined the strike. In South Yorkshire, 'The Great Lockout' as it was known, lasted five months and was one of the most violent and bitter disputes in mining history. Author David Hey wrote that in some villages, including Hoyland and Orgreave, the militia were called out to quell the disturbances. Four squadrons of Dragoons and a squadron of Lancers were stationed at Wentworth Woodhouse on the Earl Fitzwilliam's estate on standby to maintain order. The Earl, a joint owner of the Rockingham mine group, was against any of his men being union members. The Riot Act was read at Featherstone near Wakefield but it didn't prevent troops firing on striking miners, killing two and wounding sixteen. The bitter dispute dragged on, attitudes on both sides hardened and it descended into what became known locally as The Rockingham Riots. Platts Common was caught up in the dispute as the *Daily Commercial Advertiser* reported in November 1893:

> ... some thousands of miners proceeded to Hoyland Silkstone colliery and completely sacked the place, seriously injuring, with bludgeons, Mr Fincken the managing director and others. The vast body then proceeded to the Rockingham colliery of which Mr Chambers is managing director and made a most furious attack upon the premises as well as upon the persons found above ground. After drinking the contents of three casks of ale and availing themselves to a dray load of mineral waters, the rioters deliberately set fire to the offices and adjoining buildings.

A small boy carried the news to Hoyland Common where shopkeepers hurriedly put up shutters. The strike dragged on for four months before a meeting in late November 1893 agreed that the men could return to work at their old wages. All this provided a canvas to the conditions Pat Boyle and his family faced as they tried desperately to eke out a living underground.

Sport in Barnsley

When the shorter working week arrived in 1887, miners had long earned their Saturday afternoons off. The men could develop other interests, such as tending their allotments, racing pigeons, spending the afternoon in the pub or attending sporting events. Sunday was the Lord's Day, strictly reserved for putting on your Sunday best, going to church and serving God. Practically everywhere was shut apart from the church. After a short Saturday morning shift, the afternoon became devoted to sport. In summer the men in Platts Common would play bowls or cricket. Rabbit coursing was popular and took place in the fields next to The Royal Oak pub with larger competitions held at Queens Fields in Barnsley. And in winter there was football.

When Tommy was a year old in 1887, the twenty-four-year-old Tiverton Preedy arrived in Barnsley fresh from theological college to take up his post of assistant stipendiary curate at St. Peter's Church, just a stone's throw from Sheffield Road where the Boyle family had lived. Two years before, Preedy had trained in Lincoln under his mentor, Edward White Benson. A former assistant master at Rugby School, Benson was a contributor to the development of the Rugby School football rules and believed strongly in team sports like rugby with its morals of team spirit, fair play and 'Christian manliness'. Clearly influenced by Benson, who went on to become archbishop of Canterbury, Preedy arrived full of optimism. The Parish of St. Peter's was one of the poorest in the town. While walking back to St. Peter's one day, he passed a pub and overheard some young men talking about forming a football team. Where rugby appealed to the more affluent, football was the more popular, unruly game of the streets. Preedy realised that through football he could reach out to the young, working-class men he saw hanging around outside pubs with little to do in their spare time.

Preedy chose the name Barnsley St. Peter's Football Club for his community project and at the club's inaugural meeting on Tuesday 6 September 1887 he became the club's first financial secretary. His first priority was to find somewhere to play. From the steps of St. Peter's looking north-eastwards across Doncaster Road stood a valley of open fields, an area known as Oakwell. He approached the Senior brothers, owners of the Oakwell Brewery to which the fields belonged, and asked whether he could hire a field for a football match. After an initial refusal Preedy persisted and the brothers eventually granted his request. Eleven days after the inaugural meeting, on 17 September, Barnsley St. Peter's first match took place. Three years later, the club began its first season in the Sheffield and District League. Preedy must have been a keen footballer in his day as he is mentioned in an article entitled 'Is football dangerous' in the *Pall Mall Gazette* of March 1892:

> On December 10 (1891), the Rev. Tiverton Preedy was running in the football field at Barnsley when he struck his forehead with great violence against a wooden beam. He was felled and bled profusely from a severe scalp wound.

Fortunately, Preedy survived his run-in with the goalpost, but in 1896 he left St. Peter's for a new post in Islington where he continued his work in developing young men through sport, focusing on boxing and wrestling, with some of his protégés selected for the 1908 Olympics. His fondness for Barnsley remained throughout his life and he made regular return visits to see how his community project had developed. Following their years in the Sheffield and District and the Midland Leagues, Barnsley FC, along with Glossop North End and New

Brighton Tower, were elected to Division Two of the Football League in the summer of 1898. Arthur Fairclough became the first Barnsley secretary, staying at the club for three seasons before leaving in 1901. He then returned three years later for a second period, one that would see Barnsley reach two Cup Finals and sign a certain youngster from Platts Common.

The Barnsley and District Football Association was formed in September 1893 after breaking away from the Sheffield Association. Once again the Reverend Preedy was influential in matters. One of the new Association's objectives was to "encourage local talent". A year later at the first annual general meeting, some sixty clubs were represented and a Scholars' Cup competition for local schoolboys was established. Sadly, this competition was discontinued in 1895, the minutes reporting "the schoolmasters having insufficient time", but in its place an under-sixteens junior league was set up. Hoyland had a number of teams representing collieries, ironworks, churches and pubs and hard rivalries existed between them. Hoyland Silkstone pit had its own football team and there were five other football teams in Hoyland: Hoyland Rock, Hoyland Town, Hoyland Nether, Upper Hoyland and Hoyland Common Wesleyans. The whole area must have been football crazy!

Chapter 3: The Boy from Platts Common

Then up lads, and at it, though cold be the weather;
And if by perchance you should happen to fall,
There are worse things in life than a tumble in the heather,
For what is this life, but a game of football?

– James McConnell

It was an ordinary working day in the middle of August 1899, but a tragic day that would shape the young Tommy Boyle's future. The men from the village arrived for the morning shift as usual at six thirty a.m. Among them the Boyles; Pat, Tommy and John and the Leaches – Jimmy, his father and three brothers – all descended in the cage together. Tommy and Jimmy were best friends and were employed as rope-boys, pulling the full coal tubs along with their ponies. At the pit bottom, the men collected their tools from the blacksmith's shop and the boys went on their way to collect the ponies from the stables. A couple of hours into the shift, Tommy heard a loud rumble in the tunnel ahead where Jimmy had just taken a full load of coal. As he ran up the tunnel, clouds of smoke and dust engulfed him. He couldn't see a thing. He called out for Jimmy as the dust began to clear but he soon realised he was too late:

> Yesterday morning information reached the police authorities at Barnsley of a sad fatality which occurred at Hoyland Silkstone to a rope lad named James Leech, aged 15 of Platts Common who was twice buried alive by a fall in a colliery. He was found buried beneath a fall of dirt in the first case and was heard to moan while being extricated. Then a second fall

occurred and although 20 men were engaged in liberating him, life was extinct when the body was reached. (*Liverpool Mercury* 17 August 1899)

Jimmy Leach was trapped beneath a ton of rock. Tommy tried hard to pull his friend out, clawing at the rocks with his bare hands and shouting for help. Then the sound of splitting rock from above triggered a second fall that brought yards of the roof down on top of Jimmy Leach and crushed the life out of him. Tommy managed to escape but Jimmy did not.

The two boys lived in Hagues Yard and knew each other well. They shared common interests in running, football and playing cricket. Jimmy Leach became another mining fatality and another mother was left to grieve. His death made a big impact on Tommy, who never forgot that day and the final moments of his friend. It led him to focus more on his athletic ability and on fulfilling his dream of one day becoming a professional footballer.

Tommy was never much of a scholar and lived for sport. In summer it was cricket, playing bowls with his dad and athletics. In winter it was football. He had played with a ball that Ellen had stitched together from old coal sacking until he could get hold of a proper one. He would play for hours in Hagues Yard under the light of the gas lamp annoying the neighbours in the process. He had tried to get into the Hoyland Silkstone colliery team at thirteen but at just five feet two inches, they'd said he was too small. As a consequence, he'd concentrated more on his running. He entered local junior athletic events as a sprinter at the summer festivals, 'the Feasts' that each village held. The earliest record of Tommy entering an athletics competition was at the Platts Common Feast held on 28 July 1900. He was fourteen and came second in the under-sixteens 440 yards race.

Hoyland Star

The first pub the traveller meets when arriving at Hoyland, South Yorkshire is 'The Star'. In 1893, it had its own cycling and sports club and was home to a junior football team, Hoyland Star, affectionately known as 'The Stars'. The team played their home matches across the road from the pub at the Hoyland Town ground. Hoyland Star formed in August 1903 and was the first team to give Tommy Boyle a chance to show what he could do with a ball. Hoyland Star had its own committee, with a president, Mr G.F. Jacobs and a secretary (manager) Mr W.G. Rollinson. Press reports on junior matches were brief but the *Barnsley Chronicle* reported quite often on the progress of The Stars.

Hoyland Star began their league campaign in September 1903 with a four-three away win against Gilroyd. It's not known whether Tommy was in The Stars team during their first season as only the goal scorers were named but he could have been. The following week they trounced the same team eight-nil at home with an "unnamed visiting full-back scoring". After three games The Stars topped the Junior Division with three wins out of three. By the turn of the year, with bad weather forcing the cancellation of games, Hoyland Star had slipped to fourth in the league. On 16 January 1904 The Stars beat Wombwell Main Reserves three-nil and a fortnight later Pilley United two-nil to climb back to third in the table. On 9 April, The Stars beat Sheffield Grammar School two-one at home before ending their season with a four-nil away win at Cranemoor and a final league placing of fourth, which for their first season wasn't bad.

In June the *Barnsley Chronicle* reported that Arthur Fairclough had returned as secretary of Barnsley FC following the departure of John McCartney and a fine stand costing the sum of seven hundred pounds had been erected at Oakwell for the new season.

Tommy's name appeared as an entrant on the athletics programme at the thirty-first Stainboro' Feast that took place on 6 August 1904. Now eighteen and after six years working underground, he had filled out into quite a solid athlete. The two-day festival featured music, athletics and local-interest sports such as 'knurr and spell' and 'sparrow-shooting'. Some 4,000 people attended the event over the Bank Holiday weekend. The athletics finals were held on the Bank Holiday Monday and after Tommy had won his heat he was through to the final of the 120 yards sprint handicap for the prize of seven pounds. Lining up in the final were W. Horne (Blacker Hill), H. Mitchell (Higham) and T.W. Boyle (Platts Common). Tommy had also won his heat in the 440 yards and was in that final lining up against F. Pickering (Birdwell) and T. Eden (Barnsley). He didn't win either final, coming second that year, but it showed he had kept up a serious interest in athletics for over four years. It would stand him in good stead.

The 1904–5 season saw Hoyland Star compete in two competitions: the Junior League and Minor Cup. The Stars got off to a flyer in the League with a seven-nil home win against Ardsley Nelson with goals from Hodgson, Gedney, Bacon and Howard. The following week they won again by a single goal against Darfield United Reserves and in their next game, away at Wombwell Main Reserves, Hoyland Star went top of the League with a thumping eight-one win, with Howard scoring four more goals. In November, The Stars were away at Great Houghton FC. It was the first time Tommy's name appeared in a match report, scoring the winning goal with a header, the *Barnsley Chronicle* reporting,

> In the early stages Hoyland had the best of the game but Houghton scored after 30 minutes through Godfrey. In the last ten minutes of the first half, Kay and Bacon scored for the home side. Houghton equalised in the second half, but before the finish Boyle headed the winning goal for The Stars.

Final score: Great Houghton 2, Hoyland Star 3

The Stars were second in the table behind Ardley Nelson having played fewer games.

In the Minor Cup competition, they were beaten three-nil in a game versus Mapplewell. The club appealed to the League, claiming that Mapplewell had fielded an ineligible player, and the match was replayed the following Monday in a blinding snowstorm, The Stars winning three-one.

The *Barnsley Chronicle* reported on The Star's next away game at Pilley United on the first Saturday in February. Tommy again was the star of the show:

> During the first half, the game was evenly contested. However Boyle scored for The Stars. On resuming, the game went in favour of Hoyland and Boyle added two more goals for them. Pilley scored a consolation and the game ended − Pilley United 1, Hoyland Star with Tommy Boyle doing the hat-trick, Three!

The Stars closed the gap at the top with leaders Ardsley and had a game in hand. A week later The Stars played their game in hand against Rockingham Colliery at home. It was an even game but The Stars scored early on through Harry Kay. The Stars' defence managed to hold on to their slender lead to go to the top of the league with two games left. On 4 March, The Stars defeated Great Houghton by two goals to one to take the title and win their first honours. The *Barnsley Chronicle* reported, "In the Junior League Championship, Hoyland Star has secured the Championship of the first division with Ardsley Nelson a creditable runner-up."

The new Junior Champions had also reached the semi-final of the Minor Cup, which took place on 22 April 1905 at Darfield. The *Barnsley Chronicle* reported on the game against Mapplewell, with The Stars taking the lead in the second minute:

The game was played at a good pace with Boyle testing the goalkeeper with a fine shot. At half-time The Stars led 1-0. Mapplewell resorted to the 'one back' game at the restart to seek the equaliser with Ibbotson the Mapplewell full back and Sidebottom for The Stars going close with shots. Mapplewell then equalised through an Ibbotson header from a corner kick. Midway through the second half, the referee ordered two men off the field for ungentlemanly conduct. Hoyland now played with one back only and each goal had some narrow escapes but the game ended in a draw and a replay needed. The reporter noted that, 'Boyle, The Stars right half stood out as the finest performer in the game.'

Final score: Hoyland Star 1 v Mapplewell 1

The Stars won the replay two-nil. Sadly, no report was available, but they progressed to the final that took place on 29 April against Higham. A sunny afternoon and the Easter holiday attracted around 1,500 spectators to Dillington Park. The *Barnsley Chronicle* reporting

Most of the first half was a fairly even game with opportunities at either end, but five minutes before half-time, Higham struck. Mitchell scoring with a low shot that gave Camm in The Stars goal no chance. From the kick-off, Hoyland missed an opportunity to equalise and the referee blew his whistle for half-time with Higham leading 1-0. Further Hoyland pressure saw Wormald produce a fine save – 'with several players on him.' Hoyland were awarded a free kick in a good position and Gedney crossed for Sidebottom to equalise. Hoyland had the advantage and the wind at their backs and forced a corner and Sidebottom scored to make the score 2-1 to The Stars. Hoyland with their tails up almost went 3-1 up but Sidebottom was deemed offside.

Final score: Hoyland Star 2, Higham 1

The teams for the Final lining up,

Hoyland Star: Camm, Crane, A. Lindley, Boyle, Bawn, Guest, Gedney, Hodgson, Sidebottom, Kay, and J.T. Lindley.

Higham: C. Wormald, H. Mitchell, Womersley, Landers, Worsley, Charlesworth, Youell, Taylor, E. Mitchell, Kaye, and W. Wormald.

In only their second season, Hoyland Star, with Tommy playing at right-half, had done the double! It had been an excellent season and the boy from Platts Common had established himself.

At the meeting of the Barnsley Association held on 12 August, the junior teams taking part in the 1905–6 competitions were announced. Hoyland Star's name was not among them. For some unknown reason, the double winning 'Stars' had been disbanded. A new club, Hemingfield Victorias, had taken their place.

Tommy looked around for another club and was eventually signed on by Elsecar Athletic, who played in the Barnsley Minor League. It was a step up the football ladder. The Minor League included teams from the local collieries like Grimethorpe United, Wombwell Main, Mitchell Main, Hoyland Silkstone and Rockingham Colliery. It would be a much tougher test and he would need all his speed, skill and cunning to evade the flying tackles. He would be up against some hard nuts here. Men from the pits who didn't mind who they hurt. Pat Boyle told him to be sure to get his retaliation in first. He trained hard, stepping up the running and the ball practice after work.

Tommy started in Elsecar's reserves. The club had switched grounds for the new season and played in a field adjoining the Milton Arms pub in Elsecar, "the field having been generously granted free of charge by Mr W. Wales the proprietor". By 14 October, after a run in the reserves, Tommy had broken through to Elsecar's first team. After six games of the season, Hoyland Town topped the league on goal difference from Elsecar in second place. At Elsecar's next home game against Wombwell Main, the *Barnsley Chronicle* reported Tommy scoring the opener:

> The game was very fast at times particularly in the second half. The visitors won the toss and kicked uphill. The teams were well balanced and there was no score at half-time. Elsecar restarted with a rush and after ten minutes continued pressure, Boyle opened their score. The visitors tried hard to equalise but the Athletic succeeded in keeping the lead until two minutes from the end when Ezra Holmes scored from a corner.

> Final Score: Elsecar Athletic 1, Wombwell Main 1.

Elsecar remained unbeaten and were joint top of the League having won two and drawn four of their six games. In Elsecar's next match on 28 October, The *Barnsley Chronicle* reported on their performance in the Barnsley Minor Cup against Barnsley Volunteers. After ten minutes Athletic scored and by half-time they led Barnsley Volunteers by two goals to nil. Elsecar had much of the play and went three-nil up early in the second half, before the Volunteers pulled a goal back to make it three-one. Marsh and then Tommy scored, making the final score five-one to Elsecar.

After a promising start, Elsecar's League hopes faded, but they were going well in the Barnsley Minor Cup having won through to the Final as reported by The *Barnsley Chronicle*.

The Barnsley Minor Cup final:
Elsecar Athletic v. Rockingham Colliery, 28 April 1906

> The final was played on the Hoyland Town ground in front of 2,000 spectators. With a strong wind blowing and affecting the

quality of football, Rockingham won the toss and kicked off. Smith almost scored early on for Rockingham but Elsecar had most of the play and scored just before the interval, Gladwin finding the net through a crowd of players. Rockingham had the chance to equalise and missed other chances by Smith and Whitney. Elsecar continued to play the better game and a fine spurt by the front rank ended in Greenfield beating Fieldsend in the Rockingham goal. Overall a poor game due to the conditions with Elsecar winning the cup two goals to nil and capping a fine season.

The teams were not given in the *Chronicle*'s report but Tommy must have played well as he had caught the eye of one spectator in the crowd that day: the Barnsley secretary, Arthur Fairclough. Fairclough was impressed with the youngster from Platts Common, and a week later the *Chronicle* reported that Tommy had signed professional forms for Barnsley.

More Players signed on – During the week the Oakwell officials have secured the signatures for next season of; Bounds, Johnson, Silto, Hellewell, all old players, while on Thursday two Elsecar players, Cramp (half back) and Boyle (half) were secured.

Tommy's eight years working underground were over. The years had been the making of him as a man. He would bring the camaraderie, the teamwork and the hard graft he had experienced into his game as a professional. He could now breathe fresh air every day, work on his fitness, eat better, develop his speed and his game, and be paid twice what his father and brother earned in a week for doing something he loved more than anything. He'd also have more time and money to spend on the growing number of girls in Platts Common and beyond who were now starting to show an interest in him.

Tommy was actually twenty when he put pen to paper in May 1906, but when Arthur Fairclough asked how old he was, he told him he was only eighteen and gave his date of birth as 29 January 1888. Knocking a couple of years off their age was a common practice among players in those days according to Ian Nannestad of *Soccer History*. This practice had been repeated by other Barnsley players as Peter Holland discovered when researching the Barnsley winger Wilf Bartrop in his biography, *Swifter than the Arrow*. Bartrop signed for Barnsley from Worksop in June 1909 and gave his date of birth as two years later in order to prolong his career.

Chapter 4: Barnsley

Figure 5. Barnsley Football Club

The first week of August arrived and with his kit bag slung over his shoulder, Tommy walked the few miles from Platts Common into town to report for his first pre-season training session at Oakwell. Arthur Fairclough introduced him and the other new faces to the full-time professionals before the first training session. After lunch, as part of the training routine, the team went for a walk in the countryside.

The highest position Barnsley had reached in Division Two was eighth in 1903 and 1904, both under Fairclough's reign. The previous season the team had finished twelfth having won just twelve games out of thirty-eight. The Barnsley Board demanded a better performance this year. Like most newcomers, Tommy was eager to start and would ply his trade first in the reserves, playing at right-half against local sides like Leeds City, Sheffield United and The Wednesday in the Midland League.

The 1906–7 League season opened on 1 September at Oakwell in a match against Blackpool which Barnsley edged by three goals to two and pick up their first points. The mid-week *Barnsley Chronicle* reported that Tommy had been suspended for a month along with another player, Cooper. It is not known what offence he had committed. It's likely that it was for something that had gone on between the pair of them on the field in pre-season. Fighting warranted a month's ban, as did serious foul play. It certainly wasn't the best of starts and as a consequence, Tommy missed the whole of September's fixtures and watched the reserve games from the sidelines.

After the opening game against Blackpool, the first team went on a five-match losing streak before they thumped Burton United at Oakwell six-nil. A two-two draw against Spen Whittaker's Burnley at Turf Moor followed. It was five weeks into the reserves season that Tommy first pulled on a red shirt. On 6 October he took part in a Midland League fixture against Lincoln City reserves at Oakwell in front of around 200 spectators. Before the fixture and after a series of defeats Barnsley reserves were bottom of the Midland League, their performances eloquently summarised by the *Barnsley Chronicle* reporter:

> If their form were not so variable one would be justified in predicting a successful season for Barnsley Reserves for in their happier moments they can oblige with as sparkling and effective a game as need be desired. But when they are bad they are horrid! Of the later fact we have already – young as the season is – had some fearful examples and, therefore it was great relief

to find the boys on their best behaviour at Oakwell on Saturday against Lincoln City Reserves. At inside right, Scott was always a worker and often got through cleverly, but the wing man, Johnson was off colour. Boyle of Elsecar came into the team at right half and on Saturday's show looks like being distinctly useful. Final Result: Barnsley Reserves 3 Lincoln City Reserves 0.

The result lifted Barnsley reserves off the bottom and Tommy's inclusion had had a positive effect on the team's performance. He was finally off and running. A month later on Saturday 24 November the first team were in London to play Chelsea at Stamford Bridge. Barnsley had fallen to fourth from bottom of the Second Division on nine points, with four wins, one draw and seven defeats from twelve games. "Not good enough," the directors had said, "improvements needed." Chelsea had taken maximum points from all their home games and were third in the division. They were a solid outfit and would end the season in second place, securing promotion to Division One. Fairclough needed to act and knew it was the defence that needed fixing. Based on his half-dozen performances in the reserves and an injury to Ruddlesden, the directors agreed to give Tommy a start in the first team at right-half. It was his first trip to the capital as he met the rest of the team at Barnsley station on the Friday morning. Jackie Owen scored Barnsley's goal in a narrow two-one defeat, but his performance was overshadowed by the debut of the new Barnsley half-back.

Boyle, who came into the game owing to Ruddlesden's indisposition, played a capital game and may be unreservedly complimented on his first appearance in Second Division football – particularly against such opponents. He tackled well and fed his forwards with judgement the latter being a qualification which has been lacking in the Barnsley middle line. (*Barnsley Chronicle*, 1 December 1906)

Two more defeats followed the Chelsea game, leaving Barnsley next to bottom in Division Two, but Fairclough kept faith with his new right-half. There was something about the lad he liked: his work rate and his constant desire to win. He'd shouted his encouragement throughout to his teammates. He'd tackled well and had dominated the back line. On 15 December Gainsborough Trinity were visitors to Oakwell and were soundly thrashed six-nil. That result started a fifteen-match unbeaten run in the League and FA Cup and The Reds marched up the table.

The 1907 FA Cup

The FA Cup or 'English' Cup as it was more commonly known, was the most prestigious competition in English football. At that time the Cup was valued much higher than the League Championship in terms of club honours. Winning the Cup brought fame and fortune and gave the local community a huge interest as their team progressed through the rounds of the competition. In 1907, League clubs entered the Cup at the first round stage and Barnsley, tenth in the Second Division, were drawn away at Nottingham Forest, fourth in Division Two. It was at Forest where Tommy got his first taste of Cup football. Nottingham Forest were a strong side and enjoying an excellent season. They would become Second Division Champions in May. The tight Barnsley defence managed to shut-out the Forest forwards and game ended in a one-all draw, with Alec Hellewell scoring for Barnsley and forcing a replay at Oakwell the following week. Barnsley won the replay two-one with another goal from Hellewell and one from Hall in front of a 10,000 afternoon crowd at Oakwell. In the second round, Barnsley were drawn at home against the Southern League side, Portsmouth. In front of another good home crowd, The Reds beat Pompey one-nil, with a goal from O'Donnell who scored with a bullet header from a cross from the right supplied by Tommy.

Figure 6. Barnsley FC Team photograph 1906-7 Tommy is sat third from left, middle row.

Figure 7. Barnsley FC FA Cup Team 1907

In the League, Barnsley carried on their good form, beating Lincoln City six-two and Bradford City at Oakwell three-one. When the draw for the third round was announced, Barnsley were given a home tie against the First Division's twice FA Cup winners, Bury. Bury had last won the competition four years previously with a six-nil defeat of Derby County in the final. Bury were a very good side. Thirteen thousand packed into Oakwell to watch the underdogs take on the former Cup winners. In a hard-fought battle and with another solid defensive performance, Barnsley won again, one-nil, with a goal from Powell and the Second-Division side were through to the quarter-finals for their very first time. The Club's progress in the competition became the main topic of conversation in the Royal Oak in Platts Common and in all the pubs and clubs across the town. Barnsley had lifted the spirits of the whole community. Could they go all the way?

When the draw for the quarter-finals was made the following Monday, Barnsley's luck continued. Their name was first out of the hat and gave them a home tie against First Division side Woolwich Arsenal. Arsenal had been in the First Division for three years, having risen dramatically from the Southern League. The Londoners were eighth in the First Division and had knocked out Grimsby after a replay in the first round, followed by Bristol City in round two and neighbours Bristol Rovers in Round Three. Arsenal tried to get the game switched to their home ground, the Manor Ground in Plumstead but Barnsley refused and instead doubled the admission charge.

After a fortnight's build-up in the *Barnsley Chronicle*, Cup day arrived on March 9th and Barnsley made two changes: Hay came in at full-back and Rounds deputised for Thorpe in goal. A big local crowd of 13,871 turned out to cheer on The Reds into the semi-finals. The match got underway and after fifteen minutes O'Donnell scored from a Brookes corner to put Barnsley one-nil up. Oakwell went wild and scores of Barnsley spectators ran onto the pitch to celebrate. Barnsley held on to their slender lead until half-time with a strong defensive performance from the half-back line. Tommy was in the thick of it, winning a number of tackles against the Arsenal forwards, who were the bookies clear favourites to progress through to the semi-finals. With an hour of the match gone and with the Barnsley players tiring, a stronger, more determined Arsenal equalised. Five minutes later they added a second to make it two-one. Tommy wasn't finished: he took the ball up field and fired off a shot that ricocheted off the Arsenal post. A follow-up effort from Kettlewell hit the crossbar. Barnsley pushed hard to find the equaliser but to no avail and their Cup journey came to an end. It was Arsenal that went through to the semi-finals, where they lost to Sheffield Wednesday who later went on to become the Cup winners for 1907.

Barnsley and the boy from Platts Common had enjoyed their Cup run and all the interest it had brought with it. For Tommy, the Cup run to the quarter-final in his first full season was an amazing experience. The whole day, the atmosphere, even the crowd was different to a normal league match. They were much more vociferous than a League match. He'd got a taste for the Cup and wanted more. Barnsley's good form continued in the League with a three-one home win against high-flying Chelsea and a five-nil victory over Spen Whittaker's Burnley with Reeves scoring twice in each game to bring the curtain down on a fine first season for Tommy. Barnsley finished eighth, their best League placing for two years. Since his introduction to the first team in November, Barnsley had lost only seven games out of twenty-five in the League. It had been a very good first season in professional football for him. Tommy had established himself in the back-line and had brought some much needed stability into the Barnsley defence.

In the close season, despite the extra income the Cup run had brought in, Barnsley needed to balance the books. Three first team players, Owen, Stacey and Mordue, were all sold, bringing in funds; but in losing such experienced players, Barnsley struggled through the following season. The club finished in the bottom half of the table with only thirty points to their credit and were knocked out of the Cup at Plymouth Argyle in the first round.

Tommy was learning to take the rough with the smooth. He hated losing at anything and soon learned that most players ended up with nothing in this game and you had to fight every inch of the way to survive. His father had taught him that if he wanted to be a winner, he needed an edge. He needed to be fitter, stronger, faster and harder than his opponent. He had to get stuck in from the first whistle and fight all the way, and focus on winning. He worked hard during the summer break, working part time on the pit top and spending his afternoons working on his fitness. At the weekend and on the summer evenings he played cricket in Platts Common before the coming season beckoned.

The 1908–9 season began slowly for Barnsley. A two-two away draw in the first game at Blackpool was followed by defeats against Bolton, Tottenham Hotspur and Leeds City before The Reds picked up their first win against Hull City on 19 September. Another poor run of form, with only three wins in eighteen games, saw Barnsley stuck at the bottom of the Second Division on New Year's Day 1909.

Bert Freeman's boots

In the first round of the FA Cup, Barnsley had been drawn away to meet Everton and travelled to Goodison Park on 16 January. Everton led the First Division and had the brilliant young centre-forward Bert Freeman. Freeman was the League's leading scorer and was on the verge of breaking into the England team. Before the match, in another move to satisfy the bank, Barnsley sold centre-half Billy Silto, to Swindon. The timing of the transfer wasn't the best preparation for such an important game, but an offer had been made and finances dictated. Fairclough moved Tommy across from right-half to occupy the centre-half position and brought newcomer Bob Glendenning in at right-half as his cover. Barnsley lined up Thorpe, Little, Downs, Glendenning, Boyle, Oxspring, Coulthard, Griffiths, Lillycrop, Hellewell and Brookes.

The big concern for Barnsley was in keeping Bert Freeman quiet. Fairclough gave Tommy the job. It isn't clear whose idea the prank was, but before the game kicked off the Barnsley goalkeeper, Tommy Thorpe, went into the Everton dressing room and enquired as to the whereabouts of Bert Freeman's boots. The Everton players, puzzled by Thorpe's intrusion, pointed to the hook where the centre-forward's boots were hung up. Thorpe picked up the boots and in chalk wrote on them 'NO GOALS' before marching out. Freeman didn't score in the game; he was marked out of the game by the Barnsley centre-half who was man of the match. But sadly for Barnsley, Everton's class showed in the second half and they went on to win the match three-one.

His performance that day sealed Tommy's position as Barnsley's centre-half. He had adapted well against higher opposition and had been comfortable playing in the central position. If he could keep someone like Bert Freeman, the finest young striker in the country quiet, he could keep anyone quiet. Switching Tommy to centre-half was the best move Fairclough made.

In the League, Barnsley urgently needed to pick up points. Four straight home wins added eight points to their tally and they rose to fourteenth position in the table. Tommy took over as the chief penalty taker, converting three vital ones, away at Fulham and at home against Grimsby and Oldham, gaining valuable points. By the end of another poor season, Barnsley finished seventeenth, a place lower than the previous season.

It was only home form that had kept them up as they hadn't won away from Oakwell all season.

Despite Barnsley's average form, Tommy's performances were beginning to attract the attention of a number of scouts from other clubs. Arthur Fairclough was getting enquiries asking if the young centre-half was available and at what price. But Fairclough was a shrewd operator in the transfer market and would only sell at the right time and for the right price. In 1909 the Barnsley account book showed that Tommy was one of the club's prized assets, earning a weekly salary of three pounds and ten shillings during the season, almost the maximum wage of four pounds a week and around twice the salary of a skilled miner.

Chapter 5: A Grand Day Out

Figure 8. The Crystal Palace, Sydenham

Before the 1909–10 season got underway, Arthur Fairclough made Tommy the Barnsley captain. Under new leadership, Barnsley's season began with a two-one defeat at home to Hull City – not the best of starts to Tommy's new role. The Reds lost again away at lowly Glossop North End before gaining their first victory against Birmingham City with a five-one win at Oakwell and the new captain missing a penalty. A three-game goal drought followed before Barnsley travelled the short distance to meet their Yorkshire neighbours at Elland Road on 23 October. There Barnsley demolished Leeds City, seven-nil. It was their best ever away result in the League. And just to prove it was no fluke they repeated the performance the following week against Wolverhampton Wanderers at Oakwell. Tommy opened the scoring with a penalty. Gadesby scored two and Lillycrop and Forman made it five-nil to The Reds before half-time. In the second period, Gadesby scored to complete his hat-trick and winger Wilf Bartrop scored to make it Barnsley seven, Wolverhampton Wanderers one, to put Barnsley in ninth position in the table.

Barnsley organised special trains for supporters to the next League game at Gainsborough Trinity. The game ended in a dour nil-nil draw, but The Reds followed it with three good home wins against Grimsby, Leicester Fosse and Clapton Orient. Things were looking very good: the crowds were picking up and a settled team was getting the right results. The busy Christmas period brought four games in a week. An away game at Derby County on Christmas Day was followed by games against Stockport and Derby at home on 27 and 28 December. The Reds won the two home games and then faced Stockport away on New Year's Day.

Over Christmas, Tommy's mother was taken ill with bronchitis. Ellen had suffered from asthma all her life and her chest usually worsened in the winter. The illness had confined her to bed. At Edgeley Park on New Year's Day, Barnsley crashed to a five-nil defeat, their worst performance of the season. They were missing their captain, who was at his mother's side at the family home in Platts Common as she passed away from heart failure and bronchitis. Ellen was sixty-two years old. In his younger days, Tommy and his mother had enjoyed a special bond. Being the youngest, and while the others were out at work and school, the two of them had time alone together. Bringing up and feeding six children in a two-room house wasn't easy and Tommy thought the world of her. He helped his father make all the arrangements for the funeral and Ellen's burial took place the following week at St. Helen's Church in Hoyland.

Since the start of the competition in 1871, the FA Cup had been won only three times by teams from outside the top division. Second Division Notts County won in1894, Southern League side Tottenham Hotspur won it in 1901 and Second Division Wolverhampton Wanderers won it in 1908. Barnsley's twin neighbours, Sheffield United and The Wednesday, both had their name on the Cup – twice. The first week of January as Tommy came to terms with the death of his mother, he remembered the 1907 Cup run to the quarter-finals. He was determined that the team under his leadership would go a step further this year. He owed it to Ellen's memory.

In the first round of the Cup, Barnsley were drawn away at Blackpool. Barnsley had played at Bloomfield Road a month before in the League and had drawn there nil-nil, so Tommy was confident the team could get a result. Four special trains were chartered to carry around 2,000 Barnsley supporters over the Pennines to the seaside. The week before the Cup tie, Barnsley trained just a few miles down the coast at Lytham to take the sea air and to 'acclimatise'. The Cup tie drew a small crowd of 8,000 and ended in a one-all draw, with a goal from Tufnell for Barnsley. The replay took place the following Thursday afternoon at Oakwell and Blackpool were beaten convincingly, six-nil, in front of a crowd of 13,939, which included a penalty-kick from Tommy.

In the second round Barnsley were drawn away again against Southern League side Bristol Rovers. The *Barnsley Chronicle* reported that Barnsley bought the ground rights for five hundred pounds from Bristol and doubled the admission price from sixpence to a shilling. Barnsley hit form right from the first whistle and they led three-nil at half-time with goals from Bartrop, Gadesby and Forman and Tommy even missed an open goal. In the second half Barnsley made sure of their win with a goal from half-back George Utley to win the match four-nil and progress through to the next round.

In round three, Barnsley faced their stiffest test so far against West Bromwich Albion at Oakwell. Albion were ninth in the table and had the best away record in the Second Division having already won seven games away from The Hawthorns. Albion arrived at Oakwell on the back of a three-two League win at Burnley and were in good form for the match. Barnsley were also on good form having won eleven home games by the time Albion arrived on 19 February. In front of a huge Oakwell crowd of 18,836, Barnsley's biggest gate for years, and on a bitterly cold and blustery day, Tommy won the toss and played with the wind at their backs in the first half. It was a tightly contested game that was scoreless until the eightieth minute when Barnsley scored through Harry Tufnell. The half-backs came in for praise in the newspapers and had been "the stars of the show" in seeing Barnsley through to the quarter-finals for the second time in four years.

The quarter-final draw had given Barnsley a lucky home advantage and a tie against another Southern League side, Queens Park Rangers. Tommy was playing well and it was announced that he had been included in the England trial match to take place at Anfield the following week. Barnsley's successes in the Cup was contrasted with a string of away league defeats, the latest occurring at Turf Moor where they lost two-nil to Spen Whittaker's Burnley. One of the reasons for the defeat was that the club had fielded a weakened side and were fined by the football authorities for it.

Figure 9. Barnsley v Queens Park Rangers, FA Cup Quarter-Final 1910

The gates were closed for the quarter-final well before kick-off as 23,574 spectators squeezed into Oakwell. Tommy led the team out and won the toss. In the twenty-fourth minute, the captain passed the ball out to Wilf Bartrop on the wing who from near the corner flag attempted to cross the ball into the penalty area. As Bartrop struck the ball it spun off his boot, hit the post and dropped into the Rangers net! The crowd went wild. Despite several Rangers attacks, The Reds held on to their slender lead against the Southern Leaguers until the final whistle and Tommy and his men had a earned a place in the Cup semi-finals for the very first time.

In the hat for the semi-final draw along with Barnsley were; Southern League side Swindon Town and two First Division sides, Newcastle United and Everton. As Barnsley supporters eagerly opened their newspapers on the Tuesday morning, they learned that the draw had pitched Barnsley against Everton, while Newcastle United would take on Swindon. It would be Tommy's second encounter with Bert Freeman, now established as England's centre-forward.

The FA Cup semi-final: Barnsley v. Everton

After Everton had knocked Barnsley out of the competition the year before, the press were giving Barnsley little chance and were already talking up the prospect of an all First-Division clash at the Crystal Palace for the final. The Cup tie took place at Elland Road on 26 March. Everton complained about the venue because the ground was so close to their opponent's home ground and protested to the FA to no avail. Everton were tenth in the First Division and had beaten Middlesbrough, Arsenal, Sunderland and Coventry on their way to the semi-finals, scoring fifteen goals with only four conceded. In the League they had only one defeat in twelve games; as such, Everton were the clear favourites. Tommy would need to keep a watchful eye on Bert Freeman, who had already notched up four goals in Everton's Cup run so far.

Arthur Fairclough named an unchanged Barnsley side from the quarter-final: Mearns, Downs, Ness, Glendenning, Boyle, Utley, Bartrop, Gadsby, Lillycrop, Tufnell and Forman. Everton lined up: Scott, Clifford, McConnachie, Harris, Taylor, Makepeace, Sharpe, White, Freeman, Young and Barlow.

In front of 35,000 spectators, the game turned into an anti-climax. Everton didn't get the run of the ball or the quick win they expected and the game played out to a nil-nil draw with both defences excelling. Bert Freeman was marked out of the game by Tommy who followed him all over the pitch as he had done the year before. The replay would take place at Old Trafford in Manchester the following Thursday afternoon, 31 March.

Schoolmaster Herbert S. Bamlett, the match referee from Northumberland, again took charge of the two teams for the replay and more than 55,000 spectators missed a day's work to cheer on the two teams. The replay was only fifteen minutes old when the game was stopped. Everton's centre-half, Jack Taylor, had been hit in the throat with the ball. He couldn't breathe properly, his windpipe having become crushed and he was rushed to hospital. Everton had to play on with ten men and without their influential captain. The game restarted and on the half-hour Everton's Valentine Harris, handled the ball in the penalty area. Bamlett pointed immediately to the penalty spot. With a big responsibility to put Barnsley ahead, Tommy stepped forward to take the penalty. The Old Trafford crowd went silent, as he nervously placed the ball on the spot at the Stretford End. He stepped back his usual ten paces, ran up and rather than smacking it one as he usually did, he right-footed it, causing the ball to skew wide of the left-hand post! Hands on hips, he shook his head in disbelief. He could have kicked himself and so could the rest of his teammates. A massive opportunity to take the lead had gone.

*Figure 10. Tommy tosses up in the 1910 FA Cup
semi-final replay vs. Everton at Old Trafford.*

BARNSLEY v EVERTON AT OLD TRAFFORD. SEMI-FIN

Figure 11. Barnsley Score in the FA Cup semi-final replay.

Bamlett restarted the game and just before half-time it was
Barnsley's turn to concede a penalty as Everton's Sandy Young
was bundled over in the penalty area. Barnsley had blown it,
Tommy certainly thought so. He couldn't look as Sharp, the

Everton outside-left, stepped up to take the penalty. Mearns, the Barnsley keeper, judged the direction of Sharp's kick and pounced on the ball smothering it with his body as Sharp ran in for the rebound. The game remained nil-nil. Barnsley were off the hook as referee Bamlett blew the whistle for half-time. It was honours even as Tommy led the team off for their half-time cup of tea.

The second half was only five minutes old when Barnsley's Tom Forman collected the ball on the left and advanced over the halfway line. The Everton defenders backpedalled and spotting an opening; Forman let fly with a shot from thirty yards to test the Everton goalkeeper. Scott could only fist the ball away, which landed straight at the feet of Gadesby, who scored. One-nil to Barnsley! Everton replied straight away and with Barnsley hanging on for the next thirty minutes it looked increasingly likely that the Lancastrians would find the equaliser. With Everton making all the running through Freeman, they tired while Barnsley had energy in reserve. Then with five minutes of the game remaining, Tom Forman scored a second goal to make it two-nil. A pitch invasion followed and a half-dozen Manchester mounted police had to clear Barnsley's jubilant fans off the pitch.

Everton were done for. Bert Freeman couldn't believe it. He'd not had a sniff of the ball all afternoon. Then, straight from the restart, Barnsley won the ball in the centre-circle. George Lillycrop ran forward and crossed for Tuffnell to add Barnsley's third. Three-nil! No-one inside Old Trafford could have predicted the scoreline. The Second Division underdogs from Yorkshire had knocked out the Cup favourites Everton and they were through to their first FA Cup final. In the middle of the pitch a tired Tommy shook hands and commiserated with the man he had tormented all afternoon, Bert Freeman. Returning home from Old Trafford, the team and their jubilant fans were in seventh heaven. They were going to the Final at The Crystal Palace and it would be a truly grand day out.

Figure 12. The Barnsley team 'fly to the final.'

The Cup Final: Newcastle United v. Barnsley, 23 April 1910

The 39th FA Cup final would take place on 23 April at the Crystal Palace in South London. The final would be between Barnsley and Newcastle United, who had overcome Cup minnows Swindon Town in their semi-final, two-nil. As if to herald the coming final, from the middle of April, a new star appeared in the night sky in the form of Halley's Comet. From the Friday evening, 15 April, the comet was visible to stargazers in Barnsley and it would also be seen over the Pennines in Burnley, as the Burnley FC secretary, Spencer Whittaker waited for his midnight train to London. His train arrived on schedule but Spencer Whittaker would never reach his destination and his mysterious death would result in a new man taking the helm at the club. A man who would transform the Lancashire side into one of the finest in England. A man who would choose the boy from Platts Common to lead them.

TRAGIC DEATH OF THE BURNLEY SECRETARY

Burnley Football Club Secretary, Spencer Whittaker was killed as he fell from the carriage of the overnight London Express near Crewe station on Friday evening the 15th of April. Director R. H. Wadge has taken temporary charge of team affairs until a new man can be appointed.

Whittaker was travelling to FA headquarters in London to register the Accrington centre half Harry Swift in time for the match against Manchester City the following day. Whittaker had left Burnley Bank Top station on the overnight express and a passenger in the same compartment awoke when the train had reached Stafford and found Whittaker missing and the carriage-door open. The passenger informed the conductor and a search of the train was made. Whittaker was later found on the line near Whitmore station between Crewe and Stafford. He was taken to Crewe hospital and was operated upon but died at 2pm the following day from injuries sustained.

(The Burnley Express and Clitheroe Advertiser 20 April 1910)

In the League, Barnsley faced a bruising five games in fourteen days: home games against Manchester City and West Bromwich Albion at Oakwell and trips to Clapton Orient, Leicester Fosse and Lincoln City. A win, two draws and two defeats wasn't the best form leading up to the Cup final. Barnsley were saving themselves for the big occasion. Following their victory over Everton in the semi-final victory, Cup fever had hit the town. There was a scramble for Cup-final tickets and extra trains were chartered to take thousands of Barnsley supporters down to The Palace.

Barnsley's opponents, Newcastle United, were fourth in the First Division and had won the Football League Championship in 1905, 1907 and 1909. They were one of the best sides in England. But the Cup, football's glittering prize, had escaped them. On the morning of the final the *Daily Mirror* mentioned that The Magpies had been in three Cup finals and had lost on each occasion. This was their fourth Cup final in six years. Could they overcome their 'Palace hoodoo' and win it this year?

Tommy's opposite, the influential Newcastle captain Colin Veitch, certainly thought so. Veitch was a clever tactician and thinker. He was active in the players' union and in his spare time enjoyed writing and acting. Respected, intelligent and with his own column in *Thompson's Weekly News,* a leading sports paper, Veitch's views on the game were often sought and he was one of the best-known footballers of the day. Yet despite his boyish looks, public charm and popularity, Veitch had been the losing captain in the final three times running. Tommy aimed to make it a fourth. Newcastle had a team of great players. At centre-half was the Scot, Wilf Low, nicknamed 'The Laughing Cavalier', who smiled at opposing centre-forwards before putting the boot in. On the wing was Jackie Rutherford, known for his speed and control as 'The Newcastle Flyer' and another England international. Inside him was James Howie, known as 'Gentleman Jim' and at centre-forward was Albert Shepherd, a big fee-player from Bolton who possessed a cracking shot. The team were a mix of half Scots, half English and a South African, the Newcastle full-back Tony Whiston. By contrast, Barnsley were an all-English side, mainly from the north, the midlands and Yorkshire, including George Utley and Tommy.

Newcastle's journey to the final had seen them beat Stoke City, Fulham, Blackburn Rovers, Leicester Fosse and Swindon in their semi-final at White Hart Lane. They had scored fifteen goals with three conceded. By comparison, Barnsley had scored

sixteen goals and their defence had conceded just once, all the
way back in the first round at Bloomfield Road in January. It
promised to be a tight, defensive contest.

The three-thirty kick-off in South London gave the supporters
of both teams plenty of time to arrive and enjoy the
attractions of London's Sydenham Park, and wander through
the Crystal Palace exhibition halls. It was a cold day, but
from two-thirty pm the football arena began filling up with
spectators to watch and listen to the marching bands. Just
before three-thirty the two captains led their teams out and
lined up in front of the pavilion to meet Viscount Gladstone
and the FA officials and sing the national anthem. Barnsley,
in red shirts, white shorts and red socks, lined up Mearns,
Downs, Ness, Glendenning, Boyle, Utley, Bartrop, Gadesby,
Lillycrop, Tuffnell and Forman. Newcastle, in their familiar
black-and-white stripes, lined up Lawrence, McCracken,
Whiston, Veitch, Low, Howie, McWilliam, Rutherford,
Shepherd, Higgins and Wilson.

Figure 13. The Barnsley Cup final team

Figure 14. The 1910 Cup Final programme featuring Tommy and Colin Veitch

Figure 15. Tommy shakes hands with Colin Veitch at the start of the Cup final. (Courtesy of Paul Joannau)

The game got underway, and as they had done in their previous Cup games Barnsley took the game to their opponents. Tommy took an early grip on the game, shouting his instructions to the Barnsley forwards and feeding long passes down the wings to Bartrop and Forman. For the first quarter of an hour Veitch's Newcastle were happy to sit back and see what their opponents could do as the two sides had never met before. Barnsley continued to hammer at the Newcastle defence keeping them on the back-foot. Tommy stamped his authority on the game, calling throughout to his defenders and forwards. Barnsley passed the ball around well and kept hold of it. Then, with just over half an hour of the game gone, a crack appeared in the Newcastle back line.

> With eight minutes of the first half remaining, Bartrop picked up a pass from the Barnsley full- back and ran up the pitch, passed McWilliam and crossed the ball into the Newcastle penalty area. Lillycrop rushing forward tried to score, but missed the ball. It appeared Barnsley had missed their chance, but Tufnell, the left inside forward, managed to get a toe to the ball and put it in the net. (*Manchester Guardian*)

Barnsley's goal rattled their opponents, who were clearly shocked for a minute, and for the next ten minutes Newcastle attacked. But Barnsley held on to their lead until referee Ibbotson blew his whistle for half-time. They were halfway there. A nervous captain jogged off the field to enjoy the coolness of the dressing room and a well-earned mug of tea. Fairclough told them all they'd done well and they just needed to hold it together for another forty-five minutes. That was the plan: hold what they had. At four-twenty-five p.m., as he led the Barnsley team out for the second half, fingers crossed, heart thumping, wishing to God, Tommy, who rarely prayed, muttered, 'Forty-five minutes left, forty-five minutes from immortality.' And for the first thirty minutes of the second half the team managed to do hold back the Newcastle flood. The

Manchester Guardian reported: "After half-time Barnsley sat back and defended but it was not until the final 15 minutes that Newcastle were able to mount an effective attack."

The minutes counted down. Fifteen, then fourteen, the hands of the huge clock in the Crystal Palace moved slower and slower. The Barnsley defence fought off wave after wave of attacks from Newcastle, their defence holding up well. Seeing his fourth Cup final slipping away, the Newcastle captain changed the teams tactics. "Newcastle abandoned their 'clever' football and took on Barnsley by running at them. Shephard had a goal disallowed apparently for offside." (*Manchester Guardian*)

Newcastle were coming closer to scoring but Barnsley held their nerve and their slender lead. Tommy shouted instructions to the Barnsley forwards to get back and defend. They were almost there as the minutes ticked on. Twelve minutes left. In the stand John Boyle nervously checked his pocket watch. Over in the Pavilion, the Barnsley secretary's wife was certain of victory. She removed the red ribbon from her umbrella and tied it to one handle the Cup. It was a premature move. The game wasn't won, God had yet to hand them victory.

With eight minutes left Newcastle's Rutherford headed the ball into the Barnsley net, but wait a minute, was he offside? Tommy thought so and he and several of the Barnsley players ran over and remonstrated with the referee, claiming Rutherford had scored from an offside position. But referee Ibbotson raised his arm and pointed to the centre-circle. The goal stood. Play re-started and Newcastle bombarded a shocked Barnsley defence trying to seek a winner. Finally, referee Ibbotson blew his whistle for full-time. Tommy stood in the centre-circle, disbelieving the result. Like the rest of the Barnsley players, he felt robbed of the win. The Barnsley players couldn't believe that after holding out for so long they'd been robbed of victory in the final minutes. Veitch still hadn't won at The Palace, and as the two teams shook hands at the end it was the Newcastle skipper who was the more relieved captain. His men had escaped to fight another day.

The replay was scheduled for the following Thursday afternoon, 28 April, at Goodison Park. Both clubs faced a fixture pile-up. Newcastle had two League games against Bristol City away on the Monday and Aston Villa away on Wednesday, just twenty-four hours before the Cup final replay. Barnsley also had a League match to fit in, away at Grimsby Town on the Tuesday afternoon. Newcastle won at Bristol City three-nil but then went down four-nil at Villa Park having played a weakened team. At Cleethorpes, Barnsley were hammered seven-nil by Grimsby as Arthur Fairclough rested some of his key players.

Thursday morning dawned and supporters of both clubs missed a day's pay and set off early for Merseyside via scores of trains. Around 20,000, it was estimated, were travelling over from Barnsley. Sixty-nine thousand crammed into Goodison Park before the gates were locked with thousands still outside. Some supporters managed to break into Goodison, only to be driven back by a dozen mounted constables and "a posse of men on foot" said the *Manchester Guardian*. Both teams and their supporters must have been exhausted after the weeks travelling to and from matches.

Newcastle made one change from the first game, Jack Carr replacing the injured Tony Whiston in defence, while Barnsley were unchanged from the first game. The weather in the afternoon turned awful; heavy showers made the pitch heavy and would strain every sinew. Before the match began the overcrowding caused by thousands of gatecrashers caused the crowd to spill onto the pitch. The crowd problems went on well into the game, with mounted police patrolling the perimeter of the pitch to keep the spectators away. The same referee as the Final, Mr Ibbotson, got the replay underway, and the

TOMMY BOYLE − BROKEN HERO

Manchester Guardian's reporter noted that Newcastle were a transformed side:

> The Newcastle half-backs held the Barnsley forward line throughout the match. Their defence was also improved with Carr playing much better than Whiston. Lawrence in goal was troubled only once, when caught off his line he was forced to make a diving save when Bartrop broke through. The Newcastle forward line was also considerably improved. Barnsley played their hard, rough game but they were defeated by a rejuvenated Newcastle team who despite the heavy, wet ground played a mixed game blending long passes with dribbling and runs forward.

After a goal-less first half with chances for both sides, it was Newcastle who broke the deadlock in the second half with a goal from centre-forward Albert Shepherd. Then, ten minutes later, a second goal from Shepherd sealed the victory for United. Fred Mearns in the Barnsley goal had stopped most of what came his way and Tommy had twice cleared efforts off the line. After four Cup finals, Colin Veitch had finally got his victory and later commented in his column "only miracles prevented us from scoring".

Having collected their runners-up medals, Tommy and his teammates stood together and looked on as the Cup was presented to the winners by Lord Derby and the Lady Mayoress of Liverpool. The MP for Barnsley, F.E. Smith, thanked both the teams, but his speech was drowned out by the cheering of thousands of jubilant Geordies who now occupied most of the Goodison pitch.

Hands on hips, Tommy looked on as Veitch and his team mates posed for photographs and paraded the Cup around Goodison Park, to the delight of their supporters, a hollow feeling in his stomach. Defeat at this level was hard to take. He had felt robbed after the first game at The Palace and hadn't forgotten it. A feeling of ambition unfulfilled, so near and yet so far, mortality and not immortality. Another season with bugger-all to show for it apart from a runners-up medal. *A losers medal.* He hated losing. He hated losing at anything, to anybody. It showed in his mood and his temper. He wanted to be first and the best. Second place counted for nothing. Only winning the Cup made you immortal, as Veitch had now become, after his fourth final! *What in Christ did you have to do to win the bloody thing?* He looked across the pitch at the Newcastle captain. The celebrity, the hero, the man of the moment was being carried shoulder-high around the pitch by scores of joyous Newcastle supporters. His picture would be in every paper tomorrow. Thousands of happy Geordies struck up 'The Blaydon Races', their caps thrown in the air in mutual celebration. Tommy took a final look around Goodison Park through gritted teeth. Shaking his head briefly, he sought the embracing darkness of the players' tunnel and a fast train home to Yorkshire. It was a bitter conclusion to the season for Barnsley, sweetened only by the one-hundred-pound bonus the team were awarded a share in for reaching the final.

But despite the disappointment of losing the Cup replay, a wound which would take a long time to heal, Tommy had shown what he was capable of. He didn't know it, but a number of club secretaries and scouts were present at Goodison. Some of them had been at the Palace a few days before and would be filing their reports the following day. Tommy's name would be mentioned in several of them. Barnsley had played to more than 150,000 people in their Cup run. They had battled their way through to the Cup final, against all the odds, a major feat for a Second Division team. They had nearly pulled it off in the first match and had taken Newcastle to a replay only to lose at the end of a long, tiring season.

The 1910 Barnsley Continental Tour

After a long season of forty-seven games in the League and Cup, the Barnsley Board had also been busy organising an eleven-match European tour taking in France, Germany, Austria and Hungary that departed just a week after the Cup replay on 4 May.

*Figure 16. Barnsley in Budapest on their summer
European tour 1910*

*Figure 17. The Dubonnet Cup competition in Paris 1910.
(Both pictures courtesy of David Wood)*

The first match of the tour took place in Paris for the Dubonnet Cup against the losing FA Cup semi-finalists Swindon Town on 5 May. The match was played at the Parc des Princes Stadium in front of around 5,000 spectators.

> The Frenchmen seem to have been highly delighted with the match, which was not in any sense a "holiday game." Barnsley played vigorous football, but completely lost their heads towards the finish, when the Town led by two-one, especially after Boyle had missed a penalty. The kick was given against Tout for handling, but Boyle shot straight into Skiller's hands. (*Swindon Advertiser*)

The Reds lost two-one, the Barnsley goal scored by George Lillycrop and with Tommy missing the penalty to equalise it had been close. The Barnsley captain was unhappy at losing another trophy in such quick succession.

> Mr Allen, the Swindon secretary, did not hide from me, after the match, the pleasure it gave him to take this magnificent Cup back to Swindon. Boyle, the efficient Barnsley captain, could not conceal his disappointment of not winning the Cup. "Allow us to play the return match next year," said he to me. Fear not brave Tommy, the applause of the public will console you. (*Swindon Advertiser*)

After Paris, the Barnsley party travelled on to Germany where they got the Swindon defeat out of their system. They beat Karlsruhe six-nil and followed that performance with a stunning twelve-two victory over AK Graz where the local press said the Reds had played "like one of the finest teams in the world". The team received the news of the death of His Majesty the King, Edward VII on 6 May and that his son, the forty-four-year-old George V, had taken the throne as the new King. Tommy managed to find the net in the next game with a penalty against the Budapest Gymnastic Club in a five-one win and the following game Barnsley scored seven in a game against the Hungarian Gymnastic Club.

Boyle kicks the bucket

In their sixth game of the tour, Barnsley were up against the Francestown (Ferencvaros) Gymnastic Club, the current Hungarian champions. This was a much more tightly contested affair. On a hot day and in front of a partisan crowd of 12,000, Ferenc took an early lead only for Wilf Bartrop to equalise. But in the afternoon heat, Tommy lost his temper. David Wood describes the scene:

> The home trainer had placed a pail of cool lemon water by the touchline to quench the thirst of his team in the heat of the day. Throughout the match, the Ferenc players were constantly leaving the field for refreshment while Barnsley soldiered on in the heat manfully. Eventually the injustice became too much for captain Tommy Boyle who walked over to the Ferenc bench and with a huge kick sent the juice flying in all directions. (*Lifting The Cup: The Story of Battling Barnsley, 2010*)

All hell broke loose among the two teams. It upset the home crowd, who were only happy when Ferenc scored a second goal which prevented a full-blown riot starting.

At the end of a gruelling tour, Barnsley had played eleven, won nine and lost only twice in the games against Swindon and to the Hungarian Champions. They could go home feeling a sense of achievement having played good football throughout and had proudly represented their country.

The 1910–11 season started for Barnsley with a two-all draw at home to Wolves in a run that brought only three wins before Burnley arrived at Oakwell on 26 November. Tommy knew Burnley reasonably well. Uncle John and his family lived at Worsthorne, a small village just outside the town and he visited them whenever Barnsley were in town. It was the first time that the new Burnley secretary, John Haworth, had visited Oakwell, and the first time he had seen the Barnsley captain in the flesh. Haworth's Burnley won the match one nil, but throughout the game Howorth's attention was drawn to the Barnsley captains prescence, his constant running and desire to be in the thick of the action the whole game. He had never shut up throughout the whole game, barking his instructions to his players, loud enough for the Oakwell turnstile attendants to hear his running commentary.

Up to Christmas, Barnsley had won just four games. Tommy had missed a number of matches through illness. He suffered with his chest in the wintertime, taking after his mother in that respect, and his old job at the pit wouldn't have helped. The team clearly missed their leader and struggled without him. Arthur Fairclough knew that Barnsley needed strengthening but the Board were again struggling to make ends meet, despite the income from the Cup run the previous season. Tommy's health got better over Christmas and he was back louder than ever and ready for another crack at the Cup in January.

In the first round of the competition, Barnsley travelled to Watford's Cassio Road ground and won two-nil with George Lillycrop and Tommy scoring the goals. In the second round Barnsley had been drawn away against Lancashire rivals Burnley at Turf Moor on 4 February. Barnsley lost the match two-nil and their Cup quest was over for yet another year. During the game, the Burnley secretary, John Haworth was again struck by the performance of the Barnsley centre-half. He noticed that he certainly wasn't tall for a central defender at five foot seven, but he made up for height with his speed. He was quick, the thick calf muscles giving him good traction and acceleration over short distances in the mud. He could head, pass accurately and run with the ball. He looked a bit comical with his shirt tucked into the long shorts that looked ten sizes too big, but no one laughed at him. No one dared. In fact, he'd handed out several rollickings to his own players during the game and none of them had offered a word in reply. They were scared to death of him.

Howarth's mind was made up. Shortly after the match, he met with the Burnley chairman Harry Windle who had also witnessed Boyle's performance from the stand. After their meeting an offer for Tommy was put to the Barnsley board over the after-match drinks. Burnley's offer was turned down. Fairclough claimed that other clubs were interested, bigger clubs, and Barnsley could demand a big fee for their prize asset. Burnley would have to up the price if they wanted Tommy Boyle.

Back in the League, Barnsley found themselves bottom of the Second Division by 11 March. Their fortunes picked up, winning two games and then going on a nine-game unbeaten run. Going into the final game against Derby at the Baseball Ground, Barnsley were fourth from bottom on twenty-eight points. They had to win the match to avoid re-election to the League. They lost, five-one, and were at the mercy of the League's selection committee at the end of May.

Chapter 6: Burnley

Figure 18. The Mitre, Burnley

After securing the votes they needed for another season, Barnsley lost their first game of the 1911-12 season at Huddersfield, then won three games on the trot including away games against Birmingham City and Glossop North End. The previous season had seen just one away win all season. The Reds had doubled that tally and the season was only a fortnight old. Barnsley were bang on form. After four games, they were third in the table behind early League leaders, Burnley.

During the summer break, Arthur Fairclough had been busy in the transfer market. A new reserve centre-half, Ernest Hanlan, had arrived at Oakwell from Darlington. After Tommy had read the story of his arrival in the newspaper he knew he was on his way. He'd seen it happen with Billy Silto and all the others. The decision to sell him had already been made and it was just a matter of time, but where would he be going? At least the bank would be happy and the club could balance its books again. A big factor in selling Tommy was that he was due a benefit after five years' continuous service at Oakwell. The benefit fee for players in Division Two at that time was around two hundred and fifty pounds, a tidy sum for a struggling football club, equal to around half the gate receipts for a match. The Barnsley board had a choice. They could hold on to their inspirational captain and lose two hundred and fifty pounds, or sell him and raise as much money as possible and get the buying club to pay Tommy two-hundred-and-fifty-pounds as a cut of the proceeds.

Hull City were visitors to Oakwell on Saturday 23 September. On the Friday night before, Tommy had gone to bed around eleven when he heard a car pull up outside the house. Cars were a rare sight in Platts Common; only the local doctor and colliery manager had one. Along Hawshaw Terrace, curtains twitched to see who was outside at that hour. Three smartly dressed men emerged from the car. From the upstairs window, Tommy could make out his boss, Arthur Fairclough, but the other two men he'd never seen before. He went downstairs and let them in. Pat Boyle was still up and put the kettle on the range. Arthur Fairclough introduced the two men to Tommy as John Catlow and James Harrison. Both men were directors from Burnley Football Club and had come over to talk to him about a transfer to Burnley. A meeting to discuss the transfer had already taken place at Oakwell that had gone on from five p.m. until almost eleven. The five men talked long into the night. It was four in the morning when finally a deal was struck, signatures made on contracts, hands shaken and all parties were happy. It was agreed Tommy could play against Hull City in the morning and he would become a Burnley player from the following Monday morning.

In a village like Platts Common it was hard to keep anything a secret, especially something that was going on outside number fifty-four Hawshaw Terrace where the whole village knew the Barnsley football team captain lived. The word got around. Rumours spread. By Saturday afternoon, half the crowd at Oakwell knew something was going on. Tommy turned out against Hull City. There he was, the captain in a red shirt. Leaving? Nay, he can't be. With captain Tommy Boyle in charge of his last game for Barnsley, they proceeded to lose to Hull by two goals to one. No announcement was made to the crowd in the match programme and the Oakwell faithful all thought Tommy was still a Barnsley player. But by Monday morning the news presses in Burnley were rolling with the story. The fee Burnley had paid was reported as one thousand one hundred and fifty pounds, a club record, and the player would receive two hundred and fifty pounds as a transfer fee to offset the benefit he would have received. When the story broke in South Yorkshire, the Barnsley supporters couldn't believe it. Some of them sent their season tickets back in disgust and Tommy's teammates announced publicly that they were saddened to lose such a great player. Arthur Fairclough said, "[Tommy] Boyle was a gem amongst jewels, and [I am] sorry to lose his services."

It was an abrupt end to Tommy's five years at Barnsley. There he'd learned his trade as a professional footballer at his home-town club, not far from where he was born and raised. Now twenty-five [though twenty-three in his own football years] he was saying goodbye to Platts Common, the village he'd lived in all his life. The place where he had tormented the neighbours kicking a rag football up and down Hagues Yard. The place where he had worked in the colliery from twelve-years-old and had seen things he could not talk about. The place where he had tasted his first pint with his dad in The Royal Oak. And in all that time, the place had hardly changed.

Just after dawn on Wednesday 27 September, wearing his Sunday suit and cap, Tommy picked up his kitbag and said his goodbyes. Pat and John told him to look after himself before he was surrounded by four distraught sisters in tears at the thought of their little brother leaving home. He told them all he'd be back on Saturday after the match and to have the tea on the table at six. As he opened the front door and stepped outside, it looked like the whole street had turned out to see him off. As he walked up the road towards town and the railway station he must have wondered whether he'd done the right thing.

The stopping train made its slow journey across the Pennines, chugging its way through the narrow valleys before finally arriving at its destination. As Tommy walked out of the station he dropped his kitbag, raised the brim of his cap and took in the scene from the railway bridge. The town rested in the base of a broad valley surrounded by farmland and rolling hills. The verdigris dome of the town hall clock tower stood out like a beacon above a thousand terraced streets, mills and factories, their jagged rooftops scattered in all directions like a sea of grey slate. This was a busy town, the place was booming. Mill chimneys and iron furnaces belched smoke and steam. Pit winding wheels spun and trams clanked up and down the main road leading into the centre of town. The smell of industry and the town breweries filled his nostrils, so thick he could taste it.

He checked his pocket watch. It was time to go to work. He picked up his bag, slung it over his shoulder and strode off down the hill towards the town centre, to his new home and teammates at Turf Moor. His signing had created a media frenzy in Burnley. News placards all over the town announced flatteringly "Burnley's Latest Capture, T. Boyle – England's Greatest Centre Half". The Wednesday issue of the *Burnley Gazette and East Lancashire Advertiser* announced "Boyle signed by Burnley", while the *Burnley Express* proclaimed "Boyle of Barnsley becomes a Burnleyite".

Football was the main sporting interest here. Nothing else mattered. Within a thirty-mile radius, there were a dozen football clubs competing in the top two divisions plus a number of strong local sides like Padiham, Nelson, Darwen and Accrington Stanley who each possessed a rich history of their own. In September 1911 Burnley had been in Division Two for ten seasons. As the town's local economy developed, the population grew, and as a consequence the crowds at Turf Moor increased. The Burnley board were ambitious and wanted their share of the limelight like neighbours and five times FA Cup winners Blackburn Rovers. The election to the board of Harry Windle, now chairman, with his business skills and modern outlook, had lifted the prospects of the club and its supporters.

John Haworth, a year into the job as Burnley secretary, was assembling a good squad of talent and was pushing for promotion. Tommy already knew a few of the Burnley players; he'd played against them several times and Haworth had cut training short so most of them could come in to meet their new teammate. Lined up were goalkeeper and local blacksmiths son, Jerry Dawson, full-back Tommy Bamford, half-back Billy Watson and forwards Dick Lindley and Teddy Hodgson. Waiting at the end of the line was his old adversary Bert Freeman, *Gentleman Bert*, who laughed when their eyes met and gave him a warm, welcoming handshake. After the welcomes and lunch, Haworth fixed Tommy up with digs in nearby Stoneyholme. He'd be rooming with Bert Freeman in Rectory Road. Then the press boys wanted a word. Questioned about his transfer he said:

> Thursday I'm Barnsley captain; Friday I'm asked what I would say to going to Burnley. Saturday, 4am my transfer is decided upon. During the afternoon I play my last match on the Oakwell ground for the Reds against the Tigers.

On Saturday I make my first appearance for Burnley against my old club. Last year Burnley came to Barnsley with an offer for my transfer but it was refused. Blackburn Rovers and Oldham came along, but the Barnsley directors refused to be tempted. After some discussions (about the transfer) the directors agreed to accept my own estimate and consequently I receive £250 in cash in place of the proceeds of the benefit. I have always regarded Burnley as the Barnsley of Lancashire. And the warm-hearted Burnley lads and lasses who follow their team through thick and thin make many visiting teams envy the Turf Moorites of their supporters." (*Thompsons Weekly*)

The fee Tommy received was a small fortune, around two years' wages for a manual worker. He could have bought a new house with it and still had change. The *Burnley Gazette* mentioned that "Aston Villa, Newcastle and Everton had also been keen to secure his signature." Why he hadn't gone to a First Division club with more resources and bigger crowds we'll never know. One reason could have been his strong family ties, with his Uncle John's family living nearby in Worsthorne providing a stabilising influence and a bed if he'd needed one.

Haworth brought Tommy straight into the Burnley team at centre-half and he pulled on the claret and blue shirt for the first time at Oakwell on the Saturday. Also making his Burnley debut that day was inside-forward Teddy Hodgson, who made the step up from the reserve team. Burnley lined up at Oakwell: Dawson, Reid (captain), Bamford, Swift, Boyle, Watson, Morley, Hodgson, Freeman, Mountford and Mayson. Barnsley lined up: Clegg, Downs, Taylor, Glendenning, Hanlon, Utley, Bartrop, Lillycrop, Cornock, Tufnell and Leavey. Taylor took over as the Barnsley captain and Ernest Hanlon came into the Barnsley team to replace Tommy at centre-half. The following Wednesday's *Burnley Gazette* headline ran, "Dawson's Brilliance and Burnley's Magnificent

Defence". At a rain-lashed Oakwell, Tommy was given a warm reception from the 8,000 Oakwell faithful when he ran out before kick-off. He responded with applause to each side of the ground and showed he hadn't forgotten where home was. After the game got underway Burnley took the lead on twenty minutes through a penalty, following a foul on Bert Freeman as he was put through with just the goalkeeper to beat. Barnsley answered with several counterattacks but were foiled by the Burnley half-back line of Swift, Boyle and Watson. Before half-time, Leavey hit the underside of the Burnley crossbar with a shot but the ball was judged not to have crossed the line and at half-time Burnley led by the one goal. Burnley controlled much of the second half with Tommy initiating several moves. Then, with ten minutes of the game left, the game came to life as Barnsley were awarded a free-kick. The five Barnsley forwards packed the Burnley penalty box and Cornock headed in for the equaliser. In the end both sides settled for the draw.

Tommy made his home debut the following week against Nottingham Forest on 7 October in front of a large crowd of 16,333 at Turf Moor who had turned out to see the new signing make his entrance. They were not disappointed. He made an instant impression in central defence as Burnley beat Forest two-nil. With eight games of the season gone, The Clarets topped the Second Division. Things were looking good and 'promotion favourites' was already being mentioned in the press. Next, Burnley travelled to Bradford Park Avenue and a huge Second Division crowd of 25,000 turned out to see what was billed as the 'Roses' battle. Burnley lost two-one, their opponents' first goal scored by Bradford's half-back, George Halley, with a screaming twenty-five-yard shot that gave Dawson no chance. Herbert Bamlett, the match referee on the day, then allowed Bradford a second goal, after a goalmouth scramble where the ball had been handled by Bradford's Little before it was eventually put into the net. After a draw against Chelsea, Burnley notched up four straight wins to go into

December sitting on top of the Second Division with twenty-two points.

Philip and Lady Ottoline Morrell

The year before Tommy arrived in Burnley, two new faces arrived in town on the local political scene, keen to make connections with the football club. Philip Morrell became the Liberal Member of Parliament for Burnley in December 1910, winning the seat after a recount with a tiny majority of just 173 votes. He was supported through his campaign by his wife, the aristocrat and society hostess, Lady Ottoline Morrell.

Figure 19. Philip and Lady Ottoline Morrell,
portraits by Henry Lamb

Ottoline Morrell cut quite a striking figure. Unusually tall at six feet, with green eyes and flame-gold hair, she was not particularly beautiful, but become the centre of attention whenever she entered a room. She wore the most flamboyant clothes: white muslin and lace flowing skirts, or Turkish harem trousers, topped off with giant feather hats, a look that wouldn't have been out of place in the hippy movement fifty years later. She would stand out a mile in Burnley, which was exactly the reaction she wanted in injecting some colour into local politics.

The Morrell's home at 44 Bedford Square, Bloomsbury became a magnet for artisans, poets, authors and aspiring politicians, including people like; D.H. Lawrence, Bertrand Russell, Henry Lamb, Siegfried Sassoon, Virginia Woolf, David Lloyd-George, Winston Churchill and Charlie Chaplin. Ottoline made regular visits to the town both during and after the election and recorded her visits in her journal. On her first impressions of Burnley she wrote,

> The blackness and ugliness of Burnley appalled me – and seemed to enter me, but soon I grew accustomed to it. The excitement and enthusiasm of the Burnley people was astonishing. They are so much more alive, vigorous and intelligent than the southerners. Apart from their work in factories, the men and women at a place like Burnley have but little mental development. There was certainly one small technical school, but to advance out into the world of science and art was very rare.

> But interesting as life on the edge of Burnley was, I found it intensely depressing. My spirit seemed to roam over that gloomy town and found no foothold, nowhere could I rest, and I felt so intensely sorry for and sympathetic with these delightful, kind and emotional people, bereft of what was to me so essential: ecstasy and all enjoyment of art and beauty. As I remember visits to great weaving-sheds, or gatherings of any sort that we attended, I have vivid recollections of excitable floods of enthusiastic affection poured out upon us. As I went through the weaving shed- the noise was so great that I could not hear what was said to me even when it was shouted quite close to my ear.

> Sometimes the girls, despairing of making me hear by words, would kiss me instead! They used to understand each other by lip-reading.

Ottoline eventually took the town to heart and later spoke of the "warm-hearted people of Burnley". The Morrell's had an open marriage. Ottoline had met Bertrand Russell in 1907 and the pair conducted a lifelong affair until she died in 1938. In Miranda Seymour's *Life on a Grand Scale*, it is said that Ottoline would wave Philip off to his constituency from King's Cross, as Russell's train would be arriving on another platform.

Two months after Tommy's arrival at Burnley, the November 1911 local tradesmen's dinner dance was held at the Town Hall. Along with several other distinguished guests, Philip and Ottoline were present and were introduced to the evenings guests, the Burnley football team. According to the *Burnley News*, she was said to have danced with "Burnley's football hero," though the report didn't name which player it was.

Billy Nesbitt

A month after Tommy's arrival, another new face arrived at Turf Moor in October. Nineteen-year-old Billy Nesbitt was from Todmorden, a few miles from Burnley and looked like he'd just left school. Billy had been deaf since birth and was serving a weaving apprenticeship at the time John Haworth saw him playing for Portsmouth Rovers, a local junior team. His speed on the wing, dribbling and ball control were amazing. It was as if with a lack of hearing, God had given him extra ability in his feet. Haworth noticed that his teammates communicated with him by either tugging his shirt or through hand signals using a kind of footballers semaphore. Nesbitt had driven the referee into fits of rage as he couldn't hear the whistle each time he'd strayed offside. When the referee called him over for a word, Billy just cupped his hand to his ear and shrugged his shoulders. Like Tommy, there was something about the lad Haworth liked – his work rate. He'd never stopped running for the whole ninety minutes, chasing every opportunity that came his way. But could he turn a lad with a hearing impairment into a professional footballer and play the game at the highest level? It was a gamble, but Haworth thought it was worth a try. He talked to the mill manager and they agreed to suspend Billy's apprenticeship for a year. Billy signed as an amateur as he was also a keen runner and was worried that becoming a professional would affect his amateur status. Later Haworth met with Billy's parents and they finally persuaded him to sign professional terms as he'd then receive a wage. Haworth had uncovered another gem. The plan forming in his mind for a team built on speed down the wings and a five-man attack backed up by a strong attacking half-back line was falling nicely into place.

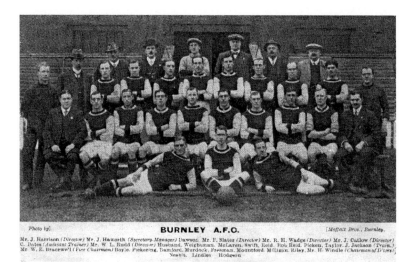

Figure 20. The Burnley team 1911

Captain Boyle and the Lancashire Cup

The Lancashire Cup competition was open to clubs at all levels in Lancashire and was organised on the lines of the FA Cup but limited to the county. Burnley's first entry into the Lancashire Cup had been in 1882, where they were soundly knocked out in the first round by Astley Bridge, eight-nil. Burnley won the Cup for the first time eight years later in 1890, beating Blackburn two-nil in the final, and had been in the final on four occasions since then but had lost each time. After a bye in round one, Tommy got his first taste of Lancashire Cup action in the second round on 9 October 1911, Burnley beating St. Helen's Town seven-nil. After a three-one away win in the third round at First Division Oldham, in a game that saw Tommy take over as Burnley team captain from full-back Henry Reid, Burnley were paired against neighbours and local rivals Blackburn Rovers in the semi-finals at Ewood Park. Rovers were a strong side and were having an excellent season in the First Division.

It would be Tommy's first taste of the oldest and most passionate local derby in English football. Tommy knew little of Rovers, except that they were in the First Division and he had never played against them before. The new captain led his team out and The Clarets went on to record a three-one victory at Ewood Park. It was Burnley's first victory over their rivals since 1899 and Burnley were through to the Lancashire Cup final. The club, the Burnley supporters and the town was ecstatic. The final of the Lancashire Cup took place on 13 December, where Burnley met First Division side Bolton Wanderers at Burnden Park. Both teams fielded a full-strength side. Bolton proved to be the superior side on the day and had the benefit of home advantage running out eventual winners, four-one. But despite the defeat, Tommy and the team had shown their mettle by putting out two First Division sides along the way and developing a passion for Cup football. It would be valuable preparation for the FA Cup competition coming up in January.

Three days after the Lancashire Cup final, full-back Dave Taylor arrived at Turf Moor, signing from FA Cup holders' Bradford City. The former Glasgow Rangers and Motherwell defender was one of the fastest full-backs in the game, having started like Tommy with a keen interest in athletics, winning races at the Highland Games. Harry Windle led the negotiations to sign Taylor that went on from "tea-time till' midnight," according to the *Burnley Express*. The fee was another four-figure sum. To begin the busy Christmas fixtures the Clarets recorded a good away win, five-one at Elland Road, and on New Year's Eve they were second in the table behind Derby County having remained unbeaten over the festive period.

January 1912 and Tommy was looking forward to the first round of the FA Cup against fellow Second Division side Fulham at Craven Cottage. After Burnley's huge spending spree on players, big things were expected. But the Cup being what it is, and home advantage being key, Fulham beat Burnley in a tight match, two-one. There would be no Cup glory for Tommy again this season. No champagne, no immortality. *Nothing for losers*. The Cup had eluded him again. Meanwhile, his old club Barnsley had done well and secured a nil-nil draw away at Birmingham City in their first-round tie. Burnley would have to put their Cup disappointment behind them and concentrate on the League. If Burnley could get promotion in Tommy's first season, that would be quite special.

Hull City were the next visitors at Turf Moor and were well beaten by five goals to one. Away at Cleethorpes in the next game, The Clarets lost to Grimsby but then went on a run of ten games undefeated. By Easter, having played thirty-four of their thirty-eight games, Burnley were six points clear at the top of the Second Division and promotion looked a certainty. Burnley had stayed undefeated at home all season and had picked up eight victories on the road.

On the morning of 16 April, the newspapers were filled with the terrible tragedy of the sinking of the *Titanic* on her maiden voyage and the loss of more than 1,500 lives. The whole country was in shock. In nearby Colne, the town awaited news of Wallace Hartley, the *Titanic*'s bandmaster. By 20 April, with one game of their season left, Burnley had dropped to second place behind Derby County on goal difference but could still go up as champions. It was very tight at the top. Burnley had to win at Wolves and they would be promoted but Chelsea could overtake Burnley if they won all their three remaining games.

Chelsea's first game in hand was at Stamford Bridge against Blackpool, who they despatched four-one. Their next game was a visit to Oakwell. Tommy and the whole of Burnley were wishing Barnsley could do Burnley a favour and win or at least take a point. But Barnsley had had a busy week. The previous Saturday they had played in the Cup final against West Bromwich Albion, which had ended goal-less. The following Monday they had had a League fixture against Derby. The Cup final replay was on the Wednesday afternoon and Chelsea would visit Oakwell just twenty-four hours later. A punishing four games in six days.

Barnsley beat West Bromwich Albion and won the Cup replay on the Wednesday afternoon. On the Thursday afternoon before the Chelsea players came out at Oakwell, Barnsley skipper George Utley proudly paraded the Cup around the pitch to massive cheers from the home supporters. It was a carnival atmosphere. Chelsea, the more focused side, spoiled the celebrations, winning two-nil. The Londoners were now level on points with Burnley, but The Clarets still had a superior goal average. It was all down to the final game of the season. Burnley away at Wolves and Chelsea at home to Bradford Park Avenue. Both needed to win to be sure of second spot. Statistically, a one-nil win for Burnley would mean Chelsea needed ten goals to overtake them. Burnley had a slight edge going into the final day, but they were away from home. In an age with no radio or television, the solitary telephone in the secretary's office at Turf Moor was the only means of getting the result of Burnley's away matches quickly, or by waiting for 'the pinks,' the post-match sports papers. For Burnley supporters waiting eagerly outside Turf Moor after the final reserve match, it was nail-biting. When it came, it was bad news. Burnley had lost at Molineux two-nil and Chelsea had beaten Bradford Park Avenue one-nil to steal in and take second place.

If the mood outside Turf Moor was bad, it was worse in the away dressing room at Molineux. The players filed in after the match, totally dejected. No one said a word. The place was like a morgue. They all sat staring at the stone floor, unbelieving. 'No champagne tonight then,' said Tommy in an attempt to break the gloom. Again there would be nothing for the captain. *Nowt for losers.* Someone did manage to eventually rustle up a crate of beer, the corks quickly pulled and the bottles passed round. But it was small consolation. Third place, Burnley's best position in ten years, but it left a bitter taste, none more than with the captain. He had seen Barnsley covered in glory after winning the Cup and found out later that Burnley's rivals, Blackburn Rovers, had won the League Championship. The papers were full of it. Tommy knew that the team had got better: they had scored more goals than any other team in the Second Division but they had dropped points when they shouldn't have done, certainly towards the end. There was still work for John Haworth's side to do before they became the finished article.

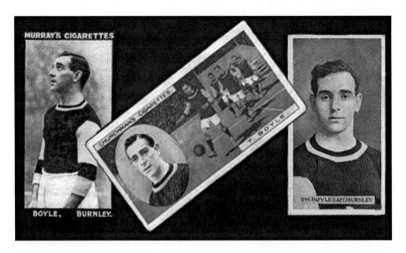

Figure 21. A selection of Tommy Boyle cigarette cards.

The players reported back for pre-season training in August in determined mood. Following the disappointment of Molineux, and after spending a fortune on players, Burnley had to deliver this season. The board demanded it, the supporters deserved it and captain Tommy Boyle was sick to his back teeth of ending up with nothing. This would be his first full-season as captain and a chance to make amends for the disappointment of the last year. The team would have to get tougher and meaner if they were to grind out the results needed to gain promotion or with the Cup. Unusually, the 1912-13 fixtures had given The Clarets four home games out of their first five matches. Burnley took points in all their home games but their away form was poor. The first win on the road came against Cup holders Barnsley with a good four-one win. That result sparked an eleven-match unbeaten run, which saw Burnley climb to the top the table by New Year's Day.

The Clapton Orient Game

Mid-table Clapton Orient were visitors to Turf Moor on 4 January 1913 for what turned into one of the ugliest games ever seen. On a heavy pitch, Tommy won the toss and defended the Bee Hole end in the first half, and after an early Orient onslaught the Burnley captain gradually took control of the game. The first incident involved Teddy Hodgson, who was badly fouled by Orient's defender Hind. A fight started, the referee stepping in to separate the two. Then someone in the crowd threw a lump of clinker at the Clapton player that hit him on the cheek. Another fight started before the referee managed to calm tempers. By half-time Burnley were three goals to the good. The referee spoke to John Haworth about the clinker-throwing incident and a policeman was despatched to that side of the ground.

Niggling kicks aimed at the Burnley players continued throughout the second half where Dick Lindley completed his hat-trick and put Burnley four-nil up. Then he received a bad cut to the head for his trouble that needed stitching off the field from Doc Hodges. Down to ten-men, Tommy went into attack and scored Burnley's fifth goal. Another bad challenge on Teddy Hodgson put Burnley down to nine men. Fists flew between Hodgson and Hind again and other players were drawn into the brawl to pull them apart. When play resumed Bert Freeman beat an Orient defender who later deliberately kicked him in an off-the-ball incident as Bert walked past him. The next time Bert beat the same defender, the Orient man threw a handful of mud, which caught Bert in the face. Ever the gentleman, Bert just laughed at him, which wound up the Orient player even more. Another brawl started, the referee losing all control as one player tried to get at another and another fist fight started. Tommy grabbed one Orient player by the throat, almost lifting him off the ground. The policeman on the far side of the pitch ran across and managed to help the referee restore order. It had been a tough scrap but they'd stuck together and slugged it out as a team. It had shown that Burnley were no push-around. The fighting spirit and rout of Orient had forged the team into a tougher, meaner outfit that was welcome preparation for the first round of the FA Cup the following week at Elland Road.

FA Cup first round: Leeds City v. Burnley, 11 January 1913

Fourteen special trains were chartered to carry Burnley supporters to the match at Elland Road on 11 January. For anyone who couldn't get to the match, they could go along and see highlights of it the following Monday at St. Andrew's Church Institute.

ST. ANDREW'S
Church Institute Commencing Monday January 13th 1913
Another Great Week of Pictures including
BURNLEY v LEEDS CITY English Cup tie at Leeds.
This topical film will be shown at every performance during
the whole of the week and can only be seen in
Burnley at St. Andrews.
(Burnley Express and Advertiser 11 January 1913)

Burnley spent the week before the Cup tie at Blackpool during a week of awful weather in the Pennines. The snow played havoc and all the chartered trains were cancelled. It still didn't stop half the 13,000 crowd making the trip over from Burnley in the snow somehow. Three members of the FA's International Selection Committee were in the stand, watching the players on display, particularly Tommy and Bert.

At half-past one, four inches of snow covered the pitch and the snow was still falling. The referee arranged for the sidelines to be swept clear and the game started on schedule at three-thirty. With four minutes gone, Teddy Hodgson scored for Burnley as snow continued to fall. Leeds equalised through McLeod, and two minutes after Tommy put Burnley back in front with a direct free kick from outside the penalty area. On twenty-four minutes, Foley equalised again for Leeds before Bert Freeman then got the better of the City defenders and scored twice to put Burnley four-two up before half-time. After the tea interval, with the snow still falling, the referee went over to consult his officials. While they deliberated, the Burnley players engaged in a snowball fight on the pitch, which entertained the crowd, and shortly afterwards the Cup tie was abandoned much to the spectators disgust. The match was replayed the following Wednesday at Elland Road, with Burnley winning three-two to progress to the second round.

The England trial

On Monday 20 January, Tommy and Bert were called into John Haworth's office. The pair had been called up for the International Trial match, England v. The North at Hyde Road in Manchester. As there were a number of injured players who didn't turn out, they had to play opposite each other, Tommy playing in The North side and Bert playing for the England XI. Reports of the match, in which The North won five-nil, told of Tommy and his men outplaying the England XI in every quarter. Tommy marked Bert out of the game, as he had done the last time they had met on opposite sides. "Freeman underwent a complete eclipse, never getting in a shot all afternoon," ran the *Yorkshire Post*. "Freeman did not get many passes but his club mate Boyle was usually too good for him," said the *Daily News*. "Boyle was too good for [Freeman] when the few chances went his way," commented the *Daily Mail*. "Boyle and Cuggy were magnificent," said the *Manchester Guardian*. With the selectors watching and a five-nil resounding victory to the 'Possibles', surely Tommy wouldn't be denied a full England call-up after a performance like that?

In the second round of the Cup, Burnley had been drawn at home against Gainsborough Trinity. Trinity had been voted out of the League at the end of the previous season to be replaced by Lincoln City. With Burnley in fine form and going for promotion, non-League Trinity were very much the underdogs and high-spending Burnley were expected to win easily. Burnley were suffering with injuries to no fewer than nine players and a cartoon of the team on crutches, swathed in bandages and walking with sticks, was displayed in the morning papers. In the first half, Burnley failed to put the ball in the net, owing mainly to the heroics of the Trinity goalkeeper, Ronnie Sewell, who was outstanding, pulling off save after excellent save. Alongside him, Trinity full-backs Sam Gunton and Cliff Jones also played brilliantly. Then, totally against the run of play just before half-time, Trinity broke away and scored. The goal stunned Burnley and the whole of the Turf Moor crowd as the teams left the field for the half-time interval.

During the break with Burnley a goal down, the Burnley chairman Harry Windle visited the Burnley changing room and met with John Haworth. Both had been impressed by the Trinity defence and a big Cup upset could be on the cards. That couldn't be allowed to happen, so Haworth changed the game plan. Whatever he said to the team at half-time worked. In the second half, two quick goals from Bert, a penalty from the captain and a Teddy Hodgson goal won the match four-one. But Trinity's defence had certainly impressed and after the match, when the Gainsborough team had already set off for home, the Burnley board called the Gainsborough officials along with Sewell, Gunton and Jones back to Turf Moor. After talks, all three Trinity players were sold to Burnley. 'Sportsman' the *Burnley Express* football correspondent couldn't believe it. The fee paid for all three players was somewhere around two thousand pounds. A letter in the following week's *Burnley Express* from a supporter calculated that Burnley had spent close to ten thousand pounds on players and ground improvements over the previous three seasons. It was a staggering amount of money for a Second Division club and many Burnley supporters were left wondering where all the money was coming from.

The British Home Championship: Ireland v. England, Windsor Park, Belfast, 15 February 1913

The recognition Tommy had waited for came in a telegram from FA headquarters on Monday 3 February. The FA selectors had selected him as centre-half for the forthcoming Home Championship match against Ireland in Belfast. Tommy became the sixth Burnley player to receive a cap by his country. He would play behind the Middlesbrough centre-forward George Elliot, who he would be defending against in the third round of the FA Cup the following Saturday. It was such an honour to play for your country in those days that the fee the players received just about covered their expenses. Players played for the honour of wearing the white shirt bearing the three lions and the matching white international cap that came with it. It was Tommy's greatest honour of his career. With a full international cap he could now add to his name, 'England International'. He was twenty-seven and at the peak of his fitness. He must have impressed the selectors well enough in the trial in order to get the call-up ahead of numerous other centre-halves playing above him in the First Division.

The British Home Championship tournament had been established in 1884 so that the home nations could compete against each other. Ireland had never beaten the English in any meeting between the countries going back thirty years. England's record was phenomenal: played thirty-one, won twenty-eight, drawn three, lost none, goals for 150, goals against nineteen. England's biggest win on home soil came in 1899, when they beat the Irishmen thirteen-two, whilst nine-one was their best win on Irish soil in a match eleven years before. When the international fixtures for 1913 had been compiled, Ireland had been given three home games. In their opening fixture against Wales, the Irish lost one-nil at Grosvenor Park in Belfast. The English were up next.

Well in advance of the match, the FA selectors thought the Irish game would be another walkover and selected seven new caps for the match. Alongside Tommy in defence and also gaining his first cap was George Utley, his old teammate and the current Barnsley captain. Five other new faces included Charles Buchan, who would later go on to establish *Charles Buchan's Football Monthly*, Frank Cuggy of Sunderland, George Elliot from Middlesbrough, Joe Smith from Bolton Wanderers and Bob Benson from Sheffield United.

England lined-up: Reg Williamson (Middlesbrough) in goal; captain Bob Crompton (Blackburn Rovers) and Bob Benson (Sheffield United) full-backs; half-backs Frank Cuggy (Sunderland); Tommy Boyle (Burnley); George Utley (Barnsley) and forwards Jackie Mordue (Sunderland); Charles Buchan (Sunderland); George Elliot Middlesbrough); Joe Smith (Bolton Wanderers) and George Wall (Manchester United).

Ireland lined up in goal Billy Scott (Leeds City); Willie George McConnell (Bohemians) and Peter Warren (Shelbourne) full-backs; Harry Hampton (Bradford City); Valentine Harris (Everton) and Willie Andrews (Grimsby) half-backs; and forwards Johnny Houston (Linfield); Denis Hannon

(Bohemians); Billy Gillespie (Sheffield United); Jim McAuley (Huddersfield); and Frank Thompson (Bradford City).

Around 22,000 noisy spectators turned out at Windsor Park on a fine Saturday afternoon. Adhering to the form book, England went ahead in the thirty-fifth minute with a debut goal by Charlie Buchan. But five minutes after the re-start it began to go wrong for the visitors. Billie Gillespie from Sheffield United, making his debut at centre-forward for the Irish, scored the equaliser to make it one-all at the interval. Gillespie caused problems all afternoon for the English defence and on the hour mark he popped up again to score a second goal to give Ireland the lead. Windsor Park erupted. Most of the home crowd had never seen their side score a goal, let alone take the lead against the English. England rallied and the home side put ten-men behind the ball. For the last half an hour to break up the play the Irish hoofed the ball into the crowd and out of the ground to wind down the clock. England tried but couldn't break through the mass of Irish defenders who booted the ball away at every opportunity.

After the match the England players were glad to get on the boat back to Liverpool. The day after the team received a mauling in the press and by the England selectors. *The Times* said "It was humiliation for England to be beaten by the Irish – a part amateur team." A jubilant *Irish Times* ran the headline "Ireland defeats England for first time". The *Daily Mirror* wrote "Ireland's Victory after 31 years – scenes of rare enthusiasm", their reporter slating the English defence. The *Manchester Guardian* led with "Great win for Ireland – England Surprised". On Tommy's performance, the *Daily Mirror* said, "Boyle in the centre, after playing finely in the first half, died away in the second. He seemed very tired long before the game finished and was always too far back." The FA's plan to play seven newcomers had backfired and their retribution was swift. Tommy, along with several of the other debutants who played that day, was never selected for England again.

They came without overcoats

FA Cup third round Burnley v. Middlesbrough, Turf Moor, 22 February 1913

In the third round of the Cup, Burnley had drawn Middlesbrough who had beaten Millwall and Queens Park Rangers in their previous rounds. The Turf Moor ticket prices went up, four shillings for the best seats and one shilling on the ground, with programmes a penny each. A big crowd was expected and the match kicked off at three-fifteen to enable all the trains to arrive. Around noon, three trainloads of Middlesbrough fans arrived at Manchester Road station and walked down the hill into town "like a regiment". Sportsman described in the *Burnley Express,*

> wearing red and white rosettes, ribbons, badges, red and white bowler hats, they made themselves heard too with bells, horns and accordions. A remarkable feature of the Middlesbrough brigade was they came without overcoats. The Northern Ironworkers are a sturdy lot.

Nearly 28,000 packed into Turf Moor, providing a noisy atmosphere on a sunny day. A clash of colours meant Burnley played in an all-white strip and they kicked off towards the Bee Hole end. After four minutes, Tommy struck a thirty-yard shot to test Williamson in the Boro' goal. It was a fast-flowing game, the first half evenly matched with opportunities for both sides. The captain managed to get more shots on target and at the interval it was honours even, one-all, with goals from Teddy Hodgson for Burnley and Carr equalising for Middlesbrough.

Thirteen minutes into the second half Burnley had a throw-in. Lindley took the ball down the wing, cut inside defender Hisbent and crossed the ball to Bert, who scored. Two-one to Burnley. The Clarets with their tails in front, continued to attack, and Williamson in goal had to handle more long-range shots from Tommy who hammered the goal at every opportunity. Ten minutes from time, Burnley were awarded a free-kick, taken by

McLaren. Teddy Hodgson passed the ball to an on-rushing Bert, who ran a good thirty yards to score a brilliant goal. Three-one to Burnley at the end and they were into the Cup quarter-finals. Sportsman in the *Express* talked of "Boyles Brilliance" in his role as an attacking centre-back, a role he had relished all afternoon, where he had added to the attacking options of the forward line.

The FA Cup quarter-final:
Blackburn Rovers v. Burnley, Ewood Park, 8 March 1913

When the quarter-final draw was made it threw up a dream tie, an East Lancashire derby. Burnley would play away at First Division and local rivals Blackburn Rovers for a place in the semi-finals. The Clarets would need to be at their best. Five times Cup winners Blackburn were mid-table in Division One and were looking forward to an eleventh semi-final appearance, whereas Burnley had never been beyond the quarter-final stage. Rovers, with home advantage, were the clear favourites and had been beaten semi-finalists in 1911 and 1912; surely with home advantage they couldn't lose out on the final three years running?

It was a glorious day and many Burnley supporters set off early, walking the twelve miles to Ewood Park. For the better-off supporter, two shillings and sixpence would get you to the match in a private wagonette. Burnley collieries closed for the day, and the iron foundries worked overtime on Friday night in order to give workers the Saturday morning off.

Sportsman in the *Express* reported it was the largest, noisiest assembly of people he had ever seen on a football ground, as 43,000 packed into Ewood Park, half of them from Burnley. An array of banners and colours from both sets of supporters decorated the ground.

The only change for Burnley was the introduction of schoolteacher and winger Eddie Mosscrop in place of Mountford. Burnley lined up Dawson, Bamford, Taylor,

McLaren, Boyle, Watson, Mosscrop, Lindley, Freeman, Hodgson and Husband. The match referee was Herbert S. Bamlett of Gateshead. Tommy won the toss and Burnley elected to play with the wind toward the Darwen End.

The game began at a frantic pace with Rovers making the early running. Jerry Dawson was in fine form, saving three consecutive efforts on goal. Burnley gradually got into their stride, Tommy feeding Mosscrop on the wing whose speed caused the Rovers full-back and England captain Bob Crompton problems all afternoon. Tommy carried on where he had left off against Middlesbrough, shooting from distance at every opportunity. In the thirty-third minute Bert Freeman got the better of the Rovers defenders and Blackburn conceded a corner. Eddie Mosscrop took the corner and Tommy ran in and leapt to meet the ball full on his forehead, the ball soaring through Robinson's fingers and into the Rovers net. Sportsman had never heard a celebration like it: "An outburst of enthusiasm the like of which I have never seen on an opponent's ground in the course of my twenty-seven years following Burnley."

Figure 22. Tommy scores against Blackburn Rovers in the FA Cup Qtr-final 1913

In the second half, Rovers fought their way back into the game and Dawson was called on several times to clear, finger-tipping the ball over the crossbar on several occasions. Burnley's defence held together and tackled well and in the latter stages of the half could have extended their lead with efforts from Bert, Eddie Mosscrop and a fine effort from Tommy. Finally after a hard-fought game, Referee Bamlett blew the whistle, and Tommy, nursing a cut forehead and black eye for his trouble, stood with his foot on the ball in the centre-circle. Ewood Park was becoming a lucky ground for him having just notched up his second victory there. Burnley were in the semi-finals of the FA Cup for the very first time. A jubilant Phillip Morrell sent a telegram to Harry Windle: "[I]t is with great delight that I have read in today's papers of the magnificent victory won by our team yesterday at Blackburn. Please accept and convey to Captain Boyle and all members of the team my warmest congratulations."

As the reality of their Cup semi-final place had sunk in, two more additions arrived at Turf Moor: right-half George Halley, signed from Bradford Park Avenue, and Tom Charlton, a centre-forward from Stockport County. There was a rumour that the club also had wanted Downs from Barnsley. The twenty-five-year old Halley's fee was another record-breaking figure of around one thousand two hundred pounds, and he had also been selected for the Scottish International trial game. John Haworth's jigsaw was almost complete.

Halley, Boyle and Watson
League Division Two: Burnley v. Bury, Turf Moor, 15 March 1913

Figure 23. George Halley, Tommy Boyle and Billy Watson

With Dawson, Taylor, McLaren and Husband all injured, George Halley came straight into the side for the important League game at Turf Moor against Bury. Ronnie Sewell deputised in goal, Cliff Jones in defence for Taylor, Halley for McLaren and Mountford for Husband.

Tommy won the toss and the team played toward the Bee Hole end. After twenty minutes Bury took the lead with a goal through Peake, after Burnley keeper Sewell slipped in the mud while jumping up to take the cross. Burnley equalised on thirty-five minutes, with Bert scoring, who then added a second goal two minutes later. Just before half-time, a corner from Eddie Mosscrop dropped nicely at Tommy's feet, who blasted in the third to give Burnley two well-earned points. "Halley made a favourable impression, he shone on Saturday," noted Sportsman in the *Burnley Express* as The Clarets ran out winners three-one. The half-back trinity of Halley, Boyle and Watson had begun in fine style.

Boyle vs. Bainbridge: Round One

Burnley travelled to the seaside on Good Friday, 21 March to meet Blackpool. With eight League games remaining, Burnley were second in the League, a point ahead of Birmingham in third place. It was tight at the top and Burnley needed to win to keep the momentum going for promotion and not to get distracted by the Cup. Blackpool were deep in re-selection trouble and were three points away from safety. They badly needed points to stay in the League. George Halley kept his place in defence and Jerry Dawson and Dave Taylor both returned. Burnley had chartered a train to bring their sixteen-man squad to the seaside for the match and then take them straight down to London for the game with Fulham the following day.

With the match twenty-five minutes old and still goal-less, the bad challenges started. Dave Taylor was first on the receiving end. Then Halley was kicked on the arm so badly he was unable to take a throw-in. After a corner to Burnley, Tommy headed the ball into the net but the goal was disallowed when the referee judged his elbows were used to gain an advantage. Tommy appealed but the referee wasn't listening. Bert Freeman was brought down in the penalty area and Jones, the Blackpool full-back, handled the ball as it was going over the line. The captain stepped up to take the penalty. He put the ball on the spot and stepped back his customary ten paces, ran in and managed to only hit the ball straight at Fiske the goalkeeper who punched the ball up into the air. Seeing an opportunity, Tommy ran forwards and knocked the goalkeeper into the net and the ball dropped over the crossbar. A fist fight started between Tommy, the Blackpool goalkeeper and his protector, the Blackpool centre-forward Joe Bainbridge. Tommy came off worst, nursing his second black eye in a fortnight, but no one was booked or sent off, the referee simply allowing play to carry on as if nothing had happened.

Two minutes before half-time winger Eddie Mosscrop scored a fine solo goal to give Burnley the lead after being put through from Dick Lindley. After the half-time break more hacking took place from the home side, but it failed to prevent Burnley going two-nil up, Bert chipping the ball cheekily over Fiske. At the end as the teams were going off the field, Tommy and Bainbridge squared up to each other a second time and both had to be restrained by their teammates.

Straight after Blackpool, the Burnley team set off for Fulham. They lost four-two at Craven Cottage but managed to hang on to second place in the table. It was getting very tight at the top. Birmingham could overtake Burnley if they won their game in hand. The cracks were beginning to show after another long season. A number of the players were nursing injuries and Burnley had six days to prepare for the biggest game in the club's history, the Cup semi-final. After returning from London on the Easter Saturday evening, the team set up their training camp back in Blackpool on the Tuesday and trained the rest of the week in the sea air.

The FA Cup semi-final:
Sunderland v. Burnley, Bramhall Lane, Sheffield 29 March 1913

The semi-final would be Burnley's biggest test. Sunderland would give nothing away. They were currently top of the First Division and had the tightest defence in the League. Their consistent performances over the season would bring them the League Championship come April. Sunderland were going for the dream double of Cup and League. But they had never won the Cup and had lost in the semi-finals before at Bramhall Lane in 1890 and '91. The mornings newspapers happily reminded their supporters that Bramhall Lane had been their graveyard in the past. Second Division Burnley would be underdogs but that meant nothing in the Cup as previous ties had shown. Tommy and the rest of the Burnley players were fired up and ready to give it everything.

It had rained in Yorkshire the previous week, and after more overnight rain, the huge pitch at Bramhall Lane was like a quagmire. The rain continued to belt down on the Saturday morning which prevented a much bigger gate turning out but it didn't put off 33,655 hardy spectators, around half of them from Burnley who had travelled down to watch the match.

The two teams lined up: Burnley - Dawson, Bamford, Taylor, McLaren, Boyle Watson, Mosscrop, Lindley, Freeman, Hodgson and Husband; for Sunderland, Butler, Gladwin, Ness, Cuggy, Thompson, Low, Mordue, Buchan, Richardson, Holley and Martin. The game began in lashing rain with a gale force wind behind it that made any attempt at football impossible. The supporters, players and even the pressmen under their oilskins on the touchline were soaked through to the skin. The bad conditions ruined what should have been an exciting game of football. Though the players' shots were on target when they left the boot, the wind and the ground conditions were so bad that the ball just took off in a direction all of its own. The game petered out into a goal-less draw, both sides happily settling for the replay that was scheduled for the following Wednesday at St. Andrew's, Birmingham.

The Burnley players went home for the weekend and regrouped on Monday morning back in Blackpool. On Monday morning eight of the players (Tommy wasn't among them) travelled over to Blackpool on the eight fifty-one train. As the train approached Kirkham station and was steaming at full speed, the players and passengers heard a loud crash of metal and then saw huge pieces of iron flying past the carriage windows. A crankshaft had broken and had almost led to the train's derailment. Tommy Bamford, joking to his colleagues, said, "Hello lads, Sunderland are going to have themselves a walkover." They were all lucky that the train had not come off the rails and no one on-board was hurt.

Semi-final replay,
St. Andrews, Birmingham, Wednesday afternoon 2 April 1913

The Sunderland squad had travelled down to Birmingham the day before, while Burnley made the decision to travel on the morning of the match, setting off on the eight-forty train. The stopping train which went via Manchester was full with few seats. Several delays took place along the way and the train finally pulled in to Birmingham at one-fifty, well over an hour late. With less than two hours to go before the kick-off, most of the Burnley players were nowhere near the ground, and by the time they had collected their kitbags and exited the station there were no taxis left. Meanwhile at St. Andrew's the gathering crowd were 'entertained', according the Sportsman in the *Burnley Express,* by "a Burnley-jerseyed youth running round the running track and onto the pitch, only to be politely asked to leave by two policemen".

Despite their travel problems, the game began on time with Burnley making one change, winger Jimmy Bellamy coming in for Eddie Mosscrop, who couldn't play due to his teaching commitments. Sunderland kicked off and, despite their exhausting journey, Burnley started well. After three minutes Teddy Hodgson had the ball in the net, only for it to be judged offside. Then from the goal kick Sunderland broke away and Martin crossed for Charlie Buchan to score with a leaping header past Dawson. One-nil to Sunderland. A minute later Buchan put the ball in the net again, only to be ruled offside. In the first half, apart from the two Sunderland goal attempts, Burnley had seen most of the ball. A foray by The Clarets in the Sunderland area led to a handball by defender Gladwin. The referee pointed to the penalty spot. Tommy picked up the ball and positioned it on the spot. *This has to go in.* He stepped back ten yards. Hands on hips, he waited for the referee to blow the whistle. He ran in and with his right foot smashed the ball past Butler in the Sunderland goal to level the scores. Cheers could be heard all around St. Andrews. Five minutes later, Burnley attacked again with Husband on the left who played a one-two with Freeman, who ran into the area to side-foot the ball past Butler. Two-one to Burnley! The crowd went wild, flags waved and hats were thrown in the air.

The first half was drawing to a close when Tommy was viscously kicked under the kneecap by Sunderland's Thompson. The referee didn't see the incident. Trying to rub some life back into his knee and with Thompson looking on, Tommy glowered at his opponent and nodded. He knew it was deliberate and would get even with him later. Pat had taught him to wait for the opportunity and when you got the chance, hit them back twice as hard. Tommy got up and limped on until the end of the half, "but he was not the same after," said Sportsman in the *Express*. The knee injury slowed him down and he soldiered on throughout the second half.

Sunderland attacked and were awarded a dubious penalty, when Holley went down after Dawson had already collected the ball. The referee whistled and pointed to the penalty spot. Jackie Mordue stepped up for Sunderland and scored. Two-all! It was turning into a classic Cup tie as both sides fought tooth and nail to win. Sunderland then claimed another penalty as Dave Taylor cleared the ball but it wasn't given. Tommy was struggling now to even run or kick the ball. He was walking around his own penalty box when ten minutes from full-time Sunderland won a throw-in. Mordue collected the ball, chipped the ball over Dave Taylor's head and passed it to Holley, who shot past Dawson to make it three-two to Sunderland. The initiative and the momentum was now all with Sunderland. In the final minutes Burnley searched for an equaliser with good chances for Lindley and Husband, but it was to no avail.

At the full-time whistle, his Cup dream over again for another year, Tommy hobbled straight off Bramhall Lane and into the dressing room. Thompson would wait; there would be another day to take his revenge on the man who had deliberately crippled him. As Burnley's Cup final dreams sank in the St. Andrew's mud, the players sat quietly, reflecting on what could have been. They stared at the dressing room floor, listening to the cheers down the corridor. *No champagne tonight, nothing for losers.* Again, they had come close, a stage further and against a top-class First Division opposition. But deep down the defeat hurt all of them. It hurt Tommy more than his knee, which was swelling up like a football. On the train home, the events of the match replaying over and over in his mind, his ambition of ever getting his hands on that damned trophy were further away than ever.

The following day John Haworth brought them all back down to earth and told them to put Wednesday's game behind them. They had to focus on the League campaign now. Birmingham City had won their game in hand and were in second place on forty-two points. Burnley had fallen to third. Burnley had to win their games in hand or the season would end again with nothing to show for it. Tommy's knee hurt like hell. It felt like his kneecap was cracked. Doc Hodges strapped it up and he was on crutches. It was clear the following day he wouldn't make Saturday's game against Bradford. But without the captain the team did well winning three-two and picking up two more precious points.

Burnley travelled to Deepdale to play the Second Division League leaders Preston North End who had played well all season. There was a suggestion in the papers that "an arrangement" had been made between Preston and Burnley on the result as both sides were vying for promotion. The FA observers at the match, however, didn't agree, yet the game ended in a one-all draw.

Leicester Fosse v. Burnley, 19 April 1913

After a four-two home victory over Wolves on 12 April, Burnley played Leicester Fosse at Filbert Street the Saturday after. George Halley deputised as centre-half for Tommy who was still out of the side and walking with crutches. Burnley led two-nil at the interval with two Teddy Hodgson goals. Nine minutes after the restart Leicester pulled a goal back, and three minutes later they equalised through Sparrow. Leicester pushed forward, and Dave Taylor was flattened when the ball hit him full in the face. Sixteen minutes from time Hodgson passed inside to Freeman, to give Burnley the lead again, and The Clarets held out for an excellent three-two away victory.

At the end of the match, in the away dressing room, the Burnley players waited eagerly for the results to come in from Birmingham and Barnsley. When it came it was excellent news: Leeds had beaten Birmingham four-nil at Elland Road and Barnsley had only managed a nil-nil draw at home to Clapton Orient. Neither Barnsley nor Birmingham could overtake Burnley now, and after thirteen seasons in the Second Division, Burnley were promoted to Division One. The player's efforts had paid off. At last they had something to celebrate. For Tommy, two seasons of hard graft had finally paid off. He'd finally won something even if it was second place. It would do for now.

On May Day, to celebrate Burnley's return to the First Division, Philip and Lady Ottoline Morrell hosted a dinner and reception for the Burnley team at the Mechanics Hall in town. Several toasts and speeches were made during the evening. As Tommy stood to respond to the toast to the team he was cheered and given a rousing reception. He said:

> On behalf of the members of the team, I beg to thank you most heartily for the toast which has been so ably proposed Alderman Whitehead and which you have all drunk with such enthusiasm. As captain of the Burnley team I feel proud to have the honour of responding to it. (Hear, Hear) Since I first joined the Burnley club it has been my ambition to see the team back

again in the First Division and I need scarcely say that it was a bitter disappointment – especially to the players when we failed in our last match at Wolverhampton last season. (Hear, Hear and applause) Our task has not been an easy one by any means for we have had many difficulties to face especially in regard to injuries but the players have shown a skill and determination which have brought us through successfully. (Hear, Hear) We also gave a good account of ourselves in the English Cup competition and the form we displayed in those matches should fill us with confidence for our fight in the First Division next season. I should also like to say how much we appreciate the kindness of Mr. Morrell in entertaining us to dinner and for the great interest he has always taken in the team, especially when we have visited London. (Loud applause)

The players' end-of-season bonus gave them a share in a pot of two hundred and twenty pounds for coming second in the League and a hundred and sixty-five pounds for reaching the Cup semi-finals. The players end-of-season knees-up would be a good one this year. Burnley were leading scorers with eighty-eight goals, and with another thirteen scored in the Cup, that made it over a hundred goals for the season. Bert was the leading scorer with thirty-one goals and Tommy had chipped in with six of his own, mainly penalties. His favourite and the one he'd remember for a long time was the header at Ewood Park in the quarter-final of the Cup. In the reserves, the youngsters had done well with Billy Pickering scoring twenty-eight goals and Milligan weighing in with another eighteen.

Throughout May, Doc Hodges worked hard on Tommy's knee. The fluid had been drained and it was repairing well. As the summer holiday period approached and the Burnley players each went their separate ways, bad news reached Tommy from Platts Common. On the morning of Monday 16 June, Pat Boyle had already started his shift at Hoyland Silkstone when he started coughing and couldn't stop. He began to cough up blood and collapsed. John Boyle and some more men managed to get Pat to the pit bottom on a makeshift stretcher. They got him into the cage, up to the surface and home. The doctor was brought out from Hoyland. Pat was in good hands, nursed by his four daughters and as soon as he received the news, Tommy travelled over to Platts Common to see how his father was. The day after Tommy got home, Pat Boyle fell into a coma and died of a brain haemorrhage. He was sixty-five.

The Boyle family was grief-stricken. Tommy's father was the strongest man he had ever known. His thoughts went back to his first day at the pit and remembered his fathers calming hand on his shoulder as the cage fell into the darkness. Just one look from his dad was all it needed to put him straight if he ever stepped out of line. He'd rarely raised a hand to Tommy; he didn't need to: the Pat Boyle stare was all it needed, the same glower Tommy had since adopted against his opponents on the field. Tommy remembered Pat taking him and John to their first football match together. He had remembered him working overtime to buy him his first pair of running spikes and watched him play for The Stars on a Saturday afternoon. The soft Irish brogue and the quiet manner contrasted with the hard-as-nails man on the outside. Patrick Boyle had lived a hard life, most of it hewing coal underground, evidenced by the tapestry of scars, the hacking cough and the fact he was hardly ever at home. He had been a good man, a good father and good family man. They would all miss him terribly.

After the funeral at St. Helen's Church, Tommy, John and the girls along with their husbands, friends and neighbours walked back to The Royal Oak for the wake and to raise a glass to their father. They sat and talked about the happy times they'd had together after which Tommy made another vow to himself. He would win that damned English Cup next year for his father, whatever it took.

League Division One

Tommy spent most of the summer of 1913 in Platts Common. He took a room at The Plough Inn on Doncaster Road and spent time with the family. His knee got better and he managed to get some light running in during July. He knew next season would be a hard one and prepared for the fight to come.

In Burnley, preparations for the club's first season back in the First Division were well advanced at Turf Moor. The new stand running the entire length of the pitch on the Brunshaw Road side with a terraced enclosure in front was finished with a total accommodation for 10,000, the facilities boasting "a nice little tea room" for spectators on the first landing. The old Star Stand opposite had been demolished and a new sloped, cinder embankment created running the length of the ground. Abel Hudson had reseeded the playing surface and Ernie Edwards had joined the club from Plymouth as first team trainer, replacing Jeremiah Jackson. Billy Nesbitt had undergone an operation on his hearing in the summer that had gone well and given him some degree of hearing in one ear. The club's quota of 1,100, twenty-five-shilling season tickets for the best seats in the new stand had all been snapped up (twenty-one shillings for ladies) and more season tickets sold on the ground than ever before.

Burnley's first match of the season was on Bank Holiday Monday, 1 September, at Goodison Park. Bert would make a return to his old club. The Burnley team sheet read: Dawson; full-backs Bamford, Taylor, Halley, Boyle and Watson; and forwards Bellamy, Lindley, Freeman, Hodgson and Husband. Before the match, the captain rallied his troops in the dressing room. He told them they had not to lose and who to look out for. He was back to his familiar self, exercising in the dressing room before they ran out. His knee was strapped but "in fine fettle", he'd told the press and he was ready for the big game. Kestrel, *The Burnley News* reporter, gave his account of the match, which ended in a one-all draw, the main incident in the match being the rough treatment meted out to Burnley goalkeeper Jerry Dawson. Tommy had shouted his commands from the first whistle as Burnley had taken an early lead through Jimmy Bellamy. Everton rallied and piled on the pressure to seek their equaliser:

> ... Dawson saving a shot from Beare knocked the ball down and rolled over it covering the ball. I could see Browell or Bradshaw rush at Dawson and kick him on the arm. [David] Taylor rushed up but he was knocked headlong into the net. Another player or two kicked Dawson in the back, and he appeared to be lifted a yard or two and almost dragged over the goal-line and over his prostrate body a rugby scrum ensued. Mr Campbell, the referee did not consider the kicking of Dawson a foul and he let the scrum develop for a time until an infringement took place. After blowing his whistle, he then threw the ball up on the goal line and as it was being cleared Browell took a pot-shot and scored.

The disputed Everton goal and the game itself was a scrap and an early wake-up call for The Clarets. It showed that this season would be no picnic and to compete they would have to fight for every inch of ground to stay in the top flight. Kestrel was sure Burnley should have won the game, but a draw away in their first game and a point was a good start. The next two games were lost before The Clarets' first win came at Turf Moor against The Wednesday. The match coincided with a visit to Turf Moor by Ottoline Morrell, who was spending a September break as a guest of Lady O'Hagan. From her seat in the new stand Ottoline observed the match and later recorded in her journal:

> On Saturday we went to the football match. About 14,000 were people there [her estimate], all packed together in the usual drizzle and veil of fog. It was mostly men who were there, their coat collars turned up against their intense faces. They make one great solid dark circle of human beings round the stadium, the only touch of colour being the red-and-white advertisement of OXO on the hoarding, and the striped jerseys of the footballers as they rushed over the black ground. I found it intensely

exciting, sitting in the cold, draughty stand with 14,000 intensely excited human beings around shouting and gesticulating wildly, so intoxicated that they had ceased to exist except as a mass, vicariously participating in the game. One was caught up into the storm of passion and found oneself contorted and wriggling with excitement, breathlessly urging on one's favourite player. One very neat, delicate little fellow with red hair called Mosscrop, who was a schoolteacher, was a pleasure to watch, so agile, so clever and precise in his movements (I heard afterwards that he was one of the few conscientious objectors from Burnley). Julian's favourite was a slim youth in a green jersey, Burnley's goalkeeper, called Jerry, who was a blacksmith.

After the match, Ottoline described her exit from the ground, which would have meant turning left and heading up Brunshaw Road hill back to Lady O'Hagan's house at Higher Brunshaw:

> It was most frightening at the end of the match when the great torrent of black-coated men poured forth into the road. Rough, pushing, jostling, to get... where? That was what I asked. After such intoxicating excitement, what was there to be done? For one was in that unsatisfactory state of having the emotions and nerves exhausted and the body unused, and one instinctively exclaimed, "What can we do now?" For it was obviously the team alone who felt decently and wholly tired. I remember this rush of strong violent men excited but rather frightened me, but still I always enjoy being in the midst of a crowd. Drink, violence, murder, seemed to be the inevitable reaction.

Ottoline Morrell was not the only woman in the ground that day. Since Burnleys' promotion, Turf Moor was attracting bigger crowds and among them a growing number of ladies who would stand in the enclosure in front of the stand to get a good view of their heroes as they came out of the tunnel. Tommy had been out with a number of girls, mainly back home in his native Barnsley, but nothing too serious. But at the end of The

Wednesday match as the players were leaving the pitch to wild applause, several of them stopped by the enclosure as they usually did to sign autographs for the youngsters. The captain as usual was in big demand. As he moved down the line of eager young faces signing their programmes, he looked up briefly to see a young woman stood in front of him with the most innocent shy smile. He smiled back to see her blush but was struck with how innocent and sweet she looked. She was with a friend and the two girls giggled as Tommy politely bowed and politely said, "ladies," before moving on down the line. As he got to the players tunnel he looked up and tried to find her again in the crowd, but she'd gone. But that face, those eyes, that smile, that innocence had made a lasting impression on him.

Burnley's next home game was against Chelsea. In front of 24,000 spectators on a glorious late autumn day, Burnley hammered The Pensioners six-one. They won without the services of Tommy, who had been in the wars again according to Sportsman in the *Express*, "suffering slight concussion during both the Bolton and Blackburn games".

The captain returned to the team the following Saturday for the trip to Boundary Park to meet Oldham and scored Burnley's goal with a right-foot thunderbolt, the game ending one-all and lifting Burnley to sixth place in the table.

A home defeat to Manchester United followed before Burnley met Spurs at home, and won three-one. Tommy was in the thick of it again. "Skipper Shines and Scores" ran Sportsman's headline in the *Burnley Express*. In the second half Tommy tested King in the Tottenham goal with a long shot, which rebounded. Running into the box for the follow-up he was hacked down from behind, "his legs kicked from under him by Collins", said Kestrel. Tommy sized up his opponent, then took the penalty and scored to give Burnley a two-one lead. Kestrel in the *Express* noted "Boyle's Great Form", and his influence in the game, spraying passes out to the wingers. Sportsman in the *Express* reported on another injury he picked up in the game, when he was, "laid out owing to the ball having struck him hard on the head".

Burnley v. Newcastle United, Turf Moor, 1 November 1913

The last occasion Tommy had met Newcastle was in the 1910 Cup final replay at Goodison Park when he had seen Colin Veitch carry off the trophy. He'd never felt so low in his life. He had waited three years to exorcise that Cup demon. Billy Nesbitt made his home debut on the right wing in place of Tom Charlton and Levi Thorpe replaced the injured George Halley. In front of a huge 30,000 home crowd, Tommy won the toss and played toward the Cricket Field end in the first half. Sportsman in the *Express*, reporting on Burnley's winning goal, said, "the ball was sent to the right and Freeman slipped the ball between two defenders to Lindley who beat Lawrence in goal amid a scene of wild enthusiasm. The shout was heard quite plainly about two miles away." The *Daily Mail* said the best players on the field were the defenders, Taylor, Boyle and Watson. At the end of the game, walking off the pitch toward the tunnel, Tommy's eye was suddenly drawn to the enclosure where the supporters were cheering them off the field. She was there again. The girl he'd seen at The Wednesday match. She was with her friend again. He was caked in mud and wiped his hands on his shorts and walked over and said, 'hello.' He gave her his best smile. "Well played Tommy," she'd said excitedly. Somehow she was different to all the other girls he'd known.

"Thank you, I'm glad you enjoyed the game," he replied. Her friend briefly introduced her, "Tommy, this is Annie, Annie Varley."

"I'm pleased to meet you Annie," he replied confidently, then said, "could I perhaps invite you both for something to eat later?" Both eagerly nodded their approval, Annie shyly saying, "yes please."

Chapter 7: The Cup

You give me your shield of victory,
and your right hand sustains me;
You stoop down to make me great.

– Psalm 18

The 1913 Christmas period brought little in the way of points for The Clarets who faced five games in eleven days. But by the first week of January 1914, Tommy and his men were looking forward to the first round of the FA Cup where they had been drawn against South Shields. Before the Cup tie, Burnley got in the winning mood at Hillsborough against The Wednesday, romping to a six-two victory, an excellent performance to start their 1914 Cup campaign.

Round One: Burnley v. South Shields, 10 January 1914

Burnley's first round opponents in the Cup, were top of the North Eastern League and played against the reserve teams of Newcastle United, Sunderland and Middlesbrough. They were a hard, semi-professional side and included, as player-manager, Arthur Bridgett, a former England international. Burnley had sent their scouts to pay them a visit over Christmas. They were a good, tough outfit and would be no pushover. Burnley lined up: Dawson, Bamford, Taylor, Halley, Boyle, Watson, Nesbitt, Lindley, Freeman, Hodgson and Mosscrop. Around 16,000 turned out at Turf Moor to see The Clarets take on the Cup minnows from the north-east. Burnley took a three-goal lead with two goals from Dick Lindley and one from Bert Freeman before South Shields came back into the game and scored themselves. Tommy missed a penalty and Bert missed an open goal that should have increased Burnley's lead. The game ended in a three-one victory for The Clarets to see them safely through and into the hat for the second round.

Wingers built like whippets

Burnley's two wingers, Billy Nesbitt and Eddie Mosscrop were both five foot seven and excellent runners. Tom Holford, the Manchester City half-back had played against Nesbitt in a recent Lancashire Cup tie and had said in the *Burnley News*,

> "...at different periods in the game I made remarks, laughed, nodded... but still he seemed to treat me with silent contempt. I could have understood it had we had any difference but there was not a semblance or unpleasantness in this game. I kept on talking but still failed to get any response. I could not make anything of him at all until I got into the dressing room. Jack Hillman said, "that is a rather good kid you were playing against, Tommy, isn't he?" I agreed he was. "But," said Jack, "he would be better still but for one thing." "What's that?" I asked. "He's deaf," said Jack...

Like Tommy, Billy Nesbitt and Dave Taylor, the red-haired Edwin (Eddie) Mosscrop began his sporting career as a sprinter and like half-back Billy Watson, he hailed from Southport. Mosscrop was a schoolmaster and would teach his class all day and then run on Southport seafront after lessons. Eddie could usually only play at the weekends and had to get special permission for time off to play in any important mid-week games from the School Board, who regularly refused to let him play. A profile of him in the *Burnley Express* described him as "clean and frail as Dresden china". 'Wick' was another word used regarding his speed. The *Burnley Express* said: "A footballer to live [through] a hard game through must have either weight and strength, or cunning – Mosscrop has little weight but much cunning. The instant he receives the ball he scampers off like a hare.'

Round Two: Burnley v. Derby County, 31 January 1914

The draw for the second round the following Monday had given Burnley another home tie against Derby County. Before the match it was announced that the Burnley board were considering an invitation they had received from the Deutscher Fussball Club in Prague to play a tour on the continent over fourteen days from the middle of May, playing six games in local towns. Burnley and Derby had never met in the Cup previously and with half the football season gone County were struggling at the wrong end of the First Division. Burnley were unchanged from the South Shields game while Derby brought in their veteran centre-forward and former England international Steve Bloomer in place of Leonard in attack. County were struggling with injuries to two other regular players, Frank Buckley (dislocated shoulder) and Betts (flu).

The attendance nearly doubled from the first Cup tie, with 29,992 paying their sixpences to witness what turned into a classic match. Before kick-off Burnley were again represented by their lucky mascot, Walter Place's son wearing the club colours, while Derby's mascot was a black and white terrier which howled at the brass band. Tommy won the toss from Bloomer and Burnley played towards the Bee Hole end with the wind. The Clarets took an early lead with a goal from Teddy Hodgson, who scored from a Billy Nesbitt cross, before Barnes equalised for Derby early in the second half. After twenty minutes of the second half, the match turned into a 'full-blooded' affair according to the Sportsman in the *Burnley Express*:

> Lindley was the first victim for after beating Waugh, the Derby player ran into him with full pace, completely knocking the Burnley player out. Waugh had previously been warned by the referee and he was moved to the outside left position by the Derby officials with the crowd calling for him to be sent off. Nesbitt was another victim of one of the most flagrant acts of the game as he was 'sandwiched' so severely that the right-

winger appeared to be badly hurt. In other incidents Mosscrop and Watson were kicked from behind for no reason. In one struggle in the Burnley goalmouth some of the players nearly got to fighting. (*Burnley Express*, 4 February 1914)

With eight minutes of the game left and the score still one-all, a replay at Derby looked to be on the cards. Teddy Hodgson then stepped up to score Burnley's second, only for Bloomer to put Waugh through a minute later to level the scores again: two-all! With just four minutes remaining, Teddy Hodgson completed his hat-trick, scoring the winner to send thousands of Burnley supporters home happy and steer Burnley through to the third round.

After the Newcastle match and his invitation to afternoon tea, Tommy and Annie started seeing each other on a regular basis. Annie was twenty-one and worked as a milliner at a shop in the town centre. The Varley family lived not far away from where Tommy and Bert were staying in digs in Stoneyholme. In early February after a brief courtship, Tommy asked Annie to marry him and the couple got engaged after he'd plucked up enough courage to ask William, Annie's father, for his daughters hand in marriage.

Round Three: Burnley v. Bolton Wanderers, 21 February 1914

The draw for the Third round of the Cup had again been kind to Burnley. The Burnley board put the admission prices up, much to the disgust of the Burnley faithful. Ground prices were doubled from sixpence to a shilling and the best seats went up from three to four shillings. That didn't stop 32,734 spectators turning out for the match on the Saturday afternoon, that was set to start at 3.15 to give around 10,000 Bolton supporters time to get to the match. The Scottish Selection Committee were also at Turf Moor checking on the progress of Burnley's Dave Taylor and George Halley.

In the week leading up to the match, Burnley had been in training at Lytham St. Anne's, as had Bolton, engaging in a variety of outdoor pursuits including brisk walks on the seafront, leapfrog, wrestling and sprinting, along with daily massage treatments and saltwater baths. Both teams travelled over to Burnley on the morning of the match. The two sides had already met twice in the League, both games ending in draws, nil-nil at Burnden Park and two-all at Turf Moor. Bolton were third in the League and were a very strong side. The furthest Bolton they had progressed in the Cup was to the 1904 final where they had lost to Manchester City. Burnley were unchanged again from the Second round and Tommy would be up against his old Barnsley colleagues, Bob Glendenning and George Lillycrop, now signed to Bolton's colours.

It had rained the Friday before and the pitch was soft but Abel Hudson had forked it and prepared a good surface. Sportsman in the *Express* mentioned the two team mascots: "a huge 'stage-dog' [a man in a dog-suit] in the Burnley colours intended to draw attention to a brand of dog biscuits was on view along with a Boltonian cyclist".

The match referee Mr T.P. Campbell, hailed from Blackburn. Tommy lost the toss and Burnley played towards the Cricket Field end in the first half. The Clarets soon settled and looked the more confident on the ball. Burnley took the lead on twenty-nine minutes with a move that started with a pass from Tommy to Bert, who dribbled his way into the penalty area and shot low past the goalkeeper. The score remained one-nil at half-time. Sixteen minutes into the second half Teddy Hodgson added Burnley's second to wild scenes among the home crowd. George Halley then added a rare goal, worthy of winning any match, where he dribbled around a defender and shot hard and low past the Bolton keeper with only nine minutes left. Halley's goal sealed it and Burnley were through to the quarter-finals. The following day the *Daily Mail* reported that "Burnley's forwards ran around the Bolton defence as they pleased – on that play the team must be a strong tip for the Palace".

Three home Cup ties had all been won and when the draw for the third round was made at FA headquarters on the Monday, it was hoped that Burnley's luck of the draw would continue.

When the draw was announced, Burnley found they were paired against their old Cup adversaries from the North East, Sunderland and would be away from home for the first time in the competition. The draw for the quarter-finals had paired,

Manchester City v. Sheffield United,
Sheffield Wednesday v. Aston Villa,
Liverpool v. Queens Park Rangers
Sunderland v. Burnley.

The Quarter final:
Sunderland v. Burnley, Roker Park, 7 March 1914

Before the Cup quarter-final, Burnley lost two-nil to Spurs in the League, and in an amazing game at Turf Moor they lost again, three-four, to a Preston side who were struggling at the wrong end of the First Division. The two defeats were not the ideal preparation for their forthcoming Cup duel against Sunderland.

Sunderland. The same side that had knocked them out in the semi-finals last season. The same side that the kneecap kicking Thompson played for. The same side Burnley had already lost to in the League at home, but who had managed a draw against at Roker Park on Boxing Day. Tommy knew they had to get a result at Roker Park. They mustn't lose there. If they could get a result, they could go all the way. After beating Burnley the previous year in the semi-final Sunderland had then lost in the final to Aston Villa and they too were determined to make amends and get their hands on the Cup for the first time.

Four thousand Burnley supporters made the long journey up to the North East. Sportsman in the *Burnley Express* describes the pre-match atmosphere:

> Most of the visitors were well behaved but of course there were the usual youthful irresponsible's who paraded the streets playing solos on whistles or 'squeakers'. Street hawkers were in great numbers selling badges, rattles, rosettes, long coloured feathers, and the ubiquitous 'squeaker', photos of popular players, colours and cards of the teams. The Burnley crowd were demonstratively vocal on the ground.

With Burnley unchanged for the fourth time in the Cup and with 34,581 spectators inside Roker Park, Bert Freeman kicked off for Burnley, who faced the sun and with a stiff sea breeze at their backs. The two captains, Thomson and Boyle, were outstanding in organising their sides, Tommy again shouting his encouragement to his men throughout the match, his voice could be heard all around Roker Park. The first half was a quite dull affair, neither side committing themselves and resorting to testing each other out.

Six minutes into the second half, Burnley had the ball in the Sunderland net through Dick Lindley that looked to have been a perfectly good goal but it was ruled offside by the referee, Mr Talks. Then a brilliant shot from George Halley hit the crossbar and should have gone in, but the Sunderland keeper jumped up and pulled the crossbar down, for which he was reprimanded by the referee. A Teddy Hodgson shot hit the side netting and Billy Nesbitt rushed at a chance that he skewed high over the bar. Bert should have had a penalty awarded after he was knocked off the ball from a Mosscrop centre. Lots of good chances came but none were finished off as Mr Talks blew the whistle for full-time. It was a fair result in the end. Burnley hadn't lost and Tommy would have taken that scoreline at the start of the game. They had another bite of the cherry and would be back on their 'lucky' home soil.

The Quarter-final replay:
Burnley v. Sunderland, Turf Moor, Wednesday 11 March 1914

With a semi-final place at stake, interest in the mid-week replay was massive as 49,737 squeezed into Turf Moor to see The Clarets aim to make the last four. The town effectively closed down. Shops, mills, foundries and factories all closed after lunch so that workers could all get to the match while some 3,000 supporters made the trip down from the North East to cheer on Sunderland. The Sunderland team had stayed in Manchester overnight and the players on both sides had recovered from the knocks and bruises from the weekend.

Tommy would give it all he had. A lot was resting on his shoulders and after a good result in the North-East he was in determined mood. He won the toss and elected to play toward the Bee Hole end. There was a slight breeze as The Clarets kicked off with the afternoon sun at their backs. In the second minute, Eddie Mosscrop, who had managed to get the afternoon off, got away from his marker, crossing the ball perfectly only to see no one on the end of it. "Push up, Bertie!" Tommy commanded.

Five minutes in, the captain sent the ball out to Billy Nesbitt who centred for Bert whose header shook the crossbar. The ball rebounded to Teddy Hodgson whose shot hit the Sunderland post. The ball continued to bounce around the penalty area and the Sunderland defenders were unable to clear it, only for Teddy Hodgson to sneak in and put the ball in the net.

A huge cheer went up on all four sides of the ground as the Burnley players rushed in to congratulate Teddy on his goal. Sunderland attacked and a chance came to Martin but Dawson was quicker to the ball, smothering it with his body. Tommy then made a perfectly fair sliding challenge from behind on Thompson to remind his adversary that he was alive and well.

At half-time Burnley led one-nil. In the dressing room Tommy told the team it wouldn't be enough. They needed a two-goal cushion at least. Sunderland were strong and would hit back at them straight from the kick-off. They had to be ready for them.

He was right. Sunderland did attack but the Burnley half-back line of Halley, Boyle and Watson held firm. Twenty minutes into the second half, Dick Lindley was fouled by Ness. The free-kick was taken and the ball was sent out to Mosscrop, whose dazzling footwork confounded Hobson. 'Mossy' centred the ball perfectly for Dick Lindley to run onto and finish with a glancing header that flicked off his forehead and sailed into the far corner of the net to make it two-nil. Sunderland looked beaten, but there were still twenty-three minutes left.

Sunderland changed their formation. Conner moved to outside-right and Mordue inside-right with Buchan in the middle. Fifteen minutes from time Cuggy went off injured and Burnley temporarily lost Billy Watson after a kick by Buchan. With both sides down to ten men Sunderland came close to scoring, but their time was short. Jerry Dawson was called on to make a good save and Taylor and Bamford blocked further Sunderland attacks on the Burnley goal-line. Then, with only two minutes left, Conner scored for Sunderland. Two-one! The Burnley supporters were hushed as Tommy roared his encouragement at the players, clapping his hands and telling them to hold the ball in the corners and run down the clock. Tommy watched referee Mr Forshaw check his pocket watch, his whistle at the ready. *Come on, come on man, have you bloody swallowed it? Blow the bloody thing.* For the final moments Burnley struggled but held out with ten men and at long, long, last, Forshaw put his whistle to his lips and blew to signal the end of the match. Huge roars and cheers were heard all over the ground from the Burnley spectators. They were through to the semi-finals for the second year running. Tommy and the rest of the team were exhausted. They'd given everything over the two games and had come through victorious in front of their own supporters. For the thousands streaming out of Turf Moor that afternoon caught up in the moment, the only question on their minds was, could The Clarets go all the way?

The day after the replay John Haworth brought the team back down to earth as they prepared for their next League encounter, a match against Liverpool, who had also made it through to the semi-finals along with Aston Villa and Sheffield United. The draw for the semi-finals had already paired;

Liverpool v. Aston Villa at White Hart Lane
Burnley v Sheffield United at Old Trafford

For the Liverpool match, Dave Taylor, Billy Watson and Bert were all unfit: Bert was suffering ligament trouble behind the knee which sounded quite serious, Billy Watson had both ankle and leg injuries and Dave Taylor had actually gone home to Scotland to nurse his badly bruised ankles. Their places were filled by Reid, Thorpe and the young Glaswegian Billy Pickering, who had been scoring well in the reserves. Liverpool were also struggling with injuries after their two-one victory over Queens Park Rangers in the Cup and rested a number of players. Despite the injuries on both sides Burnley put in an excellent performance and beat Liverpool convincingly, five-two.

A week later, three Burnley players had been selected to play for the Football League in a match which took place at Turf Moor on 21 March. Despite Burnley playing an away League fixture at fellow Cup semi-finalists Aston Villa, 35,000 spectators turned out at Turf Moor for the inter-League match between that saw The Football League take on The Scottish League. An army of 5,000 Scots made the trip south to cheer on their side.

The home supporters turned out in their masses to see three Burnley men pull on the Football League jersey for the match: Tommy Boyle, Eddie Mosscrop and Teddy Hodgson. Tommy had a chance to make amends for the Ireland defeat as the selectors would be watching him again. He was actually suffering from a chest infection but still turned out in order to get the cap that would hopefully lead to another England call up. As the two teams took to the field and lined up opposite the stand the band played the national anthem. The line-up for The Football League was as follows Hardy (Aston Villa), Crompton (Blackburn), Boocock (Bradford City), Barber (Aston Villa), Boyle (Burnley), McNeal (West Bromwich), Jephcott (West Bromwich), Stephenson (Aston Villa), Peart (Notts County), Hodgson and Mosscrop (Burnley). The line-up for The Scottish League was as follows: Shaw, McNair, Dodds, McAtee and McMenemy (Celtic), Wright (Greenock), Gordon and Reid (Rangers), Nellies (Heart of Midlothian), Croal (Falkirk) and Smith (Hibernian).

The Football League XI started well and went two goals up with a Nellies own goal and Tommy followed it with a penalty, which brought great cheers from the home crowd. If the English dominated the first half, the second half was a different matter. Croal scored twice for the Scots and then Reid gave the visitors the lead, and they were comfortable winners in the end. It looked as if the players, including Tommy, had run out of steam in the second half, letting in the Scots to score their three goals. The following week's *Burnley Express* carried a letter from The Rev. Winfield who warned of the dangers the 'pleasures' football brought. In reference to the recent Scotland–England International held at Turf Moor, he wrote:

Some five thousand [Scottish] football enthusiasts came into Burnley early on the Saturday, and for the rest of the day the town was turned into what is usually styled a pandemonium, a general assembly of evil spirits, whisky in this case appearing to be the Beelzebub... disorder, drunkenness, betting, gambling and extravagance prevailed.

The FA Cup Semi-Final:
Burnley v. Sheffield United, Old Trafford, Saturday 28 March

The Cup semi-final was a week away and the Burnley team spent the week before at their training base at Lytham. Burnley would go to Old Trafford on the back of two defeats in the League to Newcastle United and Aston Villa and Tommy would come face-to-face with his old teammate George Utley, now the Sheffield United captain. Tommy had known Utley since 1907 when he'd arrived at Barnsley a year after him. Utley had played in the same Elsecar Athletic Team that Tommy had graduated from. They had stood side-by-side in the 1910 Cup final and had also worn the Three Lions at the 1913 England v. Ireland game. They were close friends off the pitch but the Cup semi-final would be a different matter.

Tickets for the semi-final had sold well, Burnley easily selling their allocation of 14,000 tickets for Old Trafford well before the day. Burnley supporters learned on the Friday evening that Tommy may not be fit for the match. The chest infection he was suffering from the previous weekend in the international might keep him out. What the press and the supporters didn't know was that Tommy's chest infection had turned into pleurisy. But at a pre-match examination on the Saturday morning, Doc Hodges passed him fit. You can only think that Tommy had lied to Hodges about the extent of his illness in order to play.

Saturday and more than fifty trains brought fans from all over Lancashire and Yorkshire into Manchester to the match. The attendance of 55,812 was a record for a Cup semi-final and was double the attendance of the other semi-final match taking place at White Hart Lane. As Old Trafford began filling up, the *Burnley News* reporter Brunbank recorded the scene around the ground:

Fans had spent all week preparing for the day. Street vendors sold pictures of the teams and their captains, button-holes, rosettes and coloured umbrellas. One Sheffield United fan carried a huge penknife, shaped like a scythe with the blade on one end. There were fans with red and white quartered suits and faces painted. Both sets of fans sported 'fool-caps' in their club colours. Men walked around the ground throwing bags of toffee into the crowd and then caught the pennies in return.

As the Irwell Springs band played its rousing anthems, the teams came onto the field, led by the two captains. Burnley in claret and blue were unchanged from the quarter-final and lined up: Dawson, Bamford, Taylor, Halley, Boyle, Watson, Nesbitt, Lindley, Freeman, Hodgson and Mosscrop. Sheffield United, in red and white stripes, comprised Gough, Cook, English, Sturgess, Brelsford, Utley, Simmons, Gillespie, Kitchen, Fazackerley and Revill.

In the middle of the pitch, a pale-looking Tommy tossed up with George Utley and the game got underway in a stiff breeze.

Figure 24. Tommy and George Utley toss up at the start of the semi-final tie between Burnley and Sheffield United at Old Trafford 1914

Burnley had a good deal of the possession for the first twenty minutes but the Sheffield plan to stifle the creative side of Burnley's game began to work. Tommy, the Burnley engine-driver, was clearly under par as Brunbank in the *Burnley News* noticed from early on in the first half: "when not chasing the ball he was holding his side as if in great pain... he did not play like the Boyle of past Cup ties and the lack of sleep from the night before didn't help his game".

But when the ball came to Tommy, the pain seemed to melt away and he would run and pass it freely. Sheffield got their first corner after half an hour, and in going up for the corner Simmons was injured, falling badly on his ankle, and had to go off for treatment. Then George Utley was hit in the face with the ball in the Burnley penalty area, bursting his nose. Later on Lindley, Watson and Freeman were all on the receiving end of bad tackles, which all brought free-kicks. Burnley put the ball in the net on thirty-six minutes when Boyle passed through to Bert, who scored what looked a perfectly good goal, but referee Taylor ruled it offside. After the interval, Eddie Mosscrop was hurt and Fazackerley fouled Jerry Dawson, knocking him into the net deliberately and causing Dawson to wrench his knee as he landed. No foul, waved the referee. Then Bert got away and made it to just outside the Sheffield penalty area only to be brought down by Cook. Tommy stepped up for the free-kick and his shot went just over the bar. Bert was twice penalised by the referee for unfair shoulder charges. By the end of the game both Tommy and Eddie Mosscrop were clearly in pain. Each time Tommy breathed his ribs ached while Eddie Mosscrop was limping badly after suffering a dead leg.

Nil-nil and the two battle-weary teams left the field to great applause. Most of the Burnley players ended the match suffering knocks but the news on Jerry Dawson was the worst. His rib and knee injury would certainly rule him out of the replay at Goodison Park and Ronnie Sewell would have to play. There were doubts that Burnley could even field a side for the replay there were so many walking wounded. In the Burnley dressing-room after the match one of the staff had discovered that the train carrying the team down to Manchester had a coffin on board. Several of the players believed it was a bad omen and blamed the corpse for them not winning the game.

On the way home from Manchester, the captain, his lungs aching each time he breathed in, was deep in thought about the replay. *Goodison. Goodison Bloody Park where I've never won...* But after a chest poultice and decent nights sleep on Saturday night and two days rest on Sunday and Monday, Tommy's health began to pick up. The pain in his side had subsided and the coughing weakened. By Tuesday afternoon he was running around Turf Moor with Ernie Edwards for company checking on his fitness. He'd play tomorrow, whatever state he was in.

The FA Cup Semi-Final replay:
Burnley v. Sheffield United, Goodison Park Wednesday 1 April 1914

April Fool's Day and for Tommy and his teammates, a day to make history. Apart from Jerry Dawson, the rest of the team including the captain had all recovered from their knocks, and would be fit to play. Eddie Mosscrop had been given the go-ahead to play from the School Board. The only change for Sheffield United was Hall, who came in for Simmons at centre-forward.

As it was a weekday, the attendance at Goodison Park only numbered 27,266, half the crowd that had witnessed the first match. Burnley were much more on their game, Brunbank noted in the *Burnley News*, the few days' rest having done the players good. Mr Taylor took charge of the game again and was "down on rough play immediately". Sheffield's proneness to "hacking the man" was checked right at the outset by the referee, said Brunbank. The Burnley half-back line was steadier. Tommy's improved fitness since the weekend had given him another couple of yards on the pitch. The captain was everywhere. Vocally, he was louder than the rest of the players put together. Calling to Nesbitt on the wing and Bert up front, "Push up, Billy. Billy! Bertie, get hold of it…"

Eddie Mosscrop was given another dead leg by Sturgess for his trouble, but was alright after a few minutes on the side-line and a soaking from Charlie Bates's sponge. Then Bert had a shot on goal that just missed the upright. Somehow George Utley had his nose burst again and his striped shirt was a mass of red. Ronnie Sewell pulled off a fine save from the Irishman Billy Gillespie, and the first half petered out into another nil-nil stalemate. As the journalists wrote up their notes for the morning papers the match was deadlocked. Something special was needed to break the impasse.

At the start of the second half, Tommy swapped Mosscrop and Nesbitt over on the wings and they adapted better to the breezy conditions. Five minutes into the half, Eddie Mosscrop had a shot that hit the crossbar, the ball just skimming over the top, which brought groans from the Goodison crowd. Bert had an appeal for a penalty turned down after he was put through after Brelsford had fouled him in the penalty box. With time running out it looked as if the game would go to extra time when the Burnley captain decided otherwise.

Billy Nesbitt over on the left, was fouled and Billy Watson stepped up to take the free-kick a few yards outside the penalty area to the left of the Sheffield goal. Watson's free-kick hit Gough in the five-man Sheffield wall who only managed to clear the ball to Bert, who struck the ball again at Gough for him to clear a second time. The ball came out to Eddie Mosscrop who also had a shot, his effort cleared by Cook. Tommy was standing a few yards behind the Freeman and Mosscrop. Cook's clearance came straight to Tommy. "It was as if he knew where the ball would come," said Brunbank. The Sheffield defenders parted just few feet but just enough for the captain to see a gap. He ran forward and caught the ball with his right foot on the volley towards the goal. The ball flew like an arrow - straight through the Sheffield defenders and into the net as Brunbank reported:

> [T]he Sheffield goalkeeper had no chance, it was hit with such force. It crashed into the net like a projectile from a machine-gun. The net shivered and shook for several seconds as if it had been caught by a whirlwind.

A huge roar went up from the thousands of Burnley supporters. The players ran over to congratulate the captain briefly before he backpedalled to his own half. The deadlock was finally broken. Burnley had further opportunities to increase their lead through Bert and Eddie Mosscrop as Burnley sensed victory. The minutes ticked away and Sheffield made continued attacks. Tommy waited anxiously for the end. *I've scored the bloody winner...me. There can't be long left.* "How much longer ref," Tommy asked. *C'maan, blow the bloody whistle, Taylor.* The referee eventually checked his pocket-watch, and slowly raised his arm to put the whistle to his lips. On hearing the sound scores of hats were thrown in the air from the Burnley supporters. They had made it! The Cup Final! In the centre-circle, hands on muddied knees, completely exhausted, Tommy stood gasping for air before shaking hands with his old sparring partner, a bloodied George Utley. It had been a tough contest but today was his day. He would be back at The Palace again four years after he'd been there with Barnsley. Burnley were in their first ever Cup final where they would meet Liverpool in just three weeks time.

That evening a crowd of around 3,000 people gathered at Bank Top station in Burnley to welcome the team home. As the train came to a halt, Teddy Hodgson stepped out, followed by George Halley and Ronnie Sewell, who had had a marvellous game. Sewell was lifted by the crowd and carried shoulder high down Standish Street all the way to Market Place. Tommy stepped out to handshakes and congratulations from the crowd and a moment later he was hoisted up and given the 'chair' treatment before eventually escaping his captors and making his way home. A jubilant Philip Morrell telegrammed Harry Windle: "Warmest congratulations from Lady Ottoline and myself, on Burnley's great victory. Hope directors and players will honour us by dining with us here after the final on April 25th."

On the Saturday following the replay Burnley had a League game against none other than Sheffield United at Bramhall Lane. Burnley rested Bert Freeman and Teddy Hodgson and the match was officiated by Mr Taylor again, his third game between the two sides in a week; who must have been sick of the sight of each other by now. Sheffield took their retribution, punishing Burnley with a five-nil defeat. And despite reaching their first Cup final, not all Burnley supporters were happy with the standard of play on offer. 'Disgusted Member' wrote to the *Burnley Express* after the next League game, which ended in a two-one home defeat to Middlesbrough:

> I write as a disgusted member about the bill of fare that is being served up to us by the directors and players of the club who seem to think because they are in the Cup they can put anything they like on.

Disgusted Member had a point. Burnley had only picked up two points from their previous seven League games and were sliding down the table. The team had concentrated all their energies on the Cup, and League performances had suffered.

In the next two games, both at home over the Easter weekend, the team's form returned with a two-nil win over Everton on Good Friday and a five-one win against Derby County which all but secured another season in Division One. The referee for the Derby County match was Herbert S. Bamlett, and as the teams came out he was given a great reception by the Burnley crowd after being named as the Cup final referee. Bamlett was well known to the Burnley supporters. They had not forgotten the 'snowstorm' game of 1909 when Second Division Burnley were beating League champions Manchester United one-nil in the fourth round of the Cup with fifteen minutes of the game to go when Bamlett abandoned the game.

The Burnley team and its supporters could now look forward to their big day. There were two weeks of preparations left and all that stood between Burnley and Liverpool was a League match with Manchester City at Hyde Road.

Cup Fever

Since the semi-final victory, Cup fever had taken over the town. The local papers were full of stories and snippets about the Cup. Local businesses began advertising their services to those making the 'once in a lifetime trip'. For twenty-one shillings (the equivalent of a week's wages) Whittaker's were organising Cup final parties which included, "rail fare, drives, three good meals, admission to Crystal Palace and ground, conductor etc". Althams, the local tea merchants and travel agents, were offering the return rail fare to the Cup final for twelve shillings. Haffners the Pork Butchers were offering "hand made pork pies, sandwiches and everything you need for your own Cup final picnic". Madame Tussauds was offering free entry to the waxworks with production of a valid train ticket. It was a shilling to see the animals in Regent's Park Zoo and you could stay overnight at Horrex's hotel in The Strand with bed and breakfast for six shillings. It was said that some Burnley supporters had pawned their pianos and sideboards to fund the trip to London to see their team in the final.

Ten days before the final, *The Times* announced that King George would be attending the Crystal Palace to see the match. The newspaper said he might not be able to stay for the whole game, and if not Lord Derby would present the trophy to the winners and the medals at the end. The announcement fuelled a fresh wave of media interest in the match and as a consequence Cup fever hit another level. Sydenham Park needed a facelift: the pavilion needed decorating, full preparations for the royal visitors made, security arrangements tightened. The Football Association were thrown into a frenzy making adjustments to their plans to accommodate the Royal party with only over a week to go. On the game itself, there was now more at stake. History would be made. The King had attended sporting contests before, mainly rugby or the races but this would be the first time he had ever attended a football final, "a *Royal* final", the papers were now calling it. In Lytham, John Haworth stepped up the team training to get the boys in tip-top condition.

Figure 25. Burnley pose for a team photograph outside their training headquarters at Lytham, Lancashire, 1914

Figure 26. The Burnley team train on Lytham
seafront. Tommy has the ball.

Burnley's allocation of 18,500 Cup final tickets had sold out a week before the match. Ticket prices were five shillings for the best covered seats (close enough to see His Majesty) and two shillings and sixpence for the open-air seats at each end of the ground. Standing room only could be accessed on entry to the park for one shilling. Behind the stands and around one side was a raised embankment with crush barriers, and behind that six-foot high posts that people could perch on if they could keep still for long enough.

Sydenham's main attraction was the Crystal Palace that had formerly housed the Great Exhibition of 1851 in Hyde Park. The magnificent cast-iron and glass structure was moved to the park in 1854 and still attracted thousands of people annually. The football arena had been built on the site of a lake that was first used as a polo pitch. The arena provided the biggest football pitch in England and the previous year's final, in 1913, had attracted nearly 122,000 people.

After the final, sports fans could enjoy an evening of boxing where for sixpence they could see the current heavyweight champion, Bombardier Billy Wells, fight Pat O'Keefe, the middleweight champion, in an exhibition match.

Manchester City v. Burnley, Hyde Road, Saturday 18 April 1914

Seven days before the final, Burnley met Manchester City at Hyde Road in the penultimate League match of the season. The team travelled over to Manchester from their training camp in Lytham. Both sides had reached the requisite number of points to survive another season in the First Division and the match was of little interest. It was a beautiful day and the Burnley players had lunch at the Mosely Hotel in Manchester prior to the game. After lunch, the players took taxi cabs to Hyde Road. Teddy Hodgson, Tom Bamford, George Halley and Levi Thorpe, who was playing in place of Bert Freeman, were in one taxi. In the centre of Piccadilly, the taxi driver attempted to overtake a tramcar and a lorry. As the road narrowed the taxi had nowhere to go and hit the lorry before bouncing off the tramcar. Luckily, none of the taxi's occupants were hurt and the four players later joked about it, but the police were called, which led to delays in the players reaching the ground.

Jerry Dawson returned in goal and apart from Levi Thorpe in for Bert Freeman, the team was as the previous game. Tommy lost the toss and Burnley played with the sun in their faces. After fifteen minutes, Howard, for City, ran into the penalty area to meet a cross from the right. Dawson, staring into the sun, went up for the catch and didn't see the onrushing Howard coming towards him, - with his knee out. Dawson was hit in the lower ribs and went down like a sack of coal. Clearly hurt he was carried off to the side by the full-backs for treatment. Tommy put Dave Taylor in goal though five minutes later Dawson returned, saying he was all right. City's next attack came through Wynn who got into the box. Dawson, clutching his side and wincing with pain couldn't get down in time to stop Wynn's low shot fly past him and into the bottom corner of the net. Dawson couldn't continue, and with Burnley down to ten men Tommy put Taylor back in goal and Levi Thorpe switched with Tommy, who went up front to lead the attack. Burnley went a further goal behind just before half-time. After the interval Teddy Hodgson managed to pull a goal back for Burnley before City scored two more to put the game well beyond Burnley's reach.

The result mattered little. John Haworth's only concern was for his number one goalkeeper. He had been ever present in the first team for four seasons and had hardly missed a game. Would he be fit in time for the Cup final in seven days? The squad returned to Lytham on the Saturday evening and the *Burnley Express* reported on the extent of Jerry Dawson's injury:

> Dawson's injury is really to the cartilage and not actually to the ribs. There is considerable soreness but his breathing was much better yesterday in fact he was allowed to indulge in a little ball practice.

His breathing was better? It must have been a serious rib injury to have impaired his breathing. The same reporter concluded, "Trainer Edwards anticipates he will be able to play on Saturday." With a possible knee problem as well as nursing damaged ribs, Jerry Dawson masked the extent of his injury well as he kicked a ball about on Lytham seafront. Every movement made him wince in pain, but he carried on regardless. Liverpool, meanwhile, had their own share of fitness problems. Liverpool's captain, Harry Lowe, was suffering from a knee injury sustained in the previous weekend's League match at Middlesbrough. Like Dawson, it was fifty-fifty whether Lowe would be fit in time.

The eve of the Cup final: Friday 24 April 1914

By Friday morning, Burnley was in carnival mood. Workers set off to the mills and factories earlier than normal to work an extended shift so they could enjoy the Saturday off. Some supporters had already left for London on the early morning trains to make a long weekend of it. The Burnley players and club officials arrived at Bank Top station and were met by hundreds of well-wishers for their ten-sixteen a.m. train. The players looked resplendent in their matching overcoats, caps and suits, gold-watch chains and claret-and-blue ties. Tommy was asked what he thought Burnley's prospects were. He gave his answer in a few words: "I believe we shall win." The *Burnley Gazette* reporter recorded no pre-match problems regarding the squad: "[T]he men are in first-class condition, and all fit and well with the possible exception of Dawson. Jerry has been suffering of late but as his general health I thought he looked in the pink of condition."

In addition to the first eleven, three reserve players, goalkeeper Ronnie Sewell, full-back Bob Reid and forward Levi Thorpe travelled with the party. The train, with *East Lancashire's Hope* emblazoned on the front, steamed in to platform one and the players climbed on board the first carriage, the directors, the players wives and sweethearts travelling in the second carriage. When all were aboard the Burnley stationmaster blew his whistle and dropped his green flag, and amidst a cloud of steam and smoke the train slowly pulled out to waves and cheers from the packed station platform. They were off, and as the train picked up speed over the railway viaduct, detonators placed along the track went off like giant firecrackers to more loud cheers. The only person on board unable to enjoy the journey was Jerry Dawson, who felt every jolt as the train made its journey south to the capital.

East Lancashire's Hope rolled into London's Euston station at four p.m. and the team set off for their base, The Charterhouse Hotel near Smithfield Market, the same hotel they used for all their League matches in the capital. In the evening, the team, officials and wives attended the George Robey review show,

Town Topics, at the Palladium theatre in the West End. At some point that evening, perhaps just before – the exact timing is not clear – a distraught Jerry Dawson met with John Haworth. Dawson declared that he was not fit to play in the final and did not want to let the team down. His movement was restricted; even turning to his side was painful. It was a noble move by Dawson to declare his injury and put the team first, but it was a massive blow for Burnley. It would also mean Dawson would not receive a Cup medal as they were only awarded to those who played in the match. After their meeting John Haworth went along to see Tommy and told him of the news. Reserve goalkeeper Ronnie Sewell and the rest of the team were all informed before turning in for the night so they could sleep on it.

In Sydenham Park at dusk, the finishing touches were being made. The Metropolitan Police and stewards were checking the pavilion and grandstands, combing the area for anything suspicious. After the death of the suffragette Emily Davison under the King's horse at the Derby the previous summer, another possible demonstration by the suffragettes was threatened as the whole country knew the King was coming to watch the match. It was a warm evening and all was quiet in Sydenham but for the sound of the cuckoo, which had arrived early this spring.

By ten p.m. in Burnley, most workplaces had shut down until Monday. After last orders in the pubs and clubs, Burnley supporters – decked out in claret and blue and their Sunday best, carrying their picnics, flags and banners – made their way to the railway stations for the special trains that began leaving Burnley at ten minutes to midnight.

Cup Final Day
Burnley v Liverpool: Crystal Palace Sydenham, Saturday 25 April 1914

From four in the morning the first of one hundred and seventy special trains from all over Lancashire began arriving at London's Euston and St. Pancras stations. By dawn, the cafes serving breakfast on Euston Road were overwhelmed and supporters of both teams set off on foot and via the Underground to see the sights in the capital. At ten o'clock, Philip and Lady Ottoline Morrell met a number of Burnley constituents outside the Houses of Parliament to give them the guided tour.

Figure 27. Lady Ottoline Morrell outside the House of Commons with Burnley supporters before the Cup final.

In Burnley, the Saturday morning papers were in expectant mood. "Burnley Expects – The Cup" declared the *Burnley Express*, displaying a picture of Ronnie Sewell and confirming the overnight story that Jerry Dawson was injured and would not take part.

In Smithfield after breakfast, the Burnley team did some light training in Charterhouse Square, before John Haworth gathered them together to discuss tactics and the day's programme. Across London in Chingford, Tom Watson, the Liverpool manager, spent the morning giving a final fitness test to Harry Lowe. He didn't make it. Ephraim Longworth would take his place in defence and Bob Ferguson would captain Liverpool for the match. Like Burnley losing their number one goalkeeper, losing their captain at such a late stage was a massive blow for Liverpool. Their team briefings over, John Haworth and Tom Watson left for a lunch engagement with Sir Thomas Bowater, the Lord Mayor of London before finally setting off separately in taxis for Sydenham.

At FA Headquarters, the Cup final match referee, Herbert S. Bamlett, was busy making his final preparations and checking his equipment. He had a new silver whistle for the final to try out, presented to him by the boys from his old school in Gateshead. At thirty-two, he would be the youngest ever Cup final referee and was busy reading his FA rule book to be certain he would implement the law correctly.

After lunch, the Royal motorcade was preparing to leave Buckingham Palace for Sydenham. It would give His Majesty the opportunity of waving to his subjects assembled all along the eight-mile route to Crystal Palace. The King was scheduled to arrive at three-twenty to be introduced to the FA executives, match officials, civil dignitaries and the two team captains prior to the match kicking-off ten minutes later.

In Smithfield, Tommy and the Burnley players packed their kitbags, said their goodbyes to their wives and made their way to Sydenham via six hired taxicabs waiting at the front of the hotel. The directors, wives and sweethearts would follow on later.

In the back of the first cab, Tommy sat quietly. He was deep in thought, nervously contemplating the hours ahead. His lunch was churning over in his stomach. He checked his pocket watch again. It was one-fifteen. At three-twenty-five, five minutes before kick-off he would step forward and bow, touch the outstretched hand of His Majesty and then take a step backwards. That's what he'd been told to do. Then he would then play in the biggest game of his life.

As the taxi drove on, the captain looked out of the window. Across the open countryside in the far distance his gaze met on a familiar sight: the unmistakable shape of the winding gear of a Kent coalmine. His life had completely changed in the eight years he'd been a professional footballer. His years in the pit, growing up in Platts Common, the family, all seemed a million miles away. In less than two hours time he was about to be presented to the King. How he wished Pat and Ellen could have been there to see it. How they would have loved the spectacle of it all. Maybe they were watching from up there. He recalled the good times and their last times together. The joys, the laughs and at the end, the sadness. He went back four years to his last visit to the Palace and the victory that was snatched away in the final minutes. *Not again, not today.* He remembered the vow he had made last summer after the wake and felt in his pocket for the lucky sixpence one of his sisters had given him. His hope above hopes was not to let them down, not today.

And then sentimental things were put to the back of his mind. There were things still to do. He opened the newspaper and pulled out the match programme. He ran a pencil down the names of the opposition, memorising the names. Later in the dressing room he would tell the others what was at stake, who to mark and to expect no picnic. He would tell them what it felt like to be on the losing side in a Cup final, how it ate away at you for months, years, and that they might not ever get another chance. Today, it had to be today. He checked his pocket-watch again for the umpteenth time. On the cover of the match programme he wrote something in pencil, before folding the sheet and putting it into his pocket.

The taxicab turned another corner and straight ahead Tommy saw the huge vaulted glass roof of the Crystal Palace sparking in the afternoon sunshine. Inside the park, the magnolia and cherry trees were in full blossom and the floral displays were a riot of colour. The park began filling up. Football supporters of both teams decked out in their respective colours wandered around, taking in the sights or sitting around in groups on the grassy open spaces enjoying their picnic lunches. Queues formed outside the huge catering marquees and beer tents, offering food and drink of every persuasion, while others were interested to see the life-sized dinosaurs on display in the lower lake area. The keener football supporters had already taken to the stands to get a good view and watch the display of the marching bands. One young Burnley supporter, a blind paper-seller who had not missed a League or Cup match all season, took up his place behind one of the goals. Also in the crowd was Thomas Holt Freeman, Bert's father, who had made a 13,000 mile journey from Australia by steamship to see his son play in the final.

The two team colours were on display everywhere around the arena. One Liverpool fan had dressed his dog in a red suit. Street vendors were doing great business selling banners, signs, rosettes, rattles, hooters, in either red and white or claret and blue.

The match programme, 'sponsored by W.H. Smith', compared the two teams:

Burnley	Height	Weight	Liverpool	Height	Weight
	Ft. in.	St. lb.		Ft. in.	St. lb.
Ronnie Sewell	5 10	12 6	Ken Campbell	5 10	11 9
Tom Bamford	5 8	12 2	Ephraim Longworth	5 8	11 0
David Taylor	5 10	12 10	Bob Pursell	5 11	12 0
George Halley	5 8	10 10	Tom Fairfoul	5 9	11 10
Tommy Boyle (Capt)	5 7	11 3	Robert Ferguson (Capt)	5 10	11 5
Billy Watson	5 7	11 13	Donald McKinlay		
Billy Nesbitt	5 7	10 12	Jackie Sheldon	5 6	10 0
Dick Lindley	5 6	10 8	Tom Miller	5 8	11 5
Bert Freeman	5 9	13 0	Arthur Metcalf	5 6	10 11
Teddy Hodgson	5 5	10 7	James Nicholl	5 8	11 8
Eddie Mosscrop	5 7	9 8	Bill Lacey	5 8	11 9
John Haworth (Sec)			Tom Watson (Sec)		

Figure 28. The Liverpool Team

Figure 29. The Burnley Team

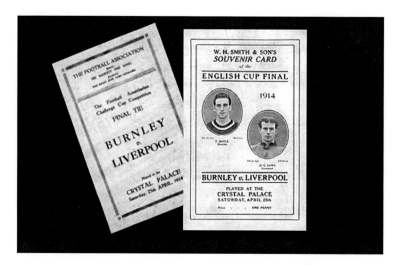

Figure 30. The 1914 Cup final programmes

Figure 31. The Cup final gets underway.
Courtesy of Eric Hebden.

After the death of suffragette Emily Davison in front of the King's horse at Epsom the year before, the police were taking no chances. Extra policemen had been drafted in and were stationed around the park entrances and the stands as a precaution against potential trouble, "the grounds [offer] a tempting mark to a suffragist with a taste for outrage," warned the Saturday edition of *The Times*.

With the afternoon temperature in the low seventies the players would soon feel the heat in their long-sleeved jerseys. The lack of rain over the week and the above average temperatures had baked the pitch hard. "There were cracks in it so wide you could get your fingers in... it looked hard as concrete," said Brunbank in the *Burnley News*

At three-fifteen, as the King was about to arrive, the Royal Standard was broken from the flagpole on top of the Royal Pavilion to great cheers from the crowd. At last, he was coming.

In the dressing room below the pavilion, Tommy and the rest of the team were getting ready: boot studs checked, liniment applied, ankles and knees bandaged. Their brand new claret-and-blue shirts hanging on their wall pegs displaying the Royal emblem. John Haworth had given the team their final instructions and wished them well. Tommy had a few words and then left and made his way to the pitch. His palms were sweating, his mind racing, nervously trying to remember the protocols he'd been told to follow when meeting His Majesty. He met the Liverpool captain who was equally nervous in the corridor and together they made their way up to the pitch.

Exactly on time at twenty past three, the Royal motorcade arrived outside the stadium. His Majesty wore a dark grey lounge suit with a red rose in his lapel, signifying the all-Lancashire final. He was met at the entrance to the pavilion by

Lord Derby and Lord Kinnaird and then escorted to the small and now brightly redecorated pavilion, decked out in flowing red velvet and freshly painted gilt handrails, displaying the colours of the two teams along with their club emblems.

The teams and three match officials, Herbert Bamlett and his linesmen Mr Talks and Mr Rogers, took to the field and lined up smartly along the touch-line directly by the pavilion. Burnley were in their claret jerseys with light-blue long sleeves, white shorts and claret-and-blue hooped stockings. Liverpool were in all-red shirts with white shorts and red stockings. The King emerged to loud cheers and applause from the pavilion and the two stands on either side and regally waved to his subjects. He was closely followed by the Lords Derby and Kinnaird. The three men descended the steps leading to the pitch. The Irish Guards and Liverpool Regiment bands struck up 'God Save the King' and everyone in the ground stood still to sing the national anthem. The two team captains then led three cheers for His Majesty before they were introduced.

Tommy swallowed and took a step forward, bowed his head, took the hand of the King and said, "Your Majesty," then he forgot to take the customary step back! The King just nodded toward Tommy and moved on to Bob Ferguson, who copied Tommy and looked the more nervous, noted Sportsman in the *Burnley Express*. The King then turned, raised his hat and climbed back up the steps, waving to the crowd before taking his seat in the middle of the pavilion, surrounded by an array of lords and ladies, Royal aides, members of the Football Association and a large contingent of policemen.

As the Burnley players broke from their line-up and took to the field to warm up, Billy Nesbitt thought he'd jump over the rope enclosing the pitch. The rope was too high and as Nesbitt jumped he caught the rope with his boot studs and collapsed on the ground in a heap to great laughter from the crowd and players. Tommy looked on and shook his head, muttering, "You daft bugger, Billy."

The sun cast long shadows across the pitch as referee Herbert Bamlett called Tommy and Bob Ferguson over to decide who would kick off. After a quick shaking of hands, Tommy won the toss and decided to change ends, Burnley taking advantage of the light breeze at their backs. He shouted one or two instructions to his men to fire them up. When the teams were in position, at three-thirty p.m. precisely Bamlett put his new silver whistle to his lips and blew to signal the start of the game.

Bert Freeman kicked off, passing the ball to Teddy Hodgson, the ball kicking up dust each time it skimmed the hard ground. The players had to cover their eyes with the bright conditions. Burnley attacked and Dick Lindley had an early shot that soared high over the Liverpool crossbar and into the stand. Liverpool counter-attacked and looked the more likely to score as a nervous Ronnie Sewell wearing his cap, twice fumbled the ball, first at the feet of Miller and then Metcalf, Dave Taylor clearing the ball away on each occasion. Tommy started shouting louder and clapping his hands at his players, encouraging them to move up the field. Liverpool attacks tested the Burnley half-back line several times before the Burnley forwards had another opportunity with a ball that ran through for Bert. The Liverpool defence cleared the danger by bundling him off the ball. "Bertie, Bertie, get hold of it!" shouted Tommy, and his captain's encouragement launched him back into action. *The Times* commented: "[Bert] Freeman stood about with an often disinterested almost detached look waiting for a chance of a single-handed attack. Sooner or later he got one, and then his fearless rush was electrifying to the spectators."

Dave Taylor, blinded by the sun, was hit square in the face with a cannonball shot from Nicholl. He was dazed for a while then alright again a few moments later after a soaking from Charlie Bates's sponge. Sewell then pulled off two fine saves from Lacey and Nicholl, Sportsman in the *Burnley Express* commenting that he "played a cat-like performance, in which he anticipated everything, towering in defence".

Tommy's voice could be heard all over Sydenham. He had toned down his normal comments, being in the presence of His Majesty, who could have easily heard him over in the Royal Pavilion. "Mossy, Mossy... Billy, Billy, Billy, hey - c'maaan..." With fists clenched and arms waving he gestured to his two wide men to get forward and told the others what to do, who to watch, where and when to get stuck in, constantly giving instructions and clapping his hands to encourage them. 'Take control early on Tommy,' that's what John Haworth had told him. 'Take control and stamp your impression on the others'. Make the opposition understand who is in charge.'

At half-time, it was stalemate and roasting hot. Bamlett blew his whistle and ended the first half of the contest. The players were drenched in sweat, covered dust, and counted their grazes from sliding tackles on the hard, dry surface. They were all ready for a mug of strong tea. Tommy's throat was as dry as a bone. "Ave you 'owt stronger, Charlie?" he asked, to break the ice. *I'll have champagne today, not beer, or water.*

John Haworth congratulated them on the work they had done so far. Each side had cancelled each other out in the heat and it would take something special to break the deadlock. Liverpool would attack, only to fail to get the ball past Sewell or be thwarted by the Burnley defenders. Bert, Dick Lindley and Teddy Hodgson looked dangerous whenever they were on the ball but they needed to see more of it to create something. The progress of Mosscrop and Nesbitt, the two wide men had been checked by the Liverpool midfield.

As the players cooled down, outside the military bands blasted out their well-rehearsed tunes, their silver and brass instruments glinting in the sun. Back at Turf Moor, the Sunday School Charity Shield match was in progress in front of a crowd of around 2,000 spectators. The first news the crowd received shortly after kick-off was that Ronnie Sewell was in goal. The crowd were updated every ten minutes with the scoreline by a boy carrying a large board around the pitch chalked with *Ten Minutes No Score, Twenty Minutes...* and so on. At least His Majesty was enjoying the match and had decided to stay until the end to see the outcome of the game.

After a final swig of tea, Tommy picked up the ball, bounced it twice and screamed his traditional "c'maaan then!", louder than ever. The game resumed and Liverpool kicked off at four twenty-five. Play carried on as the first half had ended with rushes up-field, attack and counter-attack. Twelve minutes of the second period had gone when the captain collected the ball in his own half and advanced forward just over the halfway line. He spotted Billy Nesbitt on the right who gestured to him, pointing to his feet. The pass was perfect. Nesbitt collected the ball and sped off like a hare, making progress up the wing until the Liverpool full-back, Bob Pursell, tackled him and put the ball out for a throw-in. From the throw Nesbitt collected the ball, swivelled around the defender and put in a good cross to Teddy Hodgson on the edge of the Liverpool penalty area. Hodgson went up for the header, met it first and back-headed it over Ferguson. Campbell in the Liverpool goal was watching the ball and was obstructed by one of his half-backs. He couldn't see as the ball dropped straight into the path of Bert Freeman, running toward goal about fifteen yards out from Campbell's left-hand post. As the ball bounced up, Bert met it on the volley, cutting it across Campbell's goal toward the bottom right-hand corner. Campbell, flat-footed, saw the ball flying to his right and couldn't move. He turned his head only to see the ball fly over the line and land in the back of the net.

*Figure 32. Bert Freeman scores the winning goal
for Burnley. Tommy is top left of the picture running
to congratulate him.*

As Bert turned away from goal, his arm raised in triumph,
Teddy Hodgson was the first player to congratulate him
followed by the captain. Campbell picked the ball out and
kicked it up-field in disgust. Most of the Burnley supporters,
the bulk of who were gathered at the opposite end of the
stadium, hadn't seen the ball go in. But when they saw Teddy
Hodgson, Dick Lindley, Billy Nesbitt, Bert and Tommy turn
round together, their cheers and applause started all around the
ground. Herbert Bamlett whistled and awarded the goal.
Behind the goal, the blind paper-seller asked who had scored to
be told – 'FREEMAN, BERT FREEMAN's scored son,' said all
those sitting around him.

Outside the *Burnley Express* newspaper offices in Burnley
town centre, a crowd had been gathering since kick-off and was
now so large it was stopping traffic as people waited for the
telephone to bring more news. Back at the Palace, Tom

Freeman couldn't believe it: his boy had scored to give Burnley the lead!

Ten minutes later at Turf Moor the boy with the board was proudly displaying its latest news around the pitch, *Burnley 1, Liverpool 0, Freeman Scored*. The crowd cheered wildly, any interest in the charity game now lost; it was later reported that their cheering "could be heard all over the town."

If the goal happened in a split-second, the minutes remaining seemed like hours. There was still a long-time to go. Tommy knew it. They had to concentrate now. He had been here before, seen the Barnsley lead disappear in the final minutes and could see the Liverpool players getting more of a grip on the game. From his central position he watched the action closely and bellowed his instructions to his team. Liverpool dominated for a short spell and had chances, then a shot by Eddie Mosscrop, who was having an excellent game, flaked the paint off Campbell's near post. Then at the other end, Ronnie Sewell pulled off the save of the match, stopping an almost certain goal from Lacey.

In the far distance, Sydenham's church bell struck five times. The players and the crowd knew there were around ten minutes of the match remaining. With time running out, Tom Watson pushed more Liverpool men forward to find the equaliser. Tommy, going in for a challenge with Fairfoul, was flattened. "The captain rolled about in agony," said Brunbank in the *Burnley News*, "He was carried to the sideline but refused to go off – I believe he would have had to be killed first." Teddy Hodgson then received a kick in the face and was bleeding from above the eye and had to go off for attention. Burnley were down to nine men. Could they hold on with nine? From the sideline, Tommy shouted to the forwards to get back and defend. Spectators all around the ground nervously consulted their pocket-watches. One shouted over, "Not long to go now, Tommy lad." *Ten minutes, still a long time, got to get back to help…*

Just off the pitch, sitting in front of the stand, John Haworth and Ernie Edwards couldn't keep still and checked their pocket watches. A nervous Harry Windle couldn't keep still either. He was in the pavilion, sitting four rows in front of the King, and looked over his shoulder to see His Majesty was still there and seemed to be enjoying the game. "Not long, Amelia," he said to his wife.

"Get up Tommy, or they're goin't equalise," a Burnley voice called from the crowd. Tommy turned and searched the mass of faces but couldn't find the speaker. He got to his feet, soaked himself with the cold water from the pail brought over by Charlie Bates. Refreshed and dripping with water, he returned to the fray. Back up to ten men, he had to stop Liverpool scoring in the final minutes. *Not again, not today, not bloody Newcastle all over again.* For the last ten minutes he was like a man possessed. He roared at his players, his face red, the veins in his neck fit to burst. Teddy Hodgson returned minutes later with a bandage around his head over his cut eye. Tommy shouted over to the referee, "How long left, Herbert?" Bamlett ignored him, too busy watching the play. It looked increasingly likely that Liverpool would equalise. But despite all their efforts, Burnley's defence and the half-back-line of Halley, Boyle and Watson held their ground.

Play continued. Tommy had one eye on the Liverpool centre-forward, Metcalf, whom he had just clattered after earlier picking up a long gash down his shinbone but had felt nothing, his mind totally focussed on what was going on around him. His other eye was fixed on Bamlett. The referee took out his pocket-watch to check the time. Tommy was hoping he would blow the whistle for full-time. *Surely it was time up...bloody hell Herbert?* In the eighty-ninth minute Billy Nesbitt had the ball by the corner flag, shielding it from the Liverpool defenders. Bamlett put the watch back in his pocket. *Christ, come on Herbert.* The last minute seemed like hours. Nesbitt lost the ball which was hoofed up-field into the Burnley half only to be safely taken by Sewell in the Burnley goal. "Herbert, how much longer?" Tommy shouted again. No reply.

Bamlett checked his pocket watch a second time. At twelve minutes past five he was satisfied. He slowly raised his arm and put the silver whistle to his lips, blowing it for full-time. A split-second later the sound from Bamlett's whistle had reached the players, the crowd, His Majesty and on all sides of the ground, cheers went up from the Burnley supporters. They had done it! The relief that it was finally all over was too much for some in the crowd, who ran onto the pitch. A few of Liverpool players dropped to their knees, broken, beaten. Ronnie Sewell threw his cap in the air that stuck on the goal netting and he ran over to celebrate with Dave Taylor and Tommy Bamford. Thomas Holt Freeman shed tears of joy, Annie Varley and the rest of the Burnley players wives and sweethearts were overcome with emotion, and somewhere in the crowd, John Boyle applauded the winners, his brother now the toast of Sydenham.

A hoarse and red-faced Burnley captain stood in the centre-circle, hands on his knees, his throat as dry as hell. Smiling to himself. His bloodied and bandaged knees covered in dirt, one sock cut through to the shin from Metcalf's second-half boot stud he'd never even felt. His foot resting firmly on his first prize of the day, the match ball.

"Congratulations, Tommy, well done, lad," said Bamlett.

"Thanks Herbert. I thought that bloody watch of yours had broke," Tommy replied, laughing.

Bert jogged over with a huge grin on his face. The pair burst into fits of laughter. "I see you brought your shooting boots today, Bertie," laughed Tommy as he congratulated his teammate. Then Billy Nesbitt ran over and jumped on Tommy's back. Tommy whirled him around and around just as he did in training, sending him dizzy. All the Burnley players congratulated each other, then went over and shook hands with their now sombre opponents half of who were sitting down, broken-hearted. Tommy knew exactly how they felt. It was the worst feeling in the whole world.

His whole career had been channelled to this moment, his crowning moment in football. Eight years it had taken to get here, year after year of disappointment – but not today. Today he was the King of Sydenham, and looked around the four sides of the arena surveying his kingdom. The vast cheering crowd, so many of them, their hats flung in the air, flags waving, people waving from the tall swaying trees, coloured banners of claret and blue, the smell of spring and the warmth of the late afternoon sun against a perfectly blue sky. Priceless, absolutely priceless, a golden moment no money could buy. His moment. He closed his eyes and wished it would last for ever. His place in Cup history assured. *Immortality. Champagne tonight, not beer or water.* The first Burnley captain to win the English Cup, the first captain to be given it by the King himself. The pledge he had made last summer was now fulfilled, the defeats of the past a memory. He looked upward into the clear blue sky and winked. *For you Dad.*

Over by the pavilion, the stewards were busy arranging the press and photographers into a line to take their pictures and the uniformed policemen formed a double line as the Liverpool team left the pitch to climb the steps to receive their losers medals from His Majesty. Burnley waited, and after the last Liverpool player had walked by the Cup and left the steps the stewards called Tommy forward followed by his teammates.

His heart was pounding louder than the band as he started to climb the dozen steps of the pavilion. Halfway up the steps he paused and pulled up his shirt sleeves to the elbows, exposing the elbow scrapes from where he'd fallen in battle. His Majesty was waiting. *Don't keep the man waiting.* The Cup was by his side on the table, Tommy's first sight of it. *Tell me this is real, this isn't a dream?* He stopped at the top of the steps just one step away from the King, caught his breath and bowed his head for the second time, almost cracking his head on the handrail, and took the outstretched gloved hand of the King, who congratulated him as the worthy winner and such a splendid victory. "Your Majesty," Tommy briefly looked into his eyes, bowed and thanked The King, who handed him the Cup. *Sad unhappy eyes.* The Cup was heavier than he expected, he could see the names of the winners inscribed upon its surface. Aston Villa, Barnsley, Bradford, Newcastle. Burnley's name would soon follow Villa's. He moved down the balcony to where Lord Kinnaird was standing who handed him his gold winner's medal in its case. Tommy took it and thanked him and nodded, smiling, *beaming.* He looked up to try and find Annie in the crowd. The precious trophy he had waited so long to caress, now in his hands. Below, scores of flashbulbs went off as he carried the trophy in his arms like a newborn baby, slowly and carefully down the steps. He had just joined a unique club whose members were very few. The winning captains, George Utley, Colin Veitch and Charlie Roberts. *The immortals.*

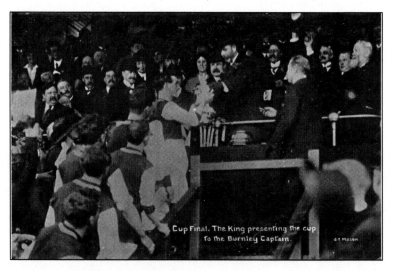

Figure 33. The winning Burnley captain is presented with the Cup by His Majesty, King George V.

The Burnley players each made their bow to His Majesty and received their medals. George Halley, followed by goal scorer Bert Freeman, Dave Taylor, a smiling Billy Nesbitt, Eddie Mosscrop the schoolmaster, Ronnie Sewell, Teddy Hodgson, Tommy Bamford, Dick Lindley and last but not least, Billy Watson, each man in turn collecting their medals. Each of them enjoying their moment of glory. Each of them looking around, trying to find a face in the crowd they knew to share the proud moment with. The whole presentation ceremony was over in seconds but what they had achieved and shared in would be re-lived over and over, every day for the rest of their lives. In that one moment at the top of those stairs they had all reached the pinnacle of their careers. This was how it felt to win football's biggest prize. It didn't get any better than this.

The two team captains were interviewed straight after receiving their medals. A proud and smiling winning captain said, "It has been a great struggle, a great game. Liverpool have striven magnificently. I think we were just the better team and deserved to win."

Bob Ferguson, the stand-in Liverpool captain, declared it to have been "a grand struggle". "Whilst I would have liked to have won the Cup," he said, "Burnley had played hard, every player was a sportsman and they each deserved their success."

That afternoon, Burnley became the most talked about team of the football world. The journalists and photographers soon left Sydenham to get back to Fleet Street and beyond to file their copy; their photographs of Tommy receiving the trophy from His Majesty would be on tomorrow's front pages. The first team to win the Cup in front of the King. The first team to defeat five First Division clubs along the way to their victory. The team that had won the Cup with only twelve players playing in the eight games. And for the second year running, a team wearing claret and blue had won the Cup, a *Royal* Cup.

In Burnley, shortly after the final whistle sounded at the Palace, and the last telephone call came through, the celebrations started. It was like no other Saturday night in town with drinking and dancing in the streets. Town-centre pubs ran out of beer before closing time and there were scenes like nothing before as the whole population joined in the celebrations. By early Saturday evening 'Funeral cards of Liverpool' were being sold in St. James's Street with the verse:

> *Ah! If they only had not fancied*
> *That football they could play,*
> *We should never had a reason*
> *For a Funeral today.*

His Majesty left Sydenham shortly after he had presented the medals. He had a number of matters preying on his mind and the match had been a welcome distraction for him in putting the affairs of state aside for an afternoon. In the dressing room, the players filled the Cup with a crate of ale and passed it round. The champagne could wait until later. They hadn't much time as dinner was arranged for seven pm up in Holborn. The Burnley team left Sydenham, with Tommy carrying the Cup, and made their way back to Smithfield in a fleet of taxicabs. Along the way, thousands of jubilant Burnley supporters cheered them on as they made their own way homeward to Lancashire. It had been a truly wonderful day. What stories they would tell when they got home. They had been there on the day and seen it with their own eyes: little Burnley, their town, their team winning the Cup in front of the King.

The Cup Final Banquet

The Cup final celebration, hosted by Lady Ottoline and Philip Morrell, began at seven p.m. at the Connaught Rooms on Great Queen Street in Holborn. Honoured guests included members of the Football Association, Lord Kinnaird and Lord Weardale, the Burnley team, their wives and sweethearts, club directors and officials. Philip and Lady Ottoline greeted them all on arrival. Tommy brought in the Cup to great applause and sat it down proudly in the centre of the top table in front of the hosts and honoured guests. Philip Morrell thanked them all for attending before everyone sat down to enjoy the dinner.

> Menu
> Connaught Rooms
> Consommé Burnley,
> Sole Florentine,
> Chicken Casserole or Saddle of Lamb,
> Mushrooms on Toast or Peaches in Ice,
> followed by coffee.

When dinner was finally over the speeches began, the first by the host Philip Morrell. Other speakers followed, and eventually, sat at the end of the table it was Tommy's turn, who was given a rousing reception when he rose to his feet. He said:

I am very pleased, seeing I am captain of the Burnley club at having won the English Cup. (Loud applause) I had hard lines at not winning it when I was with Barnsley and they won it after I left. But since I came to Burnley we only just got beaten for promotion the first year, last year we won promotion and this year we have won the Cup. (Loud Applause) I wish to thank Lady Ottoline and Mr Morrell for the kind way they have entertained us tonight and I hope and think we shall win the English League Championship next year (Applause). I sympathise with Liverpool but from the bottom of my heart I hope they may win the Cup next year. (Loud applause and cheers.)

As he sat down, the Cup was filled with champagne and passed along the top table and around the players table to great cheers. Lady Ottoline drank from the Cup and was later flattered when Bert and several other members of the team begged her to go back to Burnley with them to join in the parade on Monday afternoon.

Annie had travelled down to London with the players' wives and had watched the game from the back of the stand. It was her first visit to the capital and Tommy had bought her a new outfit for the evening and she looked splendid. The other players wives complimented the captains' fiancée on the hat she was wearing, decorated in white lace with claret, blue and white trailing ribbons, and she told them she had made it herself, especially for the occasion. As the evening progressed, Tommy winked at her assuredly from across the room.

After the speeches, there was a band and dancing and the celebrations went on long into the evening before the party eventually broke up in the early hours and the Burnley team retired to their hotel. Later, at Bedford Square, Lady Ottoline wrote to Bertrand Russell, describing the evening's celebrations and her affection for the team: "They look upon me as their mascot, but I had to decline their requests to travel back to Burnley with them."

On Sunday after church, the Burnley party enjoyed an open-topped omnibus tour of Kew Gardens, Richmond Park, Hampton Court and Windsor, and in the evening the players had free time, many of them going for an evening stroll along the Thames Embankment or taking a boat trip on the Thames.

Monday morning, and after breakfast, the team travelled by taxi to Euston for their ten-thirty train. Ottoline and Philip Morrell were waiting at the station to see them off and presented bouquets of claret carnations with blue irises to Mrs Windle and Mrs Whitehead and to a blushing Annie. The Liverpool team were also at Euston to catch their train and sportingly applauded the Burnley team as they boarded their Manchester-bound train. Tommy placed the Cup, now adorned with claret and blue ribbons provided by Annie, on the carriage table next to the window. On the way home it was filled with lemonade; the players needed to stay sober as they had their final League match to play against Bradford at Turf Moor later that evening.

The train arrived in Manchester at two-thirty, where it stopped to take on coal and water. While it was halted, the engine was decorated with claret and blue material by the engine driver and Burnley officials. The train set off from Manchester on its home leg, travelling through the East Lancashire mill towns of Bolton, Darwen, Blackburn and Accrington. Workers waved from the mill and factory windows, and people lined the station platforms all along the route to Burnley.

Sportsman in the *Burnley Express* estimated that around 10,000 people were waiting around Rosegrove station when the train arrived at five to four. The team posed for photographs on the platform and then they all boarded a charabanc with Tommy in front holding the Cup aloft. He had hardly let go of it the whole weekend. Thousands of people lined the road all the way to the town centre in order to get a look at their Cup heroes. The trams were stopped as the motorcade with players, officials and wives made its slow journey along Accrington Road to the Mitre, passing the mills and weaving sheds along Trafalgar Street. As the cars reached the junction with Manchester Road, the crowds had swelled and had to be held back by the police. It was as if royalty had come to town. Bunting and flags decorating buildings in red, white, claret and blue everywhere. In the morning's paper someone had reworded the national anthem with the words:

> *Tom Boyle, the captain then,*
> *Right ably led his men,*
> *Before the King.*
> *Royal was their display,*
> *Each man shone in the fray,*
> *On that historic day,*
> *God save the King.*

The motorcade pulled up outside the Town Hall for a reception and afternoon tea with the Mayor. Tommy and the team came out onto the balcony with the Cup and waved to the cheering thousands gathered below. Among the multitude witnessing the spectacle was a small boy who wrote over fifty years later:

> I stood as a youngster amid the mighty mass of people assembled near the Town Hall of Burnley to cheer home our Cup winners of 1914. That vast crowd was there, together with the city fathers, to welcome the Cup to Burnley for the first time. The team came out on the balcony, and there was Tommy Boyle, the captain, holding the Cup in triumph as high above his head as he could in order that all those people should see it. Even I, as a nipper of six, could see it. How I thrilled! *(R. W. Lord, 1963)*

The six-year-old Robert W. Lord never forgot what he saw that day, its lasting impression so strong that one day he too would write his own chapter in the history of Burnley Football Club. At five p.m. the players left the Town Hall to make their way by car slowly through the crowds down Grimshaw Street and Yorkshire Street and on to Turf Moor, where the Cup would reside. Strung across Brunshaw Road approaching Turf Moor a huge banner declared *Welcome to the Victors*.

As the late April sun fell toward the horizon, 35,000 people turned out at Turf Moor to see the Cup winners play their final League match against Bradford City. Prior to kick-off the two teams were led out by Tommy carrying the FA Cup. He walked to the centre-circle to show off the trophy to the crowd as the band struck up 'See the Conquering Hero Comes'. The game itself mattered little. Bradford looked like spoiling the homecoming party as they took a two goal lead through Bond and it looked as if the homecoming would end on a negative note. Burnley then rallied in the second half with a penalty from Tommy and a rare goal from Dave Taylor, scoring the equaliser with a header. At the end of the game as the players walked off, the club mascot, little Walter Place, ran to meet Tommy. He scooped the lad into his arms and lifted him shoulder high to the delight of the crowd. A pitch invasion followed as thousands of supporters tried to get as close as they could to their heroes and the Cup that was on display in the Brunshaw Road stand.

After the game the players were invited to Cronkshaw's Hotel for dinner at their 'lucky' Cup headquarters. Afterwards the team attended the Empire Music Hall where the master of ceremonies called them all up on stage to take a bow where they were given a standing ovation by the whole house and company. The following evening the Mayor held a civic reception for them at The Bull Hotel, the place where four decades before Burnley had been formed as a football club. In responding to the Mayor's toast, Tommy said:

> Thank you Mr Mayor. On behalf of the players it was a great privilege and honour to have won the English Cup. We fought hard last year but were beaten in the semi-final. This year we had got it! [Cheers] I hope that next year we will be at the top of the First Division and can I sincerely thank you for the hospitality tonight.

The last few days would live long in the memory. The photograph of Tommy receiving the Cup from King George was in every newspaper across the country. His gold Cup winner's medal hanging proudly from his watch chain. At twenty-eight, he was at the peak of his career. Life didn't get much better than this. As Tommy looked around the room, he realised that their victory had lifted the whole town; it meant so much to local people, many of whom were out of work with the recent decline in the cotton business. He had played in every game of the Cup campaign and bore the scars and bruises to prove it. As the curtain fell on football for another season, East Lancashire reigned supreme in the football world, with Burnley as English Cup winners and neighbours Blackburn Rovers, League champions.

BURNLEY
You saw Freeman score the winning goal,
FREEMAN'S
Score just the same in their Tailoring.
EVERY SUIT A WINNER
The most varied stock in East Lancashire now showing at
FREEMAN'S – Burnley's Smartest Tailors
THE CENTRE (Opposite the Hippodrome)

(Advertisement - Burnley Express, May 1914)

BURNLEY COLLIER IN TROUBLE

A Burnley collier was charged at Old Street Police Court, London on Monday with disorderly conduct and with assaulting the police. A constable stated that at 12.20 on Sunday morning the prisoner asked him the way to King's Cross Station. He directed him and without any provocation the prisoner punched him on the chest. He arrested him and then the prisoner then tried to trip him up. Prisoner said he was very sorry. He had come up from Burnley for the Cup Final and had got too much to drink.

Magistrate Mr Chester Jones: Is that the way you behave in Burnley? We do not allow such conduct in London. The prisoner murmured something about a "long day" and the magistrate imposed a fine of 10 shillings. The prisoner said he had no money left, but if allowed to return home would send the money. The Magistrate said: "Very well, you are on your honour. Pay on Saturday." *(Burnley Express, 29 April 1914)*

The Continental tour

The first the Burnley public read about a possible tour of the continent by Burnley was on 5 January following the invitation from Prague, but no further details were released on the subject until four days after the Cup final, 29 April. European tours by English clubs were not new; Tommy had toured abroad with Barnsley in 1910 and a number of other clubs had played abroad. It was already known that Glasgow Celtic, the Scottish Cup winners, were touring the Continent in May.

Political relationships between Britain, Germany and Austro-Hungary were at an all-time low when Burnley announced their tour would depart for Europe on 14 May. The Burnley board must have acted on the invitation received in January 1914, and from then would have been busy negotiating and co-ordinating the fixtures with the clubs and countries concerned. They would have had to seek permission from the FA and the Foreign Office and instructed the players to apply for or update their passports. Visas would be needed for some countries which took time to arrange. All this was going on against a deteriorating political climate and with Burnley's FA Cup campaign still progressing so there was no guarantee that they would eventually tour Europe as the eventual Cup winners. A possible explanation for the late announcement of the Burnley tour may have had a political dimension. The England national team had been expected to tour abroad, coincidentally to the same countries that Burnley announced they were going only to have their tour cancelled, as Peter Beck explains in *Scoring for Britain*:

> The early months of 1914 saw the finalisation of arrangements for a close season tour of Austria-Hungary during May and June by England's full national side. These fixtures were suggested initially at the 1913 FIFA Congress. However England's tour, replicating those made of 1908 and 1909 never took place. Even by 24th April the FA was prepared even at such a late stage to go ahead with the Austro-Hungarian tour as evidenced by the selection of the official-in-charge and 17 Players.

The tour by England had been in the planning phase for twelve months yet questions were still being asked about logistics. According to Beck, England were due to play three games on the following dates: 27 May, Vienna; 30 May, Hungarian Provincial Town; and 1 June, Budapest. Some of these dates and venues coincided with Burnley's tour dates announced on 29 April (dates that were later amended):

17 May v. Berlin Victoria FC
21 May v. Glasgow Celtic (at Ferencvaros FTC, Budapest)
24 May v. Ferencvaros (at Ferencvaros FTC)
27 May v. Hungarian Select amateur XI (at Ferencvaros FTC Budapest)
27 May v. Graz Club Vienna (original date set), fixture later cancelled after 16 May
31 May v. Vienna Rapid FC
1 June v. Austrian XI select (at Vienna Rapid FC)

Burnley's tour dates were later amended to include the Celtic game in Budapest on 21 May. As the England tour failed to get the go-ahead, whether for logistical or other reasons, the football authorities may have needed another team to take England's place and the new English Cup winners would be worthy emissaries. Beck states that there was no evidence of any government intervention in the FA's decision to cancel the England tour, but it is coincidental that Burnley's tour as the new Cup winners was initially only to Prague, but now included fixtures against three of the countries England had been going to, in the same cities and on almost the same scheduled dates. Other evidence later showed how late Burnley's arrangements were being made. On 27 May, when Burnley were already in Europe, Hugo Meisl, the Austrian coach, was in urgent communication with the Burnley directors, making the final arrangements for the two games on the Austrian leg of the tour.

Figure 34. Tommy and some of the players pose with the Cup outside the Thorn Hotel in Burnley as part of the post-match celebrations and tour of the county.

After the final League match against Bradford, Burnley spent most of the week touring Lancashire with the Cup, taking in Accrington, Blackburn and Lytham, their training headquarters. The team travelled on to Southport and Liverpool on the Wednesday afternoon before playing a charity match for the Theatrical Gala Fund at Anfield in the evening. Eight thousand people attended the game, a rerun of the Cup final, and Jerry Dawson returned in goal. Liverpool won one-nil with a deflected goal that hit Dave Taylor on the backside and went in. Tommy played well, "with his sure kicks to his wing men and his excellent heading," said Sportsman in the *Express*. But despite it being a charity game, some of the aggression of the Cup final had continued. Bert was kicked for no reason other than either being a former Evertonian or for scoring the winner at The Palace and Tommy was given a lecture by the referee for arguing over a throw-in decision.

Afterwards, both teams were photographed with the Cup and medals were presented at a dinner in Liverpool where Burnley stayed overnight. Thursday, Friday and Saturday offered more photo opportunities for the team, before the tour moved on to Rossendale, Todmorden and finally the Ribble Valley to complete a busy week. The most humorous moment was when the Burnley captain was presented with a she-goat which he said would be well looked after and kept under the stand at Turf Moor. "It will help Abel [Hudson, the Burnley groundkeeper] keep the grass down a bit," said Tommy.

WAR!

On Saturday as the Cup was passing through Nelson, two men were having a conversation when the mounted police passed by. Bill said to Joe: "Look at the Scouts." Joe said: "Get away man; can't you see those are the Mexicans and the American Cavalry. There's going to be a war!"

(Burnley Express, Jokes column, 9 May 1914)

The European Tour: May 1914

The Burnley party left Lancashire on 15 May with the full Cup team, except for Eddie Mosscrop who was not given permission by the School Board and had to report back to school for the exam period. Jerry Dawson made the trip, along with four players from the reserves, Levy Thorpe, Bob Reid, Billy Pickering and Bob Kelly. Reuben Grice, a twenty-four-year-old outside-left who had just signed for Burnley from Rotherham, travelled with the party in Eddie Mosscrop's place.

The SS Copenhagen sailed from Harwich for the overnight sail to Holland. It was a calm crossing but Bob Kelly had forgotten his sea-legs and was heaving up all night. During the following day-long train journey to Berlin, the players were engaged in learning a bit of German before arriving at tea-time, hungry and leg-weary from their trip and with Billy Pickering and Tommy Bamford suffering train sickness.

Sunday morning was spent sight-seeing around Berlin before the first match of the tour in the afternoon against the Victoria Club of Berlin. Burnley lined up: Dawson, Bamford, Taylor, Halley, Boyle and Watson, Nesbitt, Lindley, Freeman, Hodgson and Grice. Before the match began, two German players stepped forward and presented Tommy with a giant laurel wreath from the Berlin team, with a plaque stating *The Victoria Club Berlin, May 17th 1914. To the winners of the highest English football trophy.* Burnley won the match two-nil with goals from Dick Lindley and Bert, but the game itself was anything but friendly. David Taylor received a cut lip, Billy Watson a cut forehead and Reuben Grice, making his Burnley debut, was badly kicked on the ankle and knee for his trouble.

Figure 35. Tommy is presented with a giant laurel wreath by the German players before the match against the Victoria Club Berlin.

A bruised Burnley left Berlin after breakfast on a sleeper train bound for Budapest, a gruelling seventeen-hour journey. One of the Burnley party kept a journal that was published in the

Burnley Express, updating supporters on how the tour was going. "The lads are enjoying it greatly," said the anonymous author, "but the food in Berlin was too greasy and not beneficial for ball players." As the train pulled into Budapest on Tuesday morning the diarist noted, "It's very hot now and the lads are playing cards in their shirt-sleeves. We are going to the Magyar Races this afternoon." The following day the players spent the time visiting the local spa for a swim, took in the hot and cold baths, and had manicures, chiropody and a massage.

Burnley were due to play their second game against Scottish Cup winners Glasgow Celtic on Thursday. There was a trophy at stake, the jewel encrusted Budapest Cup, "shaped like a huge lighthouse" and protected throughout the match by seven policemen, "with swords, not drawn but very handy," said a reporter. The match was played at the Ferencvaros stadium. The Burnley line-up was unchanged from the first game, while Celtic played their Cup winning team of: Shaw, McGregor, Dodds, Young, Johnstone, McMaster, McAtee, Gallagher, McColl, McMenemy and Browning. Celtic lined up in green, but not their familiar green and white hoops. Instead they wore the green shirts of the home club Ferencvaros, while Burnley were told to play in blue-and-white striped shirts, the strip of local rivals and the new League champions MTK Hungaria FC. A partisan crowd turned out to witness the 'derby' dubbed in the local press, "The Battle of the Cup Winners".

The first half saw Celtic doing most of the attacking and a good shot from McAtee struck the post and rebounded to McColl, whose shot produced a good save from Dawson. Dave Taylor brought down McMenemy from behind and the Hungarian referee awarded Celtic a penalty, who converted it to take a one-nil half-time lead. In the second half Burnley were much improved and the better side. Playing with the wind swirling up from the Danube, twenty minutes into the half Burnley were awarded a penalty, which Tommy converted to put Burnley level. The reporter recalled Tommy constantly shouting at his team, encouraging them to press forward; his voice could be heard all over the ground.

The Burnley players then found themselves on the receiving end of some harsh tackling. Taylor was twice deliberately kicked on the ankle and Billy Watson was dead-legged. Billy Nesbitt was hit twice, injuring both knees and suffering 'gravel rash' on his hip and elbows. Reuben Grice was hurt in a collision with Mercer and Tommy was deliberately kicked on the shin by a Celtic player. Fifteen minutes from full-time, the game descended into a massive brawl. The *Burnley Express* noted,

> The players mistook each other for the ball and two men came to blows, [not stated who but you can guess]… the players stood shouting and arguing at each other, the hotheads wanting the match settled there and then and not too particular how the thing was done.

A pitch invasion followed. The home crowd who had not rushed onto the field were standing up yelling and cheering or stamping the planks in the stands. The match finally ended in a draw, but not before fighting broke out again on the way to the dressing rooms. The directors of the two clubs had to step in and separate the two sides from a massed punch-up. Once tempers had cooled, the teams came out and were awarded their medals. As no side had won the trophy it stayed in Budapest to be played for at a date to be decided by the two clubs and their hosts.

A two-day break followed before Burnley returned to the Ferencvaros ground on the Sunday afternoon to play the home club. Injuries forced a few changes to the Burnley line-up with Sewell deputising in goal, Taylor, Boyle (Tommy playing full-back in place of an injured Tommy Bamford), Halley, Thorpe, Watson, Nesbitt, Lindley, Billy Pickering, Bob Kelly and Grice. Ferenc took the lead early on with a shot that Ronnie Sewell couldn't stop. Then Billy Pickering had a chance to equalise with the Ferenc goal at his mercy, but nervously missed. After twenty minutes Dick Lindley equalised. Then, shortly after the restart, Lindley was tripped and fell heavily on his left arm; he heard it crack when he hit the floor. Ernie Edwards ran over and helped Dick off the field. He was in great pain and was taken to Budapest Municipal Hospital where he was treated for a fracture, coming back after the game with his arm set in plaster. He would take no further part in the tour. Bert Freeman came on in the second half but by then the home side had scored two more goals to make it three-one in favour of the home team.

On Wednesday, Burnley returned to the Ferencvaros stadium to play a select Hungarian amateur eleven. Burnley beat the amateur side two-one with goals from Freeman and Nesbitt, but the game ended with more walking wounded. Tommy had a calf strain, Billy Nesbitt a swollen ankle, Hodgson and Bamford blistered feet and Taylor a gash on his nose.

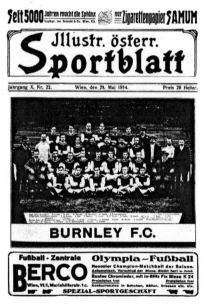

Figure 36. The Austrian sports journal, 'Presse Sportblatt'
announces Burnley's arrival.

Burnley were happy to say their farewells to Hungary on Thursday and made the eight-hour train journey to Vienna, arriving at twenty past five. The latest issue of *Sportblatt*, the Austrian sports journal, reported that the English Cup winners had arrived in town. On Friday the players left their hotel early for a guided tour of the Alps. The players thought they were being taken on a bit of a stroll and ended up climbing a 4,800-foot peak. The following morning the team were tired out, half them sporting muscle strains and more blisters. "We have two games in two days – I don't know how we shall go on," reported the anonymous diarist. "Grice cannot walk on his instep, Boyle won't play again on this trip, Bamford is doubtful and Lindley is still in plaster."

On the Sunday, Burnley played Vienna Rapid FC in front of 6,000 spectators on a gloriously sunny afternoon, Burnley winning three-one with goals from Bert, Billy Nesbitt and Bob Kelly. Then, the following evening, Burnley played the final game of their gruelling tour against an Austrian National XI, players handpicked by Hugo Meisl from three clubs; the Rapid Club, the Wiener Athletic Sportclub and the Wiener Association Football Club. Meisl had done his homework and a tired Burnley side lost the match three-nil. The team played much of the game with only ten men after George Halley picked up a thigh strain and limped off, leaving a hole in the defence which the Austrians fully exploited.

The Burnley players were simply exhausted with all the games played, the heat and the hard playing surfaces. After a long season and Cup run of forty-six matches plus another six here, the tour had turned sour. Burnley left Vienna early on Tuesday morning and the team travelled to Leipzig on another long train journey, during which a sleepy Reuben Grice fell out of his bunk and badly hurt his back. The tour had been an 'interesting' experience, one the players wouldn't forget, but every one of them bore a physical souvenir or more of the trip.

The headline in the *Burnley Express* on 6 June when they returned home read "HOME AGAIN – HAD ENOUGH OF CONTINENTAL FOOTBALL". Trainer Ernie Edwards summed up the mood in an interview:

> I would sooner have gone through half a League season than play in those conditions. There were no facilities for washing the players' kit or drying them and twice I had to go on the roof to get them dried.

When the players got back home they were given leave for the remainder of June and July and told to report back the first week of August for pre-season training. It was a glorious summer in Lancashire, eighty degrees in the shade and hotter still in the mills and factories. In Burnley's Scott Park the ice-cream sellers were doing a roaring trade and a huge flower-bed had been created commemorating Burnley's famous Cup victory, picking out the players' names and the Cup in claret, blue and gold flowers using over 2,000 plants. Tommy's name sat proudly in the centre under the King's crown.

The first Saturday of July signalled the start of the annual Wakes week holidays and Burnley like all the other Lancashire mill towns, emptied. The factories and the mills closed down for a week and the seaside resorts filled up with happy, sun-seeking Lancastrians who knew little of the events unfurling across the Channel.

Chapter 8: The Bloody War

Figure 37. The Grand International - war as sport.

On Sunday 28 June, four weeks after Burnley returned home from Austria, the heir to the Austrian throne, Archduke Franz Ferdinand and his wife Sophie were murdered after attending morning church service in Sarajevo. An already tense situation across Europe escalated and became graver by the day. The assassination set in motion a chain of unstoppable events as governments across Europe chose sides based on alliances, paper treaties and affiliations. Germany, allies of Austro-Hungary declared war on France and Belgium on Monday 3 August, the same day that the Cup-winning Burnley players returned to Turf Moor for pre-season training. The following day, as Britain was allied with France and Belgium, the British government declared war on Germany. The glorious peaceful summer was shattered.

In London, The Stock Exchange closed and all police leave was cancelled. Army and navy personnel on duty at the Royal Lancashire Show were recalled to barracks. The *Daily Mirror* carried photographs of navy dreadnoughts steaming up the English Channel in a show of sea power. Channel crossings to Germany ceased and telephone lines with the country were disconnected. The British Expeditionary Force was despatched to protect the French and Belgian ports. Across Britain, army recruiting stations opened. The price of food rose in the shops, meat by a penny per pound and a loaf of bread by three pence.

In Vienna, former Burnley footballer Jimmy Hogan, who had only taken up his post as coach to the Austrian FA in June, was followed in the streets by detectives before finally being arrested and imprisoned. His wife and children eventually managed to escape back to England with help from the American Embassy. Sam Wolstenholme, the former Blackburn Rovers player who had just started as trainer/coach with the German Football Association, and Steve Bloomer coaching at the Berlin Brittania club, were both thrown into a prisoner of war camp.

Four days after Britain declared war on Germany, the weekend *Burnley Express* carried a photograph with the caption "BURNLEY FOOTBALLERS CALLED UP". Charlie Bates, the reserve team trainer and an army reservist, was the first of the Burnley staff to get the call to rejoin his regiment. He was followed by reserve team regulars Sam Gunton and Alf Lorimer. These three Burnley men would be in it from the beginning.

Like everyone else, the Burnley players thought the fuss would all be over and done with in a few weeks and the three men would be home safely and in time to see the start of the new football season. We needed to teach Fritz a lesson and that would be that. With the start of the football season only a few weeks away and players already signed to new contracts, the FA and Football League announced that the 1914–15 football season would go ahead as planned. Cup holders Burnley would be able to defend their trophy. But the football authorities' decisions were not without their critics. Should they play their fixtures and face the wrath of some who thought that footballers should be joining the fight, or should they carry on playing and show the enemy that in Britain it was business as usual? On the Saturday of August Bank Holiday weekend, the first Saturday of the football season, the *Burnley Express* posted anonymous letters from two 'concerned citizens'. The first read:

> Sir, will you allow me as a working woman to protest against the football (FA) decision allowing play whilst our brave men are giving their lives for them and their country? If the men have not the courage to fight at least they might have the decency to keep the enemy from knowing it...

The next letter, aimed at the stay-at-home football supporter, was written by 'A Spectator for 20 years':

> What a terrible thing it must be for our gallant lads in the trenches to read of the hundreds of thousands of loungers idling their time away. Football to proceed! Good god! One reads of the unspeakable atrocities of the fiery, blood-thirsty Huns, laying waste to a peaceful country and murdering its inhabitants, committing fiendish acts on the women and children...

Letters like these appeared in newspapers all over the country and were usually anonymous. In September the football authorities announced that after the 1914–15 League season and the FA Cup competition had ended, both competitions would be suspended until the end of the war. For this season, however, clubs could honour their commitments to the players despite falling gates and revenues.

By September the war wasn't going to plan. The British Expeditionary Force, outnumbered three to one, was forced to withdraw at Mons. More men were urgently needed to shore up the front-line, so the War Cabinet called in the reserves and territorials. The initial public enthusiasm for the war started to wane as news started coming back from France that this was no picnic. The opposing armies began digging in along a 500 mile front that began at the Belgian coast and ran all the way to the Swiss border.

At Turf Moor, Cup winners Burnley hosted Bradford City in their opening League match of the 1914-15 season. Tommy missed the game due to a thigh injury picked up in training and Burnley lost one-nil, starting the season at the foot of the table. The Clarets gained their first win against Everton at home on the following Bank Holiday Monday. Then two away games followed at Manchester City and Spurs. The City match was lost one-nil, but Tommy was back in the Burnley line-up for the Spurs match at White Hart Lane. Burnley dominated the game from start to finish and won impressively, three-one, with a goal from Bert in the first half and two in the second half from Teddy Hodgson, the last one set up by Tommy for Teddy to score with a fine shot. They were back in business. Orion, the *Daily Express* reporter said of Tommy: "[H]e set about his work methodically and quietly – but stubbornly. There was purpose in his every movement and his grasp of the situation at least a couple of moves ahead of the others..."

The pressure to call a halt to professional football accelerated. In answering further public criticism, in early October 1914 the FA and the Football League proposed that players should engage in some kind of military training. In addressing the falling attendances at grounds, there would also be a player wages scheme introduced that would implement pay reductions of between five per cent for those on under three pounds per week, up to fifteen per cent for those on the top salary of five pounds per week. The money collected would be redistributed among the clubs to keep them afloat as their attendances reduced. These ideas went down like a lead balloon when the players found out. Tommy, like the other Burnley players, was outraged.

Burnley captain in 'gassing' incident

After the home match against Sheffield United, the following Monday night, the twelfth of October, was Bert Freeman's twenty-ninth birthday, and to celebrate a gang of Burnley players hit the town on a night out. Tommy and Bert got back to their digs in Stoneyholme after closing time and both of them turned in. What happened after was reported in the Burnley Express the following Friday.

> It is stated that Tom Boyle narrowly escaped an untimely end by asphyxiation early last week. He and Bert Freeman lodge at the same house in Burnley, and occupy adjoining bedrooms. After retiring on Monday night, Boyle spent some time reading and then turned out the light. What subsequently happened is a matter of surmise, but in withdrawing his hand he must have again touched the tap, and altered its position sufficiently to allow a free escape of gas.

> During the night Freeman was awakened by groans, and detecting a smell of gas, hurried into Boyle's room, to find his colleague unconscious in bed. Assistance was at once secured, and whilst measures were being adopted to restore animation, Freeman sped off for a doctor. When the latter arrived Boyle had recovered consciousness and he had recovered from the effects of the "gassing" with surprising rapidity, thanks to a strong constitution, which in the opinion of the medical man, accounts for his escape from a worse fate. Burnley supporters will wish him many happy returns of the day on which he saved the life of a club mate. (*Burnley Express*, 21 October 1914)

Both of them had been lucky. Had Bert also gone to sleep they could both have been asphyxiated or killed in a gas explosion.

The *Burnley News* carried another anonymous article that had previously been printed in the *Lancashire Daily Post*, directly attacking professional footballers, titled "SPOILT PLAYERS – MEN WHO SHIRK THEIR RESPONSIBILITIES". Though failing to name individuals or call footballers cowards directly, the tone of the article and the language used would have mortified any professional player, who was only earning a living, doing his job and fulfilling his contract until the end of the season. The players' working conditions had already been drastically affected by the war, but it would get much worse. Following the Aston Villa match, the *Burnley Express* announced that only George Halley in the Burnley squad had disagreed with the wage reduction scheme and as a consequence he had been dropped from the first team. A man of principle, Halley took his case to a League tribunal. He lost and as a result it would be a long while before he would pull on a Burnley shirt again.

The military 'training' began at Turf Moor in late October 1914. Part of the training involved target practice using air rifles, shooting at cardboard targets across the pitch. George Halley thought he would go one better and try shooting at a moving target. Fixing his sights on a bucket being carried around the ground by a workman, Halley took aim and fired. He missed the bucket by a yard and shot the poor man in the arm, the slug needing to be cut out at the infirmary. Halley clearly wouldn't make the sniper corps.

The next move from the football authorities was to announce that players would have to be engaged in war work in order to play for a League club, though it didn't state what type of work they were to do, or for how many hours a week or even when the work would begin. A number of factories in town had now switched their production facilities to war work, making shells, uniforms and medical supplies and each player would have to register their availability.

Another trophy for Burnley

On 7 December 1914 Burnley had won through to the Lancashire Cup final, where they beat Rochdale four-one in the final at Hyde Road thanks to two goals from Billy Pickering and goals from Bob Kelly and Teddy Hodgson. Tommy was absent for the match through injury but was awarded a medal for taking part in the earlier rounds of the competition.

After Christmas the 1915 FA Cup competition got underway with the holders Burnley drawn at home in round one defending their trophy against Huddersfield Town. Burnley won three-one with goals from Bert Freeman, Bob Kelly and Levy Thorpe. Despite the scoreline it was a close game, with Fayers playing an outstanding game for Huddersfield, scoring one and having two cleared off the line by Dawson and Taylor. In the second round The Clarets faced Southend United at Turf Moor and ran out easy six-nil winners. Burnley were in round three of the Cup and they were starting pick up points in the League. Things were looking promising as the season reached the three-quarter stage.

But at the end of February 1915, the positive mood at the football club was broken as the team received shocking news. Alf Lorimer, who had been one of the first three Burnley players called up the previous August, had been killed in action on 1 February in Egypt. Alf served in the Royal Army Medical Corps, helping the sick and the wounded, his unit was attached to the 2nd Battalion, the East Lancashire Regiment. Alf was only twenty-three and had a whole career ahead of him. He was buried close to where he fell in Ismailia War Cemetery on the West Bank of the Suez Canal.

John Haworth found it hard to break the news to the players. Losing one of their own hit them all hard. Up to that moment it had all been a bit of a game, it would all be over by Christmas the generals had said. Alf Lorimer's death brought home the seriousness of it all. Tommy and the rest of the team knew it wouldn't be long before they too would be engaged in the fighting. *Over by Christmas, the bloody liars.* By this stage football had descended into a surreal affair. Matches were played in front of half-full stadiums, to khaki-uniformed crowds, with growing numbers of returning wounded soldiers sitting around perimeter of the pitch swathed in bandages, maimed, crippled.

In the third round of the Cup, Burnley lost their grip on the trophy in a tight game at Burnden Park where Bolton Wanderers won two-one. The thing that had been so hard to win would now grace another clubs trophy cabinet.

After the upset of the Cup, in the remaining months of the season, Burnley almost won the League Championship in the final furlong. At the start of March, they were mid-table. Then a great run of nine straight wins rocketed Burnley up the table and in the end any one of six sides could have won the title. Burnley finished the season in fourth place, only two points behind champions Everton, followed by second place Oldham and Blackburn in third. The top six clubs were separated by just two points, the closest ever finish to a League season. As the curtain came down on League football at the end of April, Tommy's old mate George Utley won his second FA Cup winners medal as his Sheffield United side won the Cup at Old Trafford.

In April 1915 the Germans began using a new weapon against the allies. Chlorine gas caused panic as its green-yellow cloud rolled across no-mans land. If the soldiers didn't get their gas-masks on in time, they choked to death where they stood. As the football season ended and players were released from their contracts, their futures were uncertain. The players were now actively seeking full-time work in local mills and factories to support themselves and their families.

Football continues

League Football started up again in September with the formation of the Lancashire Section, with fourteen clubs represented: Burnley, Stockport County, Bolton Wanderers, Stoke, Bury, Rochdale, Preston North End, Oldham, Liverpool, Blackpool, Manchester United, Southport Central, Manchester City and Everton. Blackburn Rovers did not compete in the new League in 1915–16; instead, several of their players signed on with Burnley or other clubs in order to play and keep fit. The Burnley squad that started the 1915–16 campaign included Dawson and Langtree (goalkeepers), Bamford, Taylor and Wild (full-backs), Boyle, Watson, Shaw, Hampson and Brown (half-backs), Nesbitt, Kelly, Freeman, Hodgson, Mosscrop, Stevens and Lindley (forwards). Five Blackburn players joined the Burnley ranks: Cowell, Walmsley, Orr, Byrom and Scholes.

As the new season was about to start, John Haworth told the team of another casualty of the war. Charlie Bates the Burnley reserve team trainer serving with the South Staffordshire's in France had been captured and taken prisoner. He was being held in a prisoner-of-war camp in Germany. Tommy, along with most of his teammates, now found themselves working forty-eight hours a week in local factories making munitions. The contractual changes that had come into effect at the end of April decreed that in order to play for a club, players had to be either enlisted or engaged in war work of some kind. Bert Freeman was working on munitions in his native Birmingham, Levy Thorpe was up in Newcastle, Billy Pickering and Jimmy Lindsay were working in the Glasgow shipyards, Ronnie Sewell was apparently running a pub in Lincoln and Cliff Jones was working in Sheffield. Several Burnley players had already joined the ranks. George Halley had enlisted as a sapper in the Royal Engineers, reserve team player George Thompson joined the Pioneer Corps Special Mining Group, Bill Clarkson joined the Royal Artillery's Howitzer Brigade and John Mitton joined the Coldstream Guards. Only Eddie Mosscrop carried on in his old day job, teaching in Southport, and that wouldn't be for long.

The final insult from the football authorities was that players in England were to receive nothing for playing, expenses only, though in Scotland the Scottish Football Association had said players could earn a pound a week. Professional football contracts became outlawed in England and the players were paid solely from their jobs in the factories or from the armed forces. Football training took place two evenings a week with matches held only on a Saturday afternoon or a Bank Holiday. With no say in the matter and the players' union powerless, the players were forced to comply and play for nothing or forego their long-service record in the hope of reaching the required five years for a benefit match when the war ended. Players were still tied to clubs for registration purposes and could claim expenses up to a maximum of two shillings and sixpence a day for meals and third class rail fare when travelling to training and to away matches. All this had to be funded up front by the players, who could then claim back the money. Football club management and ground staff could continue to be paid, but the most galling for the players was that match referees and officials could still be paid their appearance fee.

The government was determined to make soldiers of them. At this rate, conscription was only a matter of time, so from the players' point of view, why rush to the ranks now? Look what had happened to Alf Lorimer and Charlie Bates. From the players view, they may as well work in the factories and play out the 1915–16 season; after all, it might be all over by Christmas, but which one?

The Burnley players then found out that John Heaton, a former Burnley player from Padiham who had volunteered for the

Coldstream Guards, had been killed in action. The *Burnley Express* said he had died "somewhere in France, at the front". Heaton had played in the Burnley reserve team and gone on later to play for Padiham FC. He was only twenty-one. Then, another tragedy when just a few days later, Harry Langtree, Burnley's new reserve goalkeeper, who was in Blackpool on holiday was suddenly taken ill and died in hospital following an emergency operation. He was only twenty-three. When the Club heard the news they lowered the flag to half-mast as a mark of respect.

The weather for the first weekend of September was glorious and large numbers of locals made their exodus to the coast for a short break. The first Saturday of September saw Burnley begin the new League against Rochdale in fine style at Turf Moor with a thumping six-one victory. "Boyle in rare fettle," said the *Express*, "Tommy was up to his usual tricks and sending old time passes out to the wings."

The same week brought more news from the war with the sinking of the passenger liner the *Royal Edward*. The liner had been converted to a troopship and had set sail from Alexandria bound for Gallipoli on 13 August. On board was a crew of 220, with 31 officers and 1,335 men. After setting sail at midnight, the ship had been shadowed by a German U-boat. The *Edward* was hit by a single torpedo fired from a mile away, which tore off the ships' stern. The decks were awash in three minutes and the *Royal Edward* went to the bottom three minutes later. The first reports stated that 132 men were lost, but as the days went by the death toll rose. *The Times* on 17 August reported that one thousand were now listed as missing. Of the various regiments on board was a company of seventy-two men from the 2nd East Lancashire Field Ambulance Territorials: local men, volunteers who had signed up in 1914, not to kill but to help the sick and the wounded – doctors, nurses, medics and stretcher bearers.

Half of the company was listed as missing. The whole town was in mourning for the missing men.

The Ministry of War kept up its request for more volunteers, "We must have more men," ran the adverts in the press. After the loss of a number of local men, the numbers of volunteers slowed to a trickle; just fourteen men signing up for the whole of the last week of September 1915, whereas a year before the queues circled the Town Hall.

BURNLEY RECRUITING CAMPAIGN OPENS TODAY
MEN URGENTLY WANTED
5th East Lancashire's.
Recruiting at the Drill Hall, Keighley Green. Open daily
from 9am to 9pm
Men wanted from five feet two inches, chest $33^{1}/_{2}$ inch
Ages 19–40 untrained and up to 45 trained.

JOIN AT ONCE AND HELP YOUR PALS
GOD SAVE THE KING

*(Army Recruitment Advertisement, Burnley News,
September 1915)*

On a much happier note, Billy Watson married Miss Lily Sanderson in Southport and the couple bought a house in the town. A two-all draw in the Burnley's next game against Bury at Turf Moor set up a big game against Manchester United at Old Trafford on 9 October. Burnley started like a house on fire. At half-time Burnley led United six goals to two. In the second half The Clarets increased their lead and the final score was seven-three to Burnley. Another good win at home to Blackpool followed: after Burnley were initially two-nil down, they went on to win five-two. Yet even though the team were winning games with ease looking at the results, Kestrel the sports correspondent in the *Burnley Express* had noticed the players were beginning to lose their fitness as the season progressed:

> [O]ne hears of the falling away of the men in the matter of physique, the effect of the indoor occupation in overheated rooms and in an impure atmosphere. The healthy looks and the springy step are beginning to go and the men are losing that elasticity of body and limb...

Gunner Boyle

At a meeting of the local Parliamentary Recruiting Committee at Burnley Town Hall on 19 October, the issue of the 'Lord Derby Canvass' was the subject of much controversy. The 'Canvass' or 'Group Scheme' was put forward as a means of categorising men if and when a call-up was needed. The Burnley players knew it was just conscription by another name. The number of volunteers had dwindled and drastic action was needed to get more men into uniform. The Derby Canvass followed on from two government moves in the summer. First, the upper age limit for war service was raised from thirty-eight to forty, but this only brought in a few thousand extra recruits and was later extended to fifty-one. Then the government passed the National Registration Act to find out how many men between the ages of fifteen and sixty-five were engaged in a trade and how many men they could call on. All men who were not already in the forces were obliged to register and give details of their employment details. Locally, men were given until late August to register their professions at Burnley Town Hall. Nationally the survey found that some five million men of military age aged between eighteen and forty were available to join the armed forces, of which one point six million were in the 'starred' category, meaning the higher skilled jobs. Footballers were not included in the starred category, though a player could be term ' starred' if he held a skilled trade. Lord Derby, one of the FA officials who had handed out the medals at the Cup Final the previous year, was appointed Director-General of Recruitment by the government in early October. It would eventually fall to him to raise the required numbers.

> The men who registered under the Derby Scheme were classified into married and single, and into 23 groups according to their age. Group 1 was for single 18 year-olds, then by year up to Group 23 for single 40's. Group 24 was for married 18 year-olds up to Group 46 for married 40's. (*www.1914-18.net*)

Most professional footballers were young, single, in good health and of average height and weight. They would make class A1 recruits in army fitness terms and 'excellent soldiering material.' Tommy, Bert and Bob Kelly were placed in the same group, as they were all single. Tommy would be in Derby Group number ten or twelve, depending on what age he gave the recruiting officer. The lower the group number, the earlier would be their call-up. Under the Derby scheme, Tommy could have been attested at either Burnley Barracks, former home of the Cavalry, on Padiham Road, or at the Town Hall, where he would have a medical and swear allegiance to the King. Burnley Barracks were home to the local Royal Field Artillery (RFA) under the command of Major Smythies, the officer commanding 30th Regimental District recruiting area. Men could give a preference to the recruiting officer and their wishes were carried out as far as possible. As Tommy joined the Royal Field Artillery, it is most likely he was attested at Burnley Barracks as his wishes to join the RFA were granted, as were Bob Kelly's. Pay was one shilling and two and a half pence per day for a gunner, one shilling and nine pence for an acting bombardier, and two shillings and three pence for a bombardier. It was a heck of a lot less than the five pounds a week Tommy was used to as a footballer with bonuses on top. He'd have to cut his cloth accordingly.

FOOTBALLS FOR SOLDIERS

Private J.F. Bradshaw of the 10th East Lancashire Regiment based at Wareham says: "When I received the ball today and opened it everyone jumped for joy. I am sure if you could have seen them you would have known that you had not spent time and trouble for nothing. We are practically all supporters of Burnley FC and wish you and the club the best of luck." (*Burnley Express, 17 November 1915*)

Back in football action, Burnley drew one-all at Haig Avenue with Southport Central in late October to put them third in the Lancashire League on eleven points, behind joint leaders Manchester City and Everton. "A weak display by the forwards," was Spectator's assessment in the *Burnley News*. Tommy and Bob Kelly were both missing, receiving their day-under-the-colours induction in Preston at the Royal Field Artillery Barracks in Fulwood. By November 1915 the attendances at Turf Moor had dwindled. The club had brought in only five hundred pounds in gate receipts from their first four home matches, compared to two thousand seven hundred and fifty pounds for five games in the 1913–14 League season. That figure equated to around 5,000 paying people per match, but the attendance figures would have varied due to the free access to men in uniform and ladies.

Christmas 1915

As the second Christmas of the war arrived for many men it would be the last they would enjoy at home with their families. In France there would be no repeat of the previous year's Christmas Day truce when the two opposing sides met in no-man's land to play football. The generals had put a stop to all that nonsense. For the men registered under the Derby Scheme it would be only a matter of months before they would get the call. Derby Groups six to thirteen, including Tommy, Bob Kelly and Bert Freeman who had joined the Royal Flying Corps, received their call-up in late February 1916.

The first mention of Tommy's rank/position was given in the *Burnley Express* in March; he was named as 'Driver Boyle' on the Burnley teamsheet. Shortly after, he became Gunner Boyle, Service Number 118158, and was based in Preston, like Bob Kelly, at Fulwood Barracks.

As some of the local wounded men started returning home, Miss Aitken, matron of the Ellerslie Auxiliary Military Hospital at Blackburn, wrote to John Haworth:

> We have 27 wounded soldiers here at present but by Christmas Day I may have 34. Would it be possible to reserve 34 good seats for the Burnley v. Liverpool match at Turf Moor? I will send them in a char-a-banc with one orderly.

John Haworth wrote back promising free seats in a good position for all the men. The game itself ended in a three-all draw in front of a crowd of around 12,000, bringing in two hundred and sixty-three pounds, the best gate receipts of the season. The result put Burnley top of the Lancashire League. After the turn of the year Burnley's good form continued with one of the most exciting games ever seen at Turf Moor when Burnley met Manchester United on 12 January. The first half saw eight goals and Burnley were five-three up at the interval. The final result was seven - four to Burnley. The Clarets followed up the high-scoring victory over United with a five-nil win over Southport Central. With the former Claret goalkeeper Jack Hillman playing in place of Jerry Dawson, Burnley were four-nil up inside thirty-three minutes. "It was a treat to see Boyle looking more like his old self and giving a display worthy of his reputation and it was great to see his two goals," reported Kestrel in the *Express*. The result could have been in double figures but for Drabble in the Southport goal.

One of the first Burnley players to receive his call-up was the young Scot Billy Pickering. Billy had been working full-time on munitions work in his native Glasgow and joined the Seaforth Highlanders, the historic, kilted Scots regiment who were bound for the conflict overseas in Mesopotamia fighting the Turks.

The following Saturday Burnley's good form in the League continued against one of the top three sides, Everton. The fine weather and good form had brought a good crowd out at Turf Moor to see the game, Burnley winning by two goals to one. With just a minute to go the sides were level at one-all when Billy Nesbitt scored a beauty, pulling down a cross-field ball, dribbling through two full-backs and shooting low to place the ball past Fern in the Everton goal. He then received a kick on the knee for his trouble and was carried off injured. Burnley were the League's highest scorers with sixty-six goals in twenty-three games and second in the table behind Manchester City. Three games remained and City were still to visit Turf Moor in a fortnight.

In the City match, the team arrived late so the referee declared there would be no half-time interval. Burnley went on to beat them by three goals to one. "It was a victory in which all departments took a share," said Kestrel in the *Express*. Teddy Hodgson and Bob Kelly were the best players on display. "It was certainly one of Boyle's best games, who kept a watchful eye on Fairclough." Burnley had been undefeated at home all season, but their away form had dipped since Christmas.

The League's deciding game took place on 26 February against Stoke City at the Victoria Ground. Going into the game, Manchester City were just a point ahead of Burnley, who had to win if they were to stand a chance of winning the title. Tommy was playing his last game before his expected call-up, but the conditions were poor with a rutted, snow-covered pitch. Burnley took a one-nil lead into the second half through Teddy Hodgson, but suffered from knocks to no fewer than eight players during a dirty, foul-strewn game. Johnny Brown, playing his Burnley debut, came off worst, suffering concussion and a bloody nose after being hit full in the face with the ball. Jerry Dawson was charged down while he was hold of the ball and was kicked on the shoulder while on the floor. Tommy got a kick on the ankle and limped off the field at the end with most of the others. The game ended in a two-all draw, which wasn't enough. It was close in the end and Burnley took the runners-up spot to Manchester City, who won the Lancashire League title by two points.

The season had seen some wonderful highs – fourteen goals scored against Manchester United, seven-three at Old Trafford and seven-four at Turf Moor. They had come back from a two-goal deficit against Blackpool to win five-two and had scored five goals or more in six matches.

The Northern Section subsidiary competition, March to May 1916

As one competition ended another one began with the League's Lancashire Northern Section - 'Subsidiary Competition,' a sort of mini-competition to lengthen the season until the summer with ten more games. Six clubs took part: Burnley, Blackpool, Preston North End, Bolton Wanderers, Bury and Southport Central. Tommy had still not received his marching orders and carried on playing, as did the others, fitting in games between their day jobs and training in the evenings. The subsidiary competition began on 8 March, and as many pubs were now closed on Saturday afternoons the football clubs hoped it would lead to an increase in attendances. There were major doubts that the new League would even last for two months and Kestrel in the *Express* noted that John Haworth was struggling to find players to cover for those who had received their call-up.

Before the new competition started the players learned that another Burnley player, Private Matt Brunton, had been wounded by shrapnel in France. Brunton wrote from his hospital bed in Leicester, "I am progressing well as can be expected, but it gets a bit tedious lying in bed so long and I look like having to stick it a while yet."

The Burnley v. Bolton game began like more of a friendly than a 'proper' League match, reported Kestrel in the *Express*. Bolton were without three of their forwards, all having been called up, and several others were not allowed to come to Burnley "because of the measles epidemic". Lance Corporal George Halley was home on leave and was back in a Burnley shirt to make his first appearance of the season. The team sheet read Dawson, Bamford, Taylor, Halley, Boyle, Brown, Kelly, Lindley, Watson, Hodgson and Mosscrop. Burnley ran out the winners, three goals to one, with a rare goal from Billy Watson playing as a makeshift centre-forward and Teddy Hodgson scoring the other two.

Eddie Mosscrop became the next Burnley player to receive his call-up. On 15 March 1916 Private Edwin Mosscrop joined his Royal Army Medical Corps unit down in Aldershot. He had previously attended a tribunal for conscientious objectors over his views whose outcome said he was exempt from military service due to his employment, but that meant little, Eddie still signed up to the RAMC and as a consequence would soon find himself posted overseas.

In the next League match, Burnley beat Blackpool at Bloomfield Road two-one and topped the League with two wins. The team then lost at Bury before returning to winning ways with a six-one win over Southport Central at Turf Moor on 29 March. The next game was the home game against Blackpool at Turf Moor on 15 April.

Boyle vs. Bainbridge: Round Two

Despite the players were not being paid and the Subsidiary League Competition may have meant little to the players, was untrue. Self-respect and pride were at stake. Before the Blackpool game, The Seasiders topped the division with ten points from six matches. Burnley were two points behind them in second place. It was three years since Tommy had met his nemesis, Joe Bainbridge, in the Second Division in March 1913. On that day, Tommy had been on the receiving end of a black eye. He hadn't forgotten it, and was determined to get even. The team list read Dawson, Bamford, Taylor, Lindley, Driver Boyle (given as Tommy's RFA rank), Brown, Kelly, Hastie, Chapman, Hodgson and Ellis. Apart from Teddy Hodgson, it was a totally new forward line. The referee, Mr Westwell of Radcliffe, had a nightmare game, particularly in applying the offside rule. The crowd got on his back from almost from the first whistle, constantly barracking him and his linesmen. After a game of niggling kicks and knocks, Kestrel of the *Express* reported that it all sparked off in the final minutes with Burnley leading two-one:

> Boyle was again engaged in what was an unseemly incident, but he was not the aggressor, though he probably was at Blackpool and it would appear that ill-feeling engendered on the previous occasion and been allowed to rankle.

> Boyle was on the ground and had no option but to collar Bainbridge by the legs and pull him down as the Blackpool back's feet were making too free with various parts of Boyle's anatomy. For a time after that fur flew, fists were busy, players were engaged in rough, hurly-burly pulling the combatants apart and incidentally developing minor engagements of their own.

The melee continued for what Kestrel said was "a brief period", and it was just as well the game was almost at an end with the referee and officials unable to control matters. No booking or sending off followed for either of them. It didn't matter who it was or how big they were, no-one crossed Tommy Boyle and got away with it.

After the final game against Southport, which ended in a four-two win for Burnley, the competition came to an end with Burnley as the 1916 Subsidiary League champions.

Burnley   P10   W8   L2   D0   F29   A12   Pts 18
Blackpool P10   W7   L3   D0   F23   A14   Pts 14
Bolton   P10   W5   L4   D1   F17   A21   Pts 11

In the two League competitions combined, Burnley had scored 100 goals over the 1915–16 season. Teddy Hodgson played in every game in both competitions, scoring twenty-three goals in thirty-six games. Billy Nesbitt had scored nineteen goals in twenty-five appearances. Tommy had made twenty-two appearances in the Lancashire league and all ten appearances in the subsidiary competition, scoring eight goals including four penalties.

After the League season finished, a number of charity games were organised to raise war funds. Tommy and a number of players were involved and on May Day 1916 he organised a match between an RFA team and a Burnley FC eleven in aid of the Mayor's war charities fund. 'The Gunners', many of them professional footballers and semi-pros, lined up Sergeant Dutton in goal, Gunners Waring and Pilling, Sergeant Sidley, Gunner Boyle and Bombardier Prince, Burnley's own Gunner Bob Kelly, Sergeant Norman, Gunner Lord, Gunner Handforth and Gunner Marsden. The Burnley XI lined up Barber in goal, Pedley, Bamford, Walders, Thorpe, Brown (Johnny was playing his last game before call-up) and up front Scholes, Jerry Dawson (playing as an inside-forward), Hastie, Dick Lindley and Teddy Hodgson.

The military were the better organised side right from the start, Tommy mustering his forces so well that the RFA took a four-nil lead into the interval. Barber, the Burnley keeper, was under constant fire from the RFA forwards. In the second half Tommy handled in the penalty area but Tommy Bamford put the penalty wide. Inside-forward Jerry Dawson helped Teddy Hodgson score a consolation goal late on, but the game ended four-one to The Gunners.

The following Saturday, another charity match took place against Blackburn Rovers at Ewood Park. Rovers hadn't played together all season, having seen their players play for a number of sides including Burnley, but they were all back together for the game. Burnley struggled to fill George Halley's slot and ended up pitching Billy Nesbitt into the role. At half-time Burnley were three-one down to Rovers with two goals from Latherton. In the second half it got worse for Burnley with no fewer than eight goals coming in quick succession including another two from Latherton. The game finally ended Blackburn Rovers nine, and a very poor Burnley three.

England v. Scotland Military International, 13 May 1916

The following weekend a military international took place at Goodison Park. Tommy and Eddie Mosscrop were both 'called up' to play, Tommy captaining the England Military XI. The England XI team lined up Private A.C. Robinson (Blackburn Rovers), Gunner L.C. Weller (Everton), Private I. Boocock (Bradford City), Corporal L. Abrams (Chelsea), Gunner T.W. Boyle (Burnley, Captain), Private J. Brennan (Manchester City), Airman F. Walden (Tottenham Hotspur), Corporal C. Buchan (Sunderland), Private H. Hampton (Aston Villa), Bombardier J. Smith (Bolton Wanderers) and Private E. Mosscrop (Burnley). The Scottish XI lined up Corporal K. Campbell (Liverpool), Trooper W. Henry (Manchester City) Farrier Sergeant Frew (Hearts), Lieutenant Logan (Raith Rovers), Sergeant J.H. Galt (Everton), Private J. Scott

(Bradford), Sergeant J.G. Reid (Airdrieonians), Private P. Dawson (Blackburn), Gunner W. Reid (Glasgow Rangers) Private P. Allan (Clyde) and Private W. Wilson (Hearts).

Eddie Mosscrop assisted with the first England goal and by half-time England were three-one ahead with goals from Smith, Abrams and Hampton. In the second half a rejuvenated Scotland came back into the game, equalising with goals from Galt and Reid. Five minutes from time, with the scores level at three-all, Airman Walden passed the ball to Eddie Mosscrop on the wing, and he cut inside the Scottish defender to score the winner. The national press reporting that both Burnley men had given a good account of themselves.

Burnley held their annual general meeting on 17 June and recorded that all its players were now either serving in the armed forces or working in munitions. Tommy Bamford and Dave Taylor were in the Army Service Corps on Motor Transport and were currently in France and London respectively. George Halley was with the Royal Engineers and serving overseas. Tommy Boyle and Bob Kelly were both with the Royal Field Artillery based in Preston and awaiting the call to go overseas. Bert Freeman was in the Royal Flying Corps and Billy Watson was expected to join him shortly. Hampson, Shaw, Brown, Thompson, Pickering, Tranter and Mitton had all joined the army and Eddie Mosscrop was in the Royal Army Medical Corps. Ernie Edwards was in the South Devon's regiment and Billy Pickering was with the Seaforth Highlanders currently serving in Mesopotamia. Jerry Dawson, Levy Thorpe, Chris Jones, Billy Nesbitt and Teddy Hodgson were all currently working on munitions, some of them awaiting their call-up. News arrived that one of the first three Burnley players to sign up in 1914 had become another casualty of the war. Sam Gunton had been invalided home after receiving wounds while fighting in Salonika. At the AGM, Director Mr J.H. Ashworth moved a vote of thanks be passed to all the players who had willingly assisted the club during the past season. He was sure they deserved all the thanks they could give them for they had given their best. As the football season wound down and sporting interests turned to cricket and the Lancashire league, the local population in Burnley were looking forward to the Wakes week holidays, starting the first Saturday of July.

Saturday 1 July 1916

In Burnley at first light, hundreds of locals were busy doing last-minute packing and preparing sandwiches before making their way to the railway stations to catch the early morning trains to Blackpool, Morecambe and Southport for the annual holiday.

Across the Channel in France, the British army were also on the move and making their final preparations. The big set-piece offensive the British had been planning for months was about to unfold. For the previous week, the Royal Artillery had been shelling the German lines along a fifty-mile front, from Gommecourt and Serre in the north, to the Somme River in the south.

The 31st Division contained the 'Pals' Battalions, formed in towns like Accrington, Barnsley, Bradford, Sheffield and Halifax, all of them volunteers. John Boyle, Tommy's brother had joined the Barnsley Pals and was now Private Boyle and part of A Company. The Accrington Pals battalion contained a company of men from Burnley, Z Company, ordinary men: – miners, weavers, husbands, brothers and sons. Men, some of whose last adventure south was to enjoy a day out at the Crystal Palace seeing their team win the Cup final. The Accrington's and the Barnsley Pals would fight side-by-side, their shared objective was to take the village of Serre and provide cover to the British right flank. They would be part of the first wave.

By seven o'clock it was daylight, the sun already up. A clear day. At seven twenty-seven a.m., British sappers detonated

TOMMY BOYLE — BROKEN HERO

a number of huge explosive mines that had been prepared under the German lines. The sound was deafening and the ground quaked beneath the Pals feet. The artillery bombardment, the mines and everything else the British had thrown at the Germans would do the trick, the generals had said confidently. The enemy had not been seen for over a week. They had withdrawn deep underground, safe in their steel and concrete-lined bunkers. Waiting. Waiting for the British artillery to fall silent. Three minutes later at seven-thirty, the British officers checked their pocket watches and drew their service revolvers. Whistles blew all along the British lines as the first wave of men went over the top. On the other side of no-mans-land on the higher ground, the Germans brought their Maxim guns up to the surface and started feeding them with cooling water and ammunition. They were amazed at what they saw coming toward them: ranks of British soldiers bolt upright, with bayonets fixed, their blades glinting in the sun. One or two of them cheekily dribbling footballs between the shell-holes as they walked.

As the British drew nearer, their advance was checked in places by thick, tangled barbed wire that was still intact. The forward officers called back for sappers to bring cutting equipment to get them through. In a few places some of the men made it to the other side. When the covering smoke barrage cleared and the front rank of soldiers were halfway through the wire, the German machine gunners picked their targets and opened fire. They couldn't miss. The Pals fell one after another like a pile of dominoes.

Thirty minutes into the advance, the first wave had been cut to pieces. The generals called in a second wave, then a third and a fourth. The Accrington's set off for Serre with a company of 720 men, and officers. By teatime on the Saturday afternoon, it had suffered 594 casualties; killed, wounded, missing or captured. The Barnsley Pals attacked with 698 men and

23 officers. Their war diary stated that the available Battalion strength had been reduced to 280 men of all ranks. By nightfall on the first of July almost 58,000 men had become casualties. Sixty battalions lost. A bloody massacre.

Two days later, on Monday 3 July, Burnley holidaymakers basking in the sun at Blackpool unaware of what was going on in France, read in the *Daily Mirror* of the 'big push' going on in France. The *Mirror's* front page ran with the headline "Allied Advance Continues, 7,000 Prisoners". Page three ran with the story of the capture of Fricourt and a headline "A very satisfactory first day". The following weekend's edition of the *Mirror*, on 8 July, showed pictures of the British wounded arriving home giving the thumbs-up. The headline ran: "A Page of Smiles from the Somme. Our Cheery Tommies Arrive Home, Wounded but Happy."

As the wounded began arriving back in Britain there were so many that the hospitals around the coastal ports were overwhelmed and so men were despatched to hospitals all over the country. Local newspapers had to stagger their reports of men killed over several months as each edition contained more details and photographs of those who had fallen.

One of the Accrington's officers to go over the top that first day of July was the proud recipient of one of the footballs Burnley had sent over. Captain Henry Davidson Riley was the secretary and leader of Burnley Lads Club, who, along with seventy of his lads, signed up in 1915 and were in D Company of the Accrington Pals. Captain Riley was shot through the head not long after the attack had begun. By the end of the war, the Burnley Lads Club lost more than a hundred members. Then one morning in late July, the Burnley secretary John Haworth's family received a knock at the door. It was a Post Office telegram boy. In his outstretched hand, a message from the War Office. The recipient knew immediately what it meant, there had been so many already that week. John Haworth's brother

Fred, who was in the East Lancashire's, had been among those killed in France. Three weeks later, in August, while Tommy was in Preston training with the Royal Artillery he received word of his brother in the Barnsley Pals. John had been machine-gunned and hit twice in the legs. He was in England recovering in a military hospital in Sunderland.

The telegram boys were busy that summer as the war raged on.

> *If you want to find the old battalion,*
> *I know where they are.*
> *They're hanging on the old barbed wire,*
> *I've seen 'em, I've seen 'em.*

> – 'The Old Battalion', a trench song

End of Part One.

Part Two:

Broken Hero

Chapter 9: Boyle's Brigade

"It is with artillery that war is made."

– Napoleon, 1809

After the brave volunteer battalions had been decimated for just seven miles of ground at The Somme, the War Cabinet moved quickly to fill the void. Lord Derby's five million conscripts would answer the call. By late summer 1916, Tommy and fellow Gunner Bob Kelly were still waiting to join the fight overseas. Over the summer Tommy had been promoted. He was now Bombardier Boyle, with a single stripe that entitled him to a raise in pay, taking his salary to two shillings and three pence per day.

At home, a new football season was about to begin. A number of fresh faces would don the Burnley colours in 1916–17, replacing those who had gone to fight. The League was run similarly to the previous season, the only change being that the subsidiary competition now ran alongside the principal competition and not tagged onto the end. Blackburn Rovers recalled their players and joined the League. Tommy played in the opening match, where Burnley won three-two against Oldham, and also the following game, a high-scoring five-four win at Deepdale taking Burnley to top of League. In the next home game, in front of a small crowd which brought in only a hundred and ten pounds to the club coffers, Burnley routed Manchester United seven-one, a match that saw Lance Corporal George Halley, home on leave in the half-back line.

In October it was announced that Phillip Morrell would be standing down as Burnley's MP at the next election. The report in the *Burnley Express* stating that, "Mr Morrell is a man of conscientious views, possessing marked sincerity of purpose as well as unquestionable ability." It would become more apparent the following spring as to the real reason why Morrell was standing down.

Kestrel in the *Express* reported on the Burnley v. Stockport match: "A Scramble at Turf Moor". The match was a full-blooded affair right from the start played in front of only 1,500 spectators. Half the Burnley team were in the Royal Artillery, who lined up Dawson, Wareing, Hastie, Yates, Boyle, Wilde, Kelly, G. Johnson, J. Barber, T. Hodgson and Kellock. A foul on Bob Kelly "seemed to upset every player and following this there were frequent evidences of desire to have a knock at some individual player". Burnley took the lead after four minutes with a goal by Kelly before Stockport equalised after twelve minutes. Teddy Hodgson scored from a header to make the score two-one and by half-time it was three-one to Burnley. Gunner Kellock scored a fourth for Burnley shortly after the interval to make it four-one. The game looked won, but with the wind at their backs Stockport stormed back into the game, scoring two quick goals to make it four-three. Bob Kelly was put through by Tommy, only for Robson to bring him down with a lunging tackle that knocked him out cold who had to be carried off. Burnley hung on for the victory, which put them second in the table, a point behind rivals Blackburn Rovers.

The Gunners

On 2 December Tommy and fellow Burnley Gunners Cook, Kelly and Kellock were playing at Manchester City in a war charity match for the Manchester Workers' Christmas Fund. The Lancashire RFA XI lined up (standing) Gunner Broad, Gunner Eccleston, Bombardier Lees (sec PNE), Gunner Sutcliffe, Gunner Kellock (Burnley), Gunner Cook, (Burnley), Gunner Bullen, Gunner Kelly (Burnley), Gunner Swarbrick, (seated) Gunner Barnes, Bombardier Boyle (Burnley), Gunner

Speak, Lieutenant Shepherd, Gunner Latherton, Gunner Walmsley and Sergeant Tootel.

Figure 38. '*The Gunners' - The Lancashire Royal Artillery Football Team at Manchester*

Burnley's 1916 Christmas programme saw Preston North End visit Turf Moor on 23 December followed by Blackpool on Christmas Day in the subsidiary competition. In the Preston game, Kestrel reported on the "fine captaincy of Boyle", Burnley winning three-one, including two goals from Tommy, one a penalty. Several Burnley 'old boys' were home on leave, including Jerry Dawson, Bert Freeman, Dick Lindley, Bob Kelly and Billy Nesbitt, who all came back into the side. In the game against Blackpool, Tommy and Bert put in "a capital exhibition", reported Kestrel. With injuries and players away fighting, Tommy reorganised the side, moving Bob Kelly to inside left and Barber over to the right. Tommy was up against his nemesis Joe Bainbridge again and it promised to be another tasty encounter. Burnley got their retribution in first, Blackpool at one point had only eight men on the pitch and as one of the injured was the Blackpool goalkeeper, Wilcox, Dunn had to replace him in goal. It was a quiet game by Tommy and Bainbridge's standards, with Tommy's adversary too busy organising the Blackpool defence. There were no punch-ups this time as the Bombardier led a strong Burnley side, now christened by Kestrel 'Boyle's Brigade', to a convincing four-nil victory.

But with too many player changes, Burnley struggled to maintain their good form going into 1917, suffering four straight defeats in January that put paid to any chance of winning the Lancashire League. Only three regular first-teamers Tommy, Bob Kelly and Dick Lindley played in a four-three victory at Gigg Lane on Saturday 27 January, which ended a bad month.

Fewer than 4,000 turned out for the Manchester City match at Turf Moor, Tommy's last game before he departed for France. Burnley lined up Pickles, Henry, Hastie, Nesbitt, Boyle, Jos Wilde, Yates, Lindley, Freeman, Roberts and Lockett. City lined up Goodchild, Gartland, Fletcher, Bottomley, Scott, Parker, Billy Meredith, Wynn, Tyler, Barnes and Cartwright. Burnley started well and had chances, Lindley with the best opportunity, before City took the lead on fifteen minutes with a cross from "Meredith the famous Welshman" for Barnes to score. In the second half, a race for the ball between Meredith and Yates saw the Burnley half-back run head-first into the railings at the Cricket Field end. Down to ten men and with Tommy also hurt, Sportsman in the *Burnley News* bade the captain a fond farewell: "Boyle was the outstanding figure in the Burnley side. It may be that the match will be memorable, insomuch as the Burnley soldier may not appear again for some time."

Wedding Bells

Having received his letter from the War Office to report to his unit, it was time for Tommy answer the call, but before leaving he had one important thing to do. After a three-year engagement, Bombardier Thomas William Boyle married Annie Elizabeth Varley at St. James Church in Burnley on Thursday 1 March 1917.

Figure 39. Bombardier Boyle and Annie Varley at their wedding on the 1st March 1917.

The *Burnley News* reported that it was a quiet affair as the bridegroom was on draft (Tommy's call-up probably pushed forward their wedding date). Tommy wore his Royal Field Artillery dress uniform, and Annie wore a navy blue outfit with a matching hat, bearing shaded roses at the side and relieved underneath with white. She also carried a spray of carnations and was given away by her father, William. Attending the couple were groomsman Arthur Haigh and the chief bridesmaid, Elsie Varley, Annie's sister.

Mr and Mrs Boyle gave their address as 20 Rectory Road, Burnley; and their ages, thirty-one and twenty-five respectively. On the marriage certificate Tommy wrote under his occupation, *Professional Footballer OHMS* and Annie wrote, *Milliner.*

The couple didn't have much time for a honeymoon. Tommy's name was down on the team sheet for the Everton match at Goodison on the Saturday afternoon but he didn't play. It was a pity, as Sportsman's headline in the *Express* ran "Turfites Towelled in Toffeeland", Burnley losing five-nil without the services of the captain.

Boyle goes to War

The FA Cup winners of 1914 were now scattered to the four corners of the world. If the players were not fighting, they were playing for a football club close to their army bases or workplaces. Football was encouraged by the military, at home and at the Front. The army handbook said it was an important morale booster, kept the men reasonably fit and gave the troops an interest. Eddie Mosscrop in the RAMC was playing part-time for Blackpool. When he wasn't driving an army truck, Dave Taylor was playing for Chelsea. Cliff Jones was playing at Chesterfield, while Levi Thorpe and Tommy Mayson were with Leeds City.

Around the time Tommy was packing his kitbag for France, news of another Burnley footballer, Dick Tranter, reached the football club.

I am now enjoying a comfortable bed in a Canadian hospital [in France]. You would be a little surprised at me being knocked out so soon. Well, it happened on February 7 and I was in the reserve trenches. As it was close on tea time the shells were whistling overhead, as is always the case at tea time. Well I was struck on the head with shrapnel and it was a good job I had my steel helmet on, for it went clean through it. I was bandaged up and carried down to the dressing station and then brought here by motor. I lost consciousness on the way and I knew nothing until the next night. Then I learned I had been under the X-Rays and an operation performed. My poor head was jumping and I've had headaches ever since though I am a lot better now. I lost the use of my right arm but have got it back again. It is very weak yet and it does not half ache with writing. The doctor said I should get to England when I'm well enough to travel.

Tranter had a stainless steel plate fitted to his skull. It had been touch and go whether he survived the operation. The delay between Tranter being wounded in France and his story appearing in the local press was around four weeks. News from the Front did not filter into the public domain quickly during wartime, the men's letters and postcards being subject to a strict censorship.

The week after Tommy set out for France, an agitated Phillip Morrell visited Ottoline in hospital, where she was recovering following a minor operation. Phillip had not been himself for some weeks and had been sent home from the House of Commons after he was seen wandering the corridors muttering to himself. At Ottoline's bedside, Phillip broke down and confessed to his wife of his infidelities. No stranger to affairs herself, Ottoline comforted her husband as his confession came out. It transpired that Philip had been unfaithful not once, but twice, and with two women Ottoline knew, very well in fact. They were Phillip's secretary, Alice Jones, and Julian's nanny, Eva Merrifield, both living under their roof in Bedford Square. If simultaneous affairs weren't bad enough, that wasn't quite the end of it. Both women were pregnant. The disclosure hurt Ottoline deeply. The couple had lost a child in infancy, Julian's twin brother, Hugh, and the couple had tried desperately to have another child of their own without success. The whole business was hushed up in the press, which ran with a story saying that Phillip was suffering from influenza which had prevented him from taking his seat in the House for a number of weeks. Ottoline stood by her husband and both of them withdrew to Garsington Manor in the South Oxfordshire countryside for most of the war. When the two children were born, both boys, Ottoline sent them gifts of books. The Morrells were never seen in Burnley again.

We are the Burnley Mashers,
When we go out at neet,
The lasses all admire us,
And think we look a treat...

– Sung by 'B Coy.' of the 2/5th East
Lancashire Regiment marching to Ypres, spring 1917

Ypres, British Sector, March 1917

In March 1917 the Belgian city of Ypres was in ruin after three years of German shelling. The medieval fortress city was a key objective for both sides in the war. The British had held the city since the start of the war and fought two major battles there in 1914 and 1915. The city had to be held to block any German advance on Paris and protect allied supplies and men arriving at Calais and Dunkirk. After the carnage of The Somme the previous summer, General Haig concluded that more guns, more ordnance and more soldiers were needed if the allies were to defeat the Germans quickly. The planning for a third major assault to strike east from Ypres had been ongoing since the previous November by Haig and his commanders. The Cabinet signed off the generals request for more men and materiel and gave him what he wanted. Armaments production increased. Munitions workers in Burnley and across the country were put on overtime, turning out an order for six million shells that the artillery would need for the summer offensive.

A week after his wedding, on 8 March 1917, Bombardier Boyle, with the rest of his gun detachment, left Fulwood Barracks in Preston. Bob Kelly travelled at the same time (he wrote later that his gun crew was located in the next field to Tommy's). After a day's train journey and a choppy sea crossing, which didn't agree with Kelly's stomach (again), the Lancastrians arrived in Calais to fine weather. As they waited in the sunshine on the docks for a troop train to take them to their destination, the Lancastrians were given a taste of what they would soon be in for. A long grey ambulance train with red crosses on the sides pulled in to the docks. The doors opened and slowly its passengers climbed down. What must have been a battalion of wounded men formed up, on their way to hospitals in England. There were men on crutches with one trouser leg pinned up, men blinded and horribly blistered, men who couldn't breathe properly, their lungs full of fluid from chlorine gas. Behind the walking wounded, a number of stretcher cases were set down – men with one or both legs blown off, or an arm and a leg gone, men with bandaged heads, some with half their faces missing. It was the Lancastrians' first sight of men trembling so violently from shell-shock they had to be strapped to their stretchers.

Conversations started between the two groups. Cigarettes were shared, stories of home exchanged, football results passed on. Where had they come from? "Wipers," they said: the same place to where Tommy and his colleagues were now travelling. No one recognised the Bombardier in his uniform. Out of his football kit he was a soldier just like the rest of them. The Lancastrians' train arrived and they all climbed onboard. They were soon underway, the carriage silent as they pulled out of Calais, the men deep in thought. The further they travelled, the more they saw of the devastating effects of the Germans' long-range artillery. A quiet rumble of thunder could be heard in the distance that increased in volume with each mile they moved closer to the Front.

Tommy gazed out of the window. The train rolled on through open countryside, through green fields of growing wheat and barley. He was no longer in control of his life, no longer able to make his own decisions or play things his way. His destiny, like every man on the train, was linked to the war and victory. He felt like part of some huge machine that needed constantly replenishing with fresh meat for the kill. His mind went back to the men on the platform he'd just met. Young lads who had seen hell, damaged for life. His mind went back to the two occasions he had met Germans, in 1910 and 1914 while on tour. He remembered the match in Berlin in 1914 when the Germans had presented him with the huge laurel wreath so big it took two of them to carry it. He remembered the warm reception the German people had given him and the team. He had been treated like a hero then. Now the same people would be trying to blow him to pieces. He was already missing Annie, wondered how John was recovering and how his sisters in Platts Common were coping. He was hungry, but more than anything, he was itching for a drink and a decent game of football.

The train lurched forward and shook Tommy from his daydream. They had arrived. As the train slowed, a buckled platform sign with the name *POPERINGHE* came into view in the window. Eight miles west of Ypres, Poperinghe was the last stop on the Hazebrouk–Ypres railway. Despite being well behind the front-line, 'Pop' was shelled regularly by the Germans. The station roof had been blown off along with half of its outbuildings and all the windows. In *Cameos of Hell*, Edward Vaughn describes what he saw on his arrival at Poperinghe, also in early 1917 like Tommy:

> A train arrived with a detachment of brand new artillery men who got out and arranged themselves in fours facing the train according to the drill book. They had just received the command 'Right' when a shell landed in the middle of them and turned to see a fountain of dust, smoke, bricks and khaki and equipment spurt up from the panic stricken column. 16 men died and many were wounded.

The Lancastrians formed up and set off on foot to their reserve area. For the next month, their task would be to acclimatise to life at the Front and the guns, their guns. Each man needed to know his gun down to its last bolt: its characteristics, how it behaved, the sound it made, how far it recoiled. They would spend day after day taking their gun to pieces, cleaning, greasing and polishing it, rebuilding it. They would do it in daytime and at night and sleep with it under the camouflage netting. Tommy was part of a ten-man gun detachment. A team. The gun was their eleventh man. By early 1917 the Royal Field Artillery had standardised on the eighteen-pounder field gun as its main weapon of choice for front-line, up-close use against the enemy. Behind these weapons came the sixty-pounders, followed by the Howitzers and furthest back of the lot, the fourteen-inch railway guns. Each eighteen-pounder and its ammunition was brought up the line by a team of six horses. The gun would be towed into position in its emplacement; a pit dug two feet deep covered by camouflage netting. Each man in the gun crew had a number, one through to ten; each number did a different job. Number one was in command, numbers two and three operated the breech and fired the gun. The others had their responsibilities, just like a football team. In firing the gun they needed to work together in harmony, in time, moving as one, aiming, loading, shooting. Each man was responsible for his team's success and in staying alive.

In helping the gun crew hit their targets, sitting out in no-man's land hidden under camouflage was the Forward Observation Post. The FOP, or OP, was used to direct the artillery fire onto the enemy and was manned by three artillerymen. The OP would be positioned around 1,500 yards in front of the guns and would relay information back to battery HQ and to the gun crews on their range, accuracy and fall of shot.

Communication was usually by a field telephone or a 'Lucas lamp' at night. If neither worked, a battery forward runner was sent back to report on the situation to headquarters. The OP team were fully armed and carried rifle grenades, twenty-four-hour rations and equipment to last them a day in the field. They needed to keep their heads down as they were prime targets for enemy snipers. The men hid underneath what was called a 'portable beehive', shaped like a large flat tin can, and observed the enemy through slits in the front. Each gunner would take their turn on OP duty. They all hated it.

Life at the Front for Tommy became routine: parade, breakfast, inspection, drill, shooting practice, mess, football, eat and sleep. To break the monotony he became the battery's chief football organiser. He organised competitions among the other gun crews in their battery. The players were provided with proper regimental football kit and full-size pitches were marked out, posts and nets erected, sometimes made from improvised camouflage netting. Tommy had been promoted on the strength of what he'd done with 'The Gunners' back in the UK and his leadership tendencies on the football field would serve him well in the Artillery. He would fit right in and would make the best of it. After a month, if the men were lucky, they might get a twenty-four-hour pass, which usually meant a visit to Poperinghe, which provided many of the comforts of home:

> Bars served Bass's Pale Ale – beer imported from home. 'Pop' even had its own brewery later in the war. [There were] Lots of English goods on sale, books, gramophone records, silk postcards of Ypres to send home, fountain pens, English cigarettes, razor blades, toothpaste, chocolate. There were English newspapers, a day old, *Daily Express*, *Mirror*, *Mail* and *Daily Sketch*. There were Patisseries and sweet shops. The hairdressers in town had a sign saying, "we do not work when the Germans are shelling." (*Cameos of Hell*)

There were other delights to behold in Poperinghe: hotels, bars and cafes where cheap wine could be drunk and *estimanets* where a soldier could get an omelette and chips for a few francs. In an army town with lots of lonely young men with money to burn, a growing number of brothels had been established.

A blue lamp outside a house signified accommodation for officers while a red lamp was the place for other ranks. The Military Police and the RAMC controlled these places, yet despite warnings from the medical officers about sexual health, venereal disease was rife amongst the troops.

Messines Ridge June 1917

After arriving in the area in March, Tommy and his gun crew were training for the set-piece battle of the coming summer. By the end of May, after nearly three months in the field, they were ready. To begin the breakout from Ypres, the prelude to battle would begin with an intense bombardment of the enemy, bigger than that at The Somme. Much bigger. By the middle of May, the six million shells ordered for the battle had arrived and were brought up the line. A total of 2,266 guns of all sizes that in some places were axle to axle would make quite an orchestra. Bombardier Boyle and his crew would be part of it all. The preliminary bombardment of Messines Ridge began on 30 May. The rapid-fire shelling then continued day and night without respite, the noise so deafening that the gunners were all issued with a new special wax to protect their eardrums.

After the Second Battle of Ypres in 1915, the generals knew they needed to concentrate on an area of the front-line three miles to the south of the city around the villages of Messines and Wytschaete. General Plumer's task was to capture the slopes and the ridge that overlooked the villages, which were heavily defended by the enemy who were well dug in on high ground. Both the British and the Germans had been tunnelling under each other's defences since the beginning of the war. By late May the British mining teams had dug twenty-one separate tunnels under the Ridge. At the end of each tunnel they created a chamber the size of a living room that was packed with tons of ammonal high-explosives. Detonators and fuses were set and the chamber backfilled with sandbags to prevent the mine backfiring and killing their own men.

By the sixth of June, as the artillery bombardment carried on overhead, the countdown began. On the eve of the battle, Major-General Sir Charles Harington addressed his commanders and uttered his famous line: "Gentlemen, I do not know whether we shall change history tomorrow, but we will certainly alter the geography."

Captain Oliver Woodward led the firing party. Twenty-one mines would be detonated simultaneously at ten past three in the morning. The 80,000 fighting troops who were going to take the Ridge were brought up to the front-line ready to go over the top once the mines had fired and the blast waves had passed over. Two minutes before the mines went off, the artillery ceased fire and everything fell silent. It was pitch black. Silent. The Germans, sensing something was wrong, came up from their bunkers, lugging their Maxim guns with them. In the darkness they fired off magnesium parachute flares to see what was going on. No advance, no movement, no noise, nothing. In the British trenches the men were ordered to cover their ears and get their heads down. At three-ten a.m. Woodward gave the command and the firing party hit the plungers, sending electrical charges into the detonators. The men couldn't agree on how many blasts they actually heard; some said three, others six, others a dozen:

> Suddenly at 3.10am, great leaping streams of orange flame shot upwards, each a huge volcano, along the front of the attack, followed by terrific explosions and dense masses of smoke and dust which stood like pillars towering into the sky all illuminated by the fires below. (Ian Passingham, *Pillars of Fire*)

Of the 10,000 Germans defending the Ridge, few complete bodies were ever found. The explosions had blown them to smithereens. Nineteen of the twenty-one mines had gone up, some creating a crater almost 100 yards in diameter. The Prime Minister David Lloyd George was quoted as having heard the sound of the explosions 150 miles away in Downing Street. Tommy certainly heard and felt it. The ground shook and lifted upwards before settling back down again like an earthquake. As the dirt and debris settled, the gunners opened up again, this time with a creeping barrage of rapid fire ahead of the advancing troops as they set off across no man's land. For once the generals had got their calculations right. The mines and the overwhelming firepower had worked this time. Enemy resistance on the Ridge was reported as 'minimal'. They were all gone.

Back in Burnley, the newspapers continued to bring more bad news. Among those who had recently been killed was another footballer. Andrew Taylor was the younger brother of full-back Dave Taylor who had played a number of games in Burnley reserves as a centre-forward. Andrew had been killed in action in France. Full-back Dave Taylor's family had already been devastated by the war. Taylor had lost two brothers-in-law, both killed in action, and another brother-in-law had been badly wounded. Now his youngest brother was dead. Andrew was a skilled carpenter and first played for Burnley reserves in February 1912, making his debut against Colne in a friendly match. The following season he had played for the reserves at Turf Moor and played in the team that reached the semi-final of the Hospital Cup.

The advantage gained by the Allies at Messines Ridge gave men like Tommy optimism that the war would soon end. But in London, arguments among the War Cabinet followed in getting approval to press home the attack. Haig was furious. At the same time, rumours circulated among the British ranks of a mutiny among the French army and there was talk of a revolution having taken place in Russia. Would the British be left to fight alone? The only positive news for the British in July 1917 was the arrival of the first of Pershing's American forces into the war. The delays gave the enemy time to pull back and build even stronger defences. As the Lancastrians waited for their next assignment, there was time for football and inter-regimental sports days. As these went on the Germans worked hard and in early July began bombarding the Allies around Ypres with mustard gas. Eventually new orders arrived and the Lancastrians moved to take up positions north of Ypres. On 11 July the RFA's forward observation teams crawled into position across no-man's land and began telephoning information back to battalion HQ on where to pick their targets. The next day the British gunners commenced firing on the enemy positions, almost a month after they'd last fired their guns at Messines.

Burnley - July 1917

Since Tommy had gone abroad, Annie had kept herself busy, working through Wakes week in her job at the mill making army uniforms. She would take her holiday when Tommy came home on his first leave. At the end of her shift, she left the mill and set off on her short walk home. As she reached the bottom of the hill and turned the corner into Rectory Road, she could see someone was waiting by the gate. A bicycle was resting against the garden wall. As she crossed the road and got closer, she saw that the visitor was wearing the dark blue uniform and crossed belt of the Post Office Telegram Office. A lump came to her throat. She began running, her heart pounding. Her first thought was that the boy must have the wrong house, but as she got to the gate he held out something his hand. The name on the telegram was hers, there was no mistake. Annie was too terrified to open it. She began to tremble, her knees buckled and she collapsed on the step. He had only been gone four months, it couldn't be, not him, not my Tommy, they'd only been married for a short while. Through tears she tore the seal and opened the telegram.

PRIORITY: (MRS) A BOYLE, RECTORY ROAD 20, BURNLEY. REGRET TO INFORM YOU YOUR HUSBAND, SERIAL NUMBER 118158 BDR T W BOYLE WOUNDED IN

ACTION ABOUT 12 JULY AND IN HOSPITAL IN ROUEN,
FR WITH LEG WOUNDS. SIGNED MILITARY REGISTRAR.

During the week that the Allied bombardment opened on 12
July, Bombardier Boyle found himself on forward observation
duty. The three of them had crawled on their bellies across no-
man's land using shell holes, smashed farm buildings and
broken trees for cover, dragging their equipment with them and
laying the field telephone cable as they went. They were due to
stay in the OP for twenty-four hours until relieved. Under the
'portable beehive', their duty was to record the co-ordinates of
enemy positions and telephone these through to Battery HQ.
As they concentrated on a section of the German line, they
heard the sound of incoming shells. The 'Whizz-Bang' high-
explosive shell was slightly smaller than the RFA's eighteen-
pounder but just as deadly. The men could hear the 'whizz' of
the shell coming as it screamed through the sound barrier at
maximum velocity, followed by the bang of the gun it had left
a fraction of a second before. The shell then exploded in mid-
air like a huge shotgun, spraying hundreds of half-inch lead
balls and brass shards as sharp as razor blades in all directions.

The shelling on both sides had been going on for quite some
hours, when at around eight-thirty p.m., a Whizz-Bang came
over and exploded short of its intended target, spraying its shot
over no-man's land, above the OP. Tommy came off the worst.
He later described that it felt as if he'd been kicked up the arse
by Joe Bainbridge, the force throwing him into the air for him
to land on his back in the bottom of a shell hole. A number of
shell splinters sliced through his tunic and trousers, shredding
the fabric and leaving cuts and scratches on his shoulders and
backside. A trickle of blood ran out of his right ear down his
neck, which looked bad. But the worst damage was a large shell
splinter that had torn a two-inch hole through the back of his
thigh. Blood ran down his leg, filling his boot. In the blackness
of the bottom of the crater, Tommy could hear nothing. He

shouted and no sound came out. He screamed for help. Nothing. His throat was as dry as hell; he was desperate for a drink. He felt for his water bottle but the shrapnel must have torn off his webbing. Looking up, he could see the stars and the moon and the red tracer fire flying in both directions against the night sky. He felt cold and began to shiver as the early symptoms of shock set in.

The other two in the OP had been lucky, receiving only mild concussion and slight scratches. The two gunners slid down the mud wall of the crater to see how he was. Tommy could see their lips moving; he strained to hear what they were saying, but heard nothing. The two had to get him out of the mud and the filth and sit him up. The leg looked bad. They comforted him, telling him he'd play again, no problem, it was only a bad scratch.

One of the gunners poured his canteen over the wound forcing out the dirt, before pressing a wad of field dressing into the hole. A bandage around the leg helped apply pressure to stop the bleeding. "Help me up, lads," Tommy asked. The blood wouldn't stop. It seeped out and soaked through the dressing into what was left of Tommy's pants. The shrapnel could have severed a major artery. The two had to get him to a forward aid post quickly before he bled to death or gangrene set in. Carefully, they raised him up to the edge of the crater. The field telephone was smashed to pieces so they couldn't call for help. They would have to keep as low as possible and not make a sound. In the darkness, with an arm around his comrades' shoulders and with shellfire coming from both directions, Tommy forced himself up on his good leg. They had to get to the aid post but where the hell was it?

The luck of Tommy's Irish ancestors was with him that evening. The three of them headed in the right direction, back to their own lines and made it home safely. They found transport that took Tommy to an advanced dressing station; the two gunners helping the driver get Tommy onto the back. He was grateful to the two men; they had put their own lives on the line for him and he owed them one. They set off back to Battery HQ to report what had happened. He would never see them again.

Lyn MacDonald, author of *The Roses of No-man's Land*, and a nurse in1915 recalls that the biggest fear for the wounded was that gas gangrene would set in:

> You got this appalling infection with anaerobic bacteria and the men just died like flies. The infection had usually set in by the time they got to us. If they had compound fractures full of mud, it was the ideal site for the bacteria to flourish, and if the men had several days on the way, the wound was simply a mass of putrid muscle rotting with gas gangrene. Eighty per cent of those getting gangrene in the early part of the war were amputees. The medical staff needed to treat the wounded as quickly as possible to kill the infection.

Speed in getting the right treatment was essential if the wounded were to make a full recovery. By mid-1917 medical and surgical procedures had improved in the three years since the start of the war and the Royal Army Medical Corps had established an efficient system of care for wounded men that began at the front-line and extended all the way back to hospitals in England. The casualty would be taken first to a front-line aid post to assess the soldier's condition. His wounds would be looked at, recorded and a label attached to his uniform. He would then be despatched to an advanced dressing station behind the lines where he would be further examined and any immediate surgery performed. For more serious wounds, the casualty would be kept at the station for twenty-four hours until after the operation, after which he was moved again to a casualty clearing station. Brandhoek clearing station was midway between Poperinghe and Ypres and the main clearing station in the area for soldiers specialising in chest and thigh wounds. It's possible Tommy was sent here as it was quite close to the area where he was wounded. It was also near to the railway station, from where the casualty could be transported to another hospital in France or via a hospital train to the docks and a ship back to England.

Following his week in Rouen, Tommy was packed on board an ambulance train and repatriated to England before the end of July. Ambulance trains arrived with regular frequency at London Charing Cross station from where the injured men would be despatched to receiving hospitals all over the country. Tommy was sent all the way to Newcastle and got a note to Annie, who came up to be with him.

The first week of August, a letter from the Burnley captain arrived on John Haworth's desk. Haworth was distraught when he read the contents. It was printed in the *Burnley Express* on 8 August 1917:

BURNLEY FC CAPTAIN
GUNNER TOM BOYLE WOUNDED

Gunner Tom Boyle, the Burnley FC captain has been wounded in France. Writing to Mr. John Haworth, secretary of the club he says: "Just a few lines to let you know that I am keeping in good spirits. I got bowled over on the 1st Ins. I got it through the thigh. It was awful at the time. I do not think it is very bad myself, but the nurses say it is, so I suppose I am trying to make little of it, but I cannot lift the leg up properly when I am on my back.

Further details of Tommy's wounds emerged the following week. In a letter to a Mr F. Slater of the Bay Horse Hotel, Northumberland, from his bed in Northumberland War Hospital, Gosforth, Newcastle-on-Tyne, Tommy wrote:

I am getting on as well as can be expected. I got a piece of shrapnel [a shell splinter more likely] about two inches long through the thigh. It went in at the back and through to the front and afterwards it was cut out. I got hit at 8.30 at night in no-man's land. It was no man's land too. We got lost when we were going to the [dressing] station, but luckily for us we came across a motor wagon and they took us through Ypres to a place beyond. We afterwards went to Rouen for a week. I lost all my kit when I got hit!

The *Burnley Express* published another letter a week later on 25 August that said Tommy had received a visit from a Burnley man, a Mr Duckworth, who had subsequently written to John Haworth:

We found Boyle all right, but he had much difficulty in hearing us as he is very deaf through shell-shock. He cannot hear at all with one ear. He says he has to stay in bed another week. The shrapnel has gone through the flesh of the thigh but it has not touched the bone. He thinks it will be all right as he walked on the leg a bit after he had been hit.

Tommy was bored to tears having to spend day after day lying face down on a hospital bed while his leg healed, not knowing if he would ever walk again let alone play football. But the Boyles were a tough lot. John, Tommy's brother, had recovered from his wounds. The doctors had fixed him up and he was passed fit for duty by the medical board despite the limp he had developed from his wounds. John Boyle was sent back to France where he joined the Labour Corps.

From his hospital bed Tommy read the sports papers and the match reports as the new season had started. Before the war, Rochdale played their football in the Lancashire Combination, but had been on the verge of gaining a Football League place. With most of players in the forces, an even more depleted

Burnley team turned out for the first game of the season with Dick Lindley, the only regular professional acting as captain. Burnley lined up Ewart (goal), Aunger and Hastie (full-backs), Lindley, Johnson and Heslop (centre-backs), Woods, Edwards, Mitton, Woodward and Cautherley. The grassy pitch at Spotland clearly suited Rochdale against a clearly unfit Burnley side who were taken apart by the 'non-Leaguers'. "The easy manner in which the home forwards got through the Burnley defence almost whenever they desired was painful to witness," wrote Sportsman in the *Burnley Express*. By half-time Burnley were four-nil down and by the close it ended the score was nine-nil, with hat-tricks for two Rochdale forwards, O'Flaherty and Halligan. The game ended as Burnley's heaviest defeat to a then non-Football League side. It was an awful start to the season.

News from abroad

Billy Watson, now a despatch rider in the Army Service Corps, wrote to John Haworth on 5 September to say that he was a member of the regimental football team which included Sergeant-Major Sams, the former Fulham goalkeeper, and John Houghton of Norwich City. Dave Taylor, also in the ASC, had been promoted to Corporal and by October he had made Sergeant. Sergeant Taylor, playing his football in the blue of Chelsea, had played for the Army v. Navy at Stamford Bridge, but had been kicked in the eye for his trouble and had been forced off injured. Taylor had also been involved in the athletics meeting at Grove Park, winning the 100 and 220 yards races and coming second in the steeplechase. Tommy Bamford was in France and playing football whenever he could get the chance. George Halley was in South Africa at a rest camp in Durban and had played in a game there, showing the natives a few football skills. Gunner Kellock wrote from his base in Salonika:

> It is awfully hot here, around 130 degrees. I wish I was playing again, but I hope to get home in time for a game, so just keep a

place in the team for some Saturday about Christmas as I am trying to get six days leave. Just fancy, Saturday afternoon and going on 48 hours guard duty in a scorching hot sun when I might be at Blackpool.

Eddie Mosscrop, also in Salonika, asked for news of the other players. Mosscrop had also managed to play a few matches in the prickly heat. He wrote:

A chap may feel all right one minute and then go down with chronic diarrhoea, dysentery or malaria. There are big black centipedes that crawl over you at night, about six inches long.

Mosscrop, ever the comedian, sent John Haworth a sketch of the beast, asking in his letter "if he'd fancy it for a bed mate!"

Gunner Yates wrote from France:

I was placed in the Royal Garrison Artillery and did the biggest part of my three months training at Bexhill. After two days at base camp in France I volunteered to come up the line. Whilst at Bexhill we had a crack football team including Joe Bainbridge (Blackpool) Mager (Manchester United), Campbell and Rigsby (Southport Central). Bainbridge has since been wounded. I also came across Harry Haworth and Shipman the Rawtenstall and Nelson cricket pros.

Teddy Hodgson had been promoted to Corporal and had played in an English XI against a team of Dutch sailors, the English winning easily with Teddy among the goals. Private Jonathan Brown, serving with the Burnley Territorials, had been involved in a wiring party one night in September when four of his team were hit and badly wounded. Brown got a 'scratch' on the leg but said it was nothing serious. Brown wrote and asked John Haworth whether the club would send them over a football.

Burnley played the return match against Rochdale at Turf Moor, determined to improve on the previous week's awful performance. With first team regulars Dick Lindley and with Levi Thorpe, Billy Nesbitt, and Teddy Hodgson home on leave, The Clarets managed a two-all draw. On 15 September Burnley travelled to Goodison Park with only nine players. They borrowed two, Everton's Kelly going in goal and Kempster at full-back. Burnley lined up Kelly, Kempster, Hastie, Lindley, Heslop, Johnson, Wood, Dunn, Mitton, Edwards and Woodward. By half-time Everton led six-nil and by the end Burnley finished up with another nine-nil drubbing. A bewildered Sportsman wrote sarcastically that "Kelly did very well in goal". After three games, Burnley had one point. They had scored two goals and let twenty in. The only happy note up to Christmas in a miserable season was a six-one victory against Blackburn.

For the Burnley men overseas things were no better, as the rain came down in the autumn in France. Billy Watson wrote to John Haworth from France:

> The weather has taken a turn for the worse. We have had a terrible lot of rain lately and it makes going on the roads pretty bad. The mud on Turf Moor is nothing compared to this. I see that you got your first victory against Blackburn Rovers, and that Bert was getting the goals. I see you are not getting well supported just now. Never mind we shall have another Cup year before many years are out. How is Boyle getting on? I hope he is getting on all right I do hope it won't interfere with his football. He takes a bit of knocking out but those pieces of shell are a lot harder than a football.

Tommy wrote briefly from Gosforth hospital on 21 November. The wound to his leg was mending nicely and he was about to undergo an operation to improve his hearing.

On 1 December 1917 Burnley were playing away at Blackpool when the club received news of another one of their players serving abroad. Billy Pickering was from Barony, Glasgow and arrived in Burnley in 1912 as an eighteen-year-old from Ashfield, a junior side from the Glasgow shipyards. In his first season he scored thirty-three goals in thirty-seven games for Burnley reserves, which included four goals against Everton and another four against Accrington Stanley. He had scored two goals in the Lancashire Cup final and had played in some of the matches on Burnley's European tour in 1914. He was destined one day to take over the centre-forward slot from Bert Freeman. In his last season before joining the 72nd Seaforth Highlanders, Billy scored twenty goals in twenty-four reserve team appearances. He loved the game, and at twenty-three his prospects looked excellent. Billy's regiment had been in action in Mesopotamia since 1915 and the Seaforth's had fought their way from Basra up the banks of the Tigris, defeating the Turkish forces for control of the Anglo-Persian oilfields. Baghdad had eventually fallen to the Allies in March 1917. Billy was killed while on active duty in Baghdad on 7 November. Reports say he was shot through the head and died instantly. The young centre-forward was buried close to where he fell in North Baghdad.

Over the winter, Tommy's leg healed and he could soon walk normally again without any crutches. The operation on his burst right eardrum had given him some degree of hearing back. He was discharged from the military hospital in Gosforth and by late January 1918 he was back in Burnley being looked after by Annie and was itching to kick a ball. John Haworth called round to see how he was. With Tommy eager to return to playing, they worked out a light training routine to get some power back to the muscles that had been unused for months. He had lost weight during his time in hospital, and started off with walking before graduating to light running around Turf Moor, then skipping with a rope. He could feel the repaired leg pulling when he kicked a ball, but it wasn't painful, not a hindrance, it just felt different. He'd been lucky. He cut out the beer and drank beef tea instead. By the first week of March he was sprinting the length of the pitch and wasn't out of breath. He borrowed a ball from the Club and got some practice in on Calder Vale recreation ground playing with the local kids.

Tommy was ready for a practice game when a letter from the War Office arrived. It told him to report to the Town Hall for a medical. He couldn't believe it. Having just got himself fit the army wanted him back. He thought he'd done his bit and had finished with the army, he had nearly lost his life in the process. But no, it wasn't enough, the War Office wanted more. Struggling for numbers, the War Office increased the maximum recruitment age to fifty-one and wanted as many men as they could lay their hands on for the next planned 'big push' in the summer of 1918. After his medical Tommy's record card was rubber-stamped fit for duty, and within a month he was transferred into the army reserve on notice for draft. Like John Boyle he was back in uniform. He couldn't believe it.

But before he was sent back to France, Tommy made his comeback on 9 March 1918 at Turf Moor against Stockport County. Around 2,000 people turned out at Turf Moor to welcome the captain back and Burnley lined up Spencer, Finney, Hastie, Hobson, Boyle, Jones, Woods, Edwards, Freeman, Lindley and Clarkson. Tommy was nowhere near his best and Burnley fell behind in the first half. The Clarets conceded a second goal with twenty minutes left with the captain struggling. But at least he had managed to last the whole match and the leg had held up well.

As he packed his army kitbag and kissed Annie goodbye for a second time, Burnley suffered their third nine-nil defeat of the season away at Stoke City. Stoke topped the Lancashire league after twenty-eight games, having scored 100 goals in the process. Burnley had let 100 goals in. Tommy shook his head when he read the result and wondered when he'd be back home and playing again. He was livid at having to go back when others had been discharged with less serious injuries than he had received. He would have to stay fit and keep his head down. There would be no heroics, no Boyle's Brigade, no volunteering. *Sod them.*

Burnley were relieved to see the curtain fall on the 1917-18 football season on 3 April. They had never been so bad. Seventy-six different faces had played in claret and blue. The club had resorted several times to borrowing players for matches at Everton, Port Vale, Oldham, Liverpool, Blackpool and Preston. It was said that the club had even asked people passing Turf Moor if they fancied a game. From the regular professionals, Dick Lindley had played in all thirty games; Bert Freeman had made fifteen appearances and Billy Nesbitt nine. There had been nine-nil hammerings by Rochdale, Everton and Stoke, an eight-nil defeat by Bolton and a seven-one loss to Liverpool. With no Halley, Boyle and Watson, forty-two goals were conceded in five games. The League table told its own horror story: Played thirty, won four, drawn four, lost twenty-two, goals for twenty nine, goals against one hundred, points twelve.

Four years of war had destroyed the best team Burnley had ever fielded. With no end of the conflict in sight and with a number of players already killed, maimed or captured, the Club would have to start all over again when the war ended. Off the field, things were so bad that Burnley announced that in order to meet some its financial liabilities, a portion of the timber forming the Cricket Field end had been taken out and sold. Could matters get any worse?

In July 1918 Tommy was in France from where he wrote to John Haworth:

I have gone up the line from base. It is a lot better up here than down. You do know when you have finished here. We have plenty of football and we play the Canadians tonight. I met Lol. Cook here and Tabby Booth from Manchester City, also J. Hay of Newcastle and Dodds from Celtic. They are in my lot so it looks like we will be having some good football.

All that mattered to Tommy was that he was playing football again. Football was his salvation and got him through his second tour of duty. Later that month, another player reported that he had been wounded in circumstances similar to Tommy's. Signaller and inside-forward Levi Thorpe wrote to John Haworth:

I got hit by shrapnel in the knee on the 23rd July [1918] and came into hospital two days later. I went through an operation and had it drawn, so have my leg in splints for a week. I shall be glad when I can get my feet on the bed and get off my back although we keep smiling. It's very warm here. We are expecting coming to Blighty in a few days.

Thorpe made in back to England and spent several weeks recovering in a London hospital.

In the last week of July 1918, a German attack along the front line to the east of Reims was countered by the Allies, now much superior in numbers with the Americans and the whole of the Commonwealth engaged in the fighting. The Second Battle of the Marne signalled the turning of the tide in the war as the Allies broke through the German lines with tanks, air support and artillery that forced the Germans into full retreat. Throughout August and September, the Allies pressed home the advantage, taking territory that the Germans had held for four years. The War Committee announced a huge morale booster for the troops. Every man was going to get a half-pound plum pudding for Christmas. Tommy and the rest of the players serving overseas would have been overjoyed and would have known exactly where the War Committee could stick it.

By the time a new football season kicked off in September 1918, Tommy was in a reinforcement camp with the 1st Army Reserve as Burnley proceeded to lose its opening match, again to Rochdale, four-two at Spotland, with Dick Lindley in command as captain. With eight games of the new season gone and with November approaching, Burnley still hadn't won. Things were as bad as the previous season: played eight, won none, drawn two, lost six, goals for six, goals against twenty, points two.

Staff Sergeant Eddie Mosscrop was reported to be ill while abroad, suffering from influenza, and Gunner Bob Kelly in the RFA wrote to John Haworth saying that he had seen and spoken to Tommy, who was managing to keep his head down. He said, "Tommy is out here again but he like me is just waiting for the war to finish."

Figure 40. Fritz is kicked into touch – another football related postcard of the time

The end of the affair

The end everyone hoped and prayed for finally came on 11 November 1918. At first the men serving overseas couldn't believe it and didn't know which side had won. The total cost of over four years of fighting around the world: thirty-seven million casualties, including nine million dead. In Burnley, street parties took place and the church bells rang. Effigies of the Kaiser, who had abdicated, were burnt in the Market Square. But despite all the flag waving, the joy and relief that it was finally all over, the Armistice was not the signal for the immediate release for the men who had fought to win the peace. It was months before they all returned home, to a *'land fit for heroes to live in'*. The demobilisation of five million British soldiers in France took time, and for men like Tommy Boyle it appeared the rule was *'last ones out, last ones home'*. There was still much for the army to do. The dead needed burying in proper graves, the materiel of war collecting, and they had to make sure that Jerry didn't start another scrap. From late November, men needed to rebuild the economy were demobilised first, followed by skilled craftsmen and then men with families. Tommy, like most other footballers, was at the end of the queue.

As the national newspapers filled with the glorious news of the Allies' victory over the enemy, the faces of men killed in action carried on appearing in the papers. Private Jonathan (Johnny) Brown had played a number of times for the Burnley first team during the war and just before the war he had played his football mainly in the reserves at left-half. Jonathan, serving in the 1st East Lancashire Regiment, was dead, killed on 6 November 1918, five days before the end of the war. He was twenty-nine and was buried at Maubeuge Cemetery in France. The day after Johnny Brown fell, another player Tommy knew well also lost his life. Wilf Bartrop the Barnsley winger who Tommy played alongside in the 1910 Cup final was like him, in the Royal Artillery and serving in Belgium when he was killed. Both footballers had gone through the whole campaign to be killed just a few days from its conclusion.

The cost locally

Some 4,500 men from Burnley and the immediate area were killed during the war: over 1,000 men for each year of the conflict. Added to this were the men who were wounded, the prisoners of war and the ones who would suffer for the rest of their lives, a combined figure nearly four times those killed.

A Roll of Honour was published by the *Burnley Express* a year after the war in 1920. It named all the local men killed in action. After only a few page turns, it moves the reader to tears. It names the thousands of men and boys who were lost from individual families. It names the 149 families that each lost two sons, the fourteen families that lost three sons, and finally, the Hall family from Padiham, who lost four sons, one for each year of the conflict. Four sons. Four telegrams. Four graves.

And for the men lucky enough to survive their experience and make it back physically unscathed, the damage they'd suffered might not show immediately. It might be months or years before a flashback or a loud noise would trigger them to do the most unusual things, like dive under a table for cover, begin trembling or burst into fits of tears for no apparent reason. According to the reports, Tommy suffered shell shock in 1917. The effects of it were varied and more complex than burst eardrums from the blast wave of a shell. It was later found that shell shock led not just to deafness but the loss of speech, epileptic fits and the loss of motor control of the limbs where the patient would shake uncontrollably. Much later it was found that exposure to shell shock could lead to the onset of mental illness.

The men who returned home tried their best to fit back into normal family life and work if they had jobs to return to. Generally, the men were proud of what they had achieved and would remember what they had done every day for the rest of their lives. It cannot have been easy living on nerve endings and adrenalin, being trained and ordered to kill, and then to simply flick a switch and return to 'normal' family mode again. Yet after demobilisation, that was what was expected. After demobilisation there was little or no support other than the soldier's family. The men who had gone through it rarely spoke of their experiences, but inside a rage tore at them. They were glad to be alive, but also bitter about the treatment their country had put them through. In his book *The Soldiers' Tale* Samuel Hynes says, "Those who survived were shocked, disillusioned and embittered by their war experiences and saw that their real enemies were not the Germans, but the old men at home who had lied to them." At night, many would lie awake, revisiting the battlefield, haunted by the faces of their lost comrades. They found it hard to let go. It ran on and on. With no post-trauma counselling, they were simply left to get on with their lives. For a great many, the pressure of coping with such an experience would build up before finally they cracked under the strain. Unable to cope they would be taken off to the local infirmary to 'get well'. And if the treatment there failed, they would be transferred to an asylum, sometimes never to be seen again.

By the time the General Election had taken place in December 1918 and Burnley elected its first Labour MP, Dan Irving, Tommy and many of his teammates were still abroad, spending Christmas 1918 in France with their War Office Christmas pudding for comfort and no sign of immediate release. Tommy wrote to John Haworth, asking him to try to get him released, which was possible if an employer made a direct plea to the War Office stating their employee was needed. The *Burnley News* reported:

Many people will sympathise with the appeal of Tom Boyle the Burnley captain to the secretary of the Burnley club to use his efforts to get him out of the army. If what he says is correct, clubs are already sending in applications to the War Office authorities for the discharge of their footballers from the army."
(*Burnley News*, 14 December 1918)

As Big Ben rang in 1919 and New Year's revellers celebrated in Trafalgar Square, millions were still overseas. In January Eddie Mosscrop, serving with the Salonika Forces, wrote, "I fancy that my group will soon be on its way home." Billy Watson was in Belgium and expected to leave at the start of February. He said, "Things around Christmas got very dismal. If it had not been for good old football, half of us would have been ill I am sure. Football has gone a long way to pass the time." George Halley was the furthest away of any of the players, serving in India with the Royal Engineers. Billy Watson and Eddie Mosscrop eventually made it home to Southport, strangely on the same train on 19 February. It took Billy nine days to get home from Belgium and Eddie, thirty-two days from Salonika who had slept on deck the whole time at sea under wet blankets night after night and was suffering from exhaustion when he got home.

Chapter 10: The Comeback

Those who hope in the Lord will renew their strength.
They will soar on wings like eagles;
They will run and not grow weary,
They will walk and not be faint.

– Isaiah 40:31

Tommy arrived back in Burnley on 5 March 1919, four months after the war had ended. His kitbag had hardly touched the floor before he was round at John Haworth's house for a talk. He told the Burnley secretary he had been playing regularly in the army and that his health was fine, and pleaded with him to give him a place in starting line-up on Saturday. Haworth agreed. He was relieved to see his captain back to his old self and was sure his inclusion would make a big difference.

On Saturday 8 March Tommy was in the starting line-up against Stockport County. A more familiar-looking Burnley side lined up: Dawson, Smelt, Brown, T. Taylor, Boyle, Watson, Kelly, Lindley, Freeman, Hodgson and Mosscrop. Stockport took the lead only for Bert Freeman to equalise. Bert then scored a second to give Burnley a two-one lead at half-time. Teddy Hodgson, home on leave from Germany, scored to make it three-one and Eddie Mosscrop passed the ball to Bert to complete a fine hat-trick. Crawshaw pulled a goal back for Stockport to make the final score four-two to Burnley. With several regulars on display, the attendance had picked up, a crowd of around 15,000 turning out, one of the best attendances for years. The captain was back.

In the wars again

On 26 March, Kestrel in the *Burnley Express* reported on the captain's contribution in a two-one defeat at Stoke City. He had been in the wars, picking up a bad head injury for his trouble:

> If anyone worked hard for a win, he did. His headers were wonderful. Many a time it seemed to be that Boyle was holding the whole of Stoke at bay. He tried to instil into the front line something of what was desirable in swinging the ball about. There were frequent unfair incidents on the part of Stoke and one does not envy Whittingham's reputation in this direction. Twice, early on, he "back-headed" Boyle when the latter had quite legitimately won the ball.

Tommy was in the thick of it again in the following game where he picked up another head injury in a three-one defeat by Preston at Turf Moor:

> It was unfortunate that Boyle was injured in the melee leading to the first goal, for after that he hardly dare use his head, suffering as he was from a cut over the right eye sustained in a collision with Broome. Before then he had given the side a hint of what they ought to do, firing at long-range, with the wind behind them. He went off temporarily to have his injury seen to but returned to the fray later.

Having impressed in the three games they had played in, Tommy and Eddie Mosscrop were selected for the inter-League match on 5 April at Hampden Park. The *Daily Mirror* reporter commented: "Tommy Boyle at centre half is playing in place of Parker. That is a wise change I think. With a hustling player like Richardson to deal with, an indefatigable worker is required and Boyle is the man."

Eddie Mosscrop scored the last goal and the winner in a three-two win for the English League. The curtain came down on wartime football on 23 April 1919. Kestrel reported that

Tommy was outstanding in the last game of the season in front of a 20,000 crowd at Turf Moor against the old enemy, Blackburn Rovers. Burnley won four-two and finished the Lancashire League season in thirteenth place on twenty-three points, with Tommy making five appearances since his return.

The football authorities announced that from August 1919 a full League programme and the FA Cup competition would return. The First and Second Divisions were to be increased from twenty to twenty-two clubs and the season extended, commencing on 15 August and closing on 15 May. The restriction on the payment of wages to players would be lifted. The players could give up their factory jobs and get back to playing full-time.

Burnley announced its admission prices for the new season. The top price season tickets in the stand cost five pounds and five shillings, double the pre-war price, though the tickets would now include twenty-one home matches plus the Central League reserve team games. Match-day prices on the ground were doubled from sixpence to a shilling and Kestrel in the *Express* asked who would pay the new prices. The maximum wages for players would be increased to seven pounds and ten shillings a week plus there would be an improved bonus scheme of two pounds for a win and one pound for a draw.

By summer 1919, Burnley had got almost all its Cup winning team back from war service apart from George Halley, who was still on duty in India, and Teddy Hodgson, who was still serving in Germany. In June, Bert Freeman married Margaret Elizabeth Whitehead, the daughter of the Burnley FC Club president, Alderman Edwin Whitehead.

At Burnley's AGM it was announced that the club had made a small profit of six hundred and seventy-seven pounds over the 1918–19 season, so selling half of the Cricket Field end timber had been unnecessary as the club's credit at the bank after four years of wartime football was a healthy six thousand five hundred and thirty-one pounds.

In late July news came in concerning the illnesses of two Burnley players. Teddy Hodgson was serving in Germany with the British forces with the 52nd Manchester Regiment as a sergeant instructor when he was taken ill and brought home to convalesce in the military hospital in Whalley near Burnley. Dave Taylor was also suffering ill health with a heart condition and was in hospital in Scotland. Kestrel in the *Express* reported that Taylor was seriously ill: "It is evident that his strength is ebbing away. It was obvious when he last visited Burnley that he was not in the best of condition. Taylor is very weak though quite conscious and is making a brave struggle."

On Sunday 3 August, just a fortnight before the return of League football, a peace celebration took place at Turf Moor. At the service, in front of a full house, choirs sang and local children were awarded a peace medal. People on the terraces sang hymns as brass bands played.

The following Tuesday morning, as the Burnley players came in for training. John Haworth asked the players not to get changed until they had all arrived as he had something to tell them. They knew it wouldn't be good news from the look on Haworth's face. When everyone had arrived, Haworth broke the sad news that Teddy Hodgson had died in Whalley the day before. The players couldn't believe it. Teddy Hodgson was thirty-three and had been an ever-present face in the team since arriving from Chorley in September 1911. He had made his debut in the match against Barnsley at Oakwell, the same game Tommy made his Burnley debut in. The dressing room was silent and no training took place as a mark of respect for their teammate.

On Friday, the day of Teddy's funeral, thousands lined the streets to pay their last respects as the funeral procession left the Hodgson family home in Haven Street not far from Turf Moor and passed by the football ground. Teddy's coffin took the same route, but in the opposite direction, the triumphant Cup winners had taken only five years before. Tommy, Bert, Tommy Bamford, Dick Lindley, Jerry Dawson and Billy Watson carried Teddy's coffin into the church at Rosegrove cemetery for the funeral service. Eddie Mosscrop who couldn't get release from school and George Halley, who was still abroad, were the only missing faces from the 1914 Cup-winning team.

Burnley FC players who served their country in the Great War, 1914–19

Killed in action

Private **Alfred Lorimer**, aged twenty-three, Service Number 240, RAMC, attached to the 2nd Battalion East Lancashire Regiment serving in Egypt. Killed on 1 February 1915. Buried in Ismailia War Cemetery, West Bank, Suez.

Private **John T. Heaton**, aged twenty-one, Service Number 13638, 1st Battalion Coldstream Guards. Killed on 16 August 1915 in France. Buried in Vermelles war cemetery near Calais.

Private **Andrew Taylor**, centre-forward, younger brother of full-back David Taylor. Played for Burnley Reserves between 1912–13. Killed in June 1917.

Private **William Pickering**, aged twenty-three, Service Number 12434, 72nd Seaforth Highlanders. Killed on 9 November 1917 in Baghdad. Buried in Baghdad North Gate war cemetery.

Private **Jonathan Brown**, aged twenty-nine, Service Number 34933, 1st East Lancashire Regiment. Killed on 6 November 1918. Buried in Maubeuge Centre Cemetery, France.

Died after the war of war-induced illness
**Sergeant Instructor/Lance Corporal Edward (Teddy)
Hodgson**, aged thirty-three, Service Number 79012, H
Company, 52nd Manchester Regiment. Served in several
theatres of war. Died of kidney failure in Whalley Military
Hospital, 4 August 1919. Buried in Burnley Cemetery.

Died
Harry Langtree, reserve goalkeeper, aged twenty-three, died
in Blackpool hospital in August 1915 from complications
following an emergency operation.

Wounded on active service
Bombardier Thomas William Boyle, received shrapnel
wounds, shell-shock and suffered deafness.
Private Levi Thorpe, received shrapnel wounds.
Corporal Dick Tranter, received shrapnel wounds.
Corporal Tom Bamford, **Private Sam Gunton** and **Private P.
Goodison**, all wounded.

Captured and taken as a prisoner of war
Burnley Trainer **Charlie Bates**, South Staffordshire
Regiment, captured near Ypres on 26 October 1914, interred
as a prisoner of war for over four years, released 1 December
1918. During his time in the camp Charlie took part in two
unsuccessful escape attempts after he and his comrades dug a
tunnel under their hut.

Received injuries while playing football in France
Gunner Walker Hampson, reserve half-back discharged
from the Royal Garrison Artillery with a knee injury sustained
while playing football in France.
Sergeant Ernie Edwards, Burnley trainer until 1918,
sustained a broken ankle while playing football in France in
1917. He later become a trainer at Swansea.

Served in various operational theatres of war

Private E. Ashworth, Private H. Hargreaves, Private J. Hutton, Private J. Podley, Private H. Shaw, Private G. Thompson, Private R. Sewell and **Lance Corporal H. Wolstenholme** all served in the army.

Lance Corporal George Halley served with the Royal Engineers,

Bombardier J. Clarkson, Gunner Bob Kelly, Gunner W. Clarkson, Gunner Cook and Gunner Kellock all served in the Royal Field Artillery.

Staff Sergeant Edwin Mosscrop served in the Royal Army Medical Corps

Sergeant David Taylor and **Trainer-Sergeant/Instructor William Watson** served in the Army Service Corps, Motor Unit.

Bert Freeman served in the Royal Flying Corps.

Dick Lindley served in the Glasgow Shipyards and also in munitions.

Jerry Dawson, Joe and James Wild, Cliff Jones and **Billy Nesbitt** all went into war munitions.

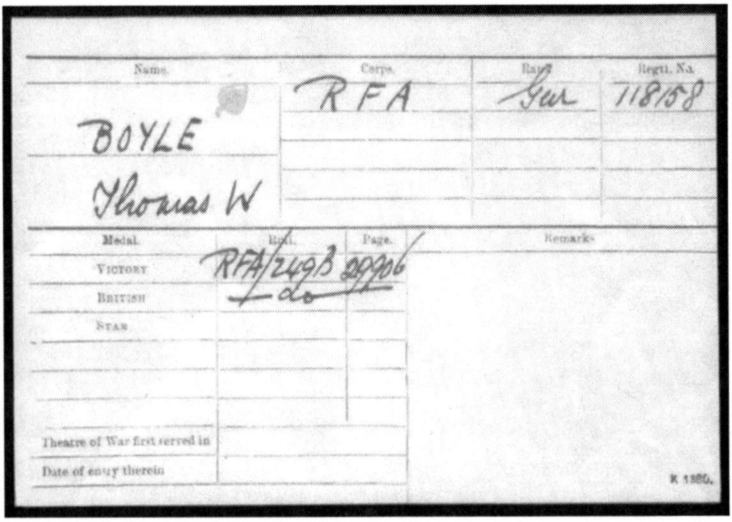

Name.	Corps.	Rank.	Regtl. No.
BOYLE Thomas W	RFA	Gnr	118158

Medal.	Roll.	Page.	Remarks
Victory	RFA/249B	29906	
British	do		
Star			

Theatre of War first served in

Date of entry therein

K 1380.

Figure 41. Tommy Boyles medal card.
(Courtesy The National Archive.)

The League returns

The Football League recommenced on the August Bank Holiday weekend with Burnley visitors to Notts County where they lost two-nil. Their first point came in the next game at Burnden Park in a one-all draw, which was followed with a return home win against Notts County, two-one.

In Burnley for the September Bank Holiday weekend was a flying circus of Australian airmen who took those who were brave enough and could afford the guinea fare on a circuit of the local area to a height of 4,000 feet. Tommy was one of the first passengers taking off from a tiny airstrip in Towneley on the outskirts of town:

> Considerable attention from those on holiday at home has been given to three Australian airmen to the town and the vicinity of the aviation ground adjoining the Co-operative Laundry has been visited by a large number of people. The aeroplanes take off and finish their flights from Towneley Holmes. Tommy Boyle, Burnley's Captain was among the passengers and the machine circled the football field. At the conclusion, Boyle expressed his delight at his experience. (*Burnley Express* September 1919)

The rarefied atmosphere must have done Tommy the world of good as Burnley won their next four games on the trot, including two victories over Blackburn Rovers three-one at home and three-two away to put Burnley joint top of the League on twelve points. After a home defeat to Chelsea, which Tommy missed due to flu, he was back in action for the next game and scored in a two-all home draw against Sheffield United.

After four years of service with the Royal Engineers, and seeing action in Mesopotamia, Egypt, South Africa and India, Lance Corporal George Halley finally took off his army uniform after arriving back in Burnley in mid-October 1919, almost a year after the war had officially ended. Halley took in the Sheffield United game as a spectator at Bramhall Lane, seeing Burnley win three-one.

As winter approached Tommy missed a number of important games through illness. By late November and with no captain, Burnley were floundering. Kestrel in the *Express* commenting on Burnley's "lack of a leader". The captain returned for the match at Bradford, Burnley winning one-nil to go back to the top of the League in early December, a point ahead of fellow League contenders West Bromwich Albion. The Halley, Boyle and Watson partnership were back in business. Kestrel in the *Express* noted "there was little doubt where Burnley's strength lay and that was in the middle division, where Boyle's return coupled with his amazingly clever generalship acted as a tonic to other members of the team and pulled them together".

On the morning of the Oldham match, Tommy received an anonymous letter, franked in Bristol, offering him a thousand pounds if the team would lose the match. He reported it straight away to the Burnley officials. It transpired that several other club captains had been offered bribes to throw games and it was later found that the letters were linked to an illegal betting syndicate.

A bad day at Boundary Park

The Oldham game on 6 December was a disgraceful display of football, according to Kestrel in the *Express*, the match descending into an undisciplined free-for-all. Tommy was hurt during what play managed to take place.

> The trouble had been brewing in this game for some time. Fouls had been fairly frequent on both sides and the Burnley men who had played a scientific game became irritated through the vigorous, unceremonious and altogether strenuous tactics of the

Oldham side. The referee should have taken action early on. Dolphin wilfully kicked Cliff Jones the Burnley full back on the calf, the Burnley man lost his temper, turned round and deliberately kicked Dolphin. The referee saw it and sent Jones to the stands. But he didn't walk immediately. Both sets of players rushed over to the spot and a fist fight ensued. One or two spectators rushed onto the field and the referee became embroiled in the middle of it all. Jerry Dawson managed to get the spectators off the field and Jones eventually left the field for the stands.

As the game progressed, Oldham became rougher in their tactics and Boyle was very nastily brought down and fell on the back of his head. He lay there while the Oldham forwards played on around him. The Burnley captain was dazed and the game was stopped for several minutes.

Jones was banned for a month for his part in the fracas at Oldham. On the same weekend, West Bromwich Albion had won three-two at Manchester City and took over at the top of the table. A week later at Turf Moor against Oldham it was both Tommy and Bert's benefit match, but both of them missed the game through injury. Wins against Preston at Deepdale and Middlesbrough followed to keep Burnley in contention for the title over Christmas, but then a disastrous sequence of seven games without a win followed, which saw The Clarets fall back in the title race.

In January the FA Cup competition returned. Burnley were pitched against minnows Thorneycroft's, a team of shipyard workers from Woolston on the Solent. The match took place at Portsmouth's Fratton Park and ended in a tight goal-less draw, Burnley bringing the shipbuilders back to Turf Moor where they won five-nil. For the second round, Burnley were drawn against their old cup adversaries Sunderland at Turf Moor.

For the Cup tie Tommy was unwell, the *Express* reporting, "[he] was confined to bed with a very severe cold accompanied with fits of shivering. A Cup tie without Boyle would be like *Hamlet* without the Prince.*" There were hopes up to the day of the Cup tie that Tommy would play, but his temperature was still high and Doc Hodges declared he wasn't fit. It was the first time the captain had missed a Cup match at Turf Moor.

In preparing for the big game it was reported that the banking on the 'Star' side of the ground had been on fire again and during the week attempts had been made to flood the fire out with hosepipes. Not much impression had been made on it, as wisps of smoke still rose through the clinker in places even though 50,000 gallons of water had been poured on it. On the positive side, Dave Taylor's health was improving and he was expected to start some light training soon.

The Cup tie ended in a one-all draw and Burnley went to Roker Park for the replay, but without their influential captain they lost two-nil. They were out of the Cup, but still had a good chance of winning the League title. By 14 February Burnley were three points behind leaders West Bromwich Albion, who were having a bad spell themselves, having lost twice to Sheffield United. But would Tommy be fit to join in the fight in time? He returned to the team a fortnight later on 28 February and faced Derby County at home, The Clarets winning two-nil. With ten games left, the title race was between two clubs, West Bromwich Albion and Burnley. The next two matches brought the title contenders head to head. In the first encounter at Turf Moor on 6 March, the game ended honours even in a two-all draw. Before the next game at The Hawthorns a week later, the team spent a few days away in Droitwich taking in the brine waters. The spa treatment did nothing to help Burnley's cause and they fell to a four-one defeat at The Hawthorns, which dented their title challenge as West Brom had two games in hand.

Joe Anderson

Since Teddy Hodgson's death, John Haworth had been searching for another goal scorer. He went to Scotland to see a promising twenty-five-year old who was scoring regularly in the Scottish League, Joe Anderson. With thirty goals in twenty-eight matches for Clydebank, Anderson had hit four hat-tricks since the start of the season. Could he continue his excellent form south of the border at a higher level? John Haworth certainly thought so. At five foot nine, Anderson had served three years in the army with the Royal Scots Fusiliers and had received a bullet wound in the wrist at Bullecort. A figure in the region of two thousand pounds was paid to secure his services.

Joe Anderson made his debut against Sunderland in the League at Turf Moor playing in Teddy Hodgson's old berth alongside Bert Freeman. Kestrel reported on another battle at the Turf:

> The game started well with good football but ended in a scrappy rabble. The referee gave the players too much latitude in the early stages and the game suffered because of it. Players on both sides were to blame. The game was only a few minutes old by which time Mosscrop had been fouled by Poole three times. A bad injury to Martin who was fouled by Smelt the Burnley full back after ten minutes. On 30 minutes, Sherwin kicked Watson's legs from under him and almost immediately afterwards Coverdale caught Mosscrop on the jump, kicked him in the legs and turned him in the air like a Catherine wheel. The result was that the referee ordered him off the field.

Despite being down to ten men, Sunderland scored first. Tommy was well below par and missed a penalty, before Burnley scored twice and won the match two-one, putting them four points behind Albion who still had two games in hand. Any hopes of winning the Championship sank in the Roker Park mud a week later. Charlie Buchan starred in a three-nil victory for the home side to leave Burnley six points adrift of West Brom with six games left. Burnley conceded the title a fortnight later after a two-nil defeat at Highbury, and West Bromwich Albion went on to take the title by nine points in the end. Burnley finished the season as runners up, their highest ever League position so it had been a good season. But runners-up wasn't good enough for Tommy, he wanted the title to add to his Cup winners medal.

He had been in and out of the team all season for some reason or another – illness, injuries, knocks. He hadn't been fully fit at the start of the season and then over the winter period his bad chest had laid him up for weeks. If he could just stay fit for a few more games next season, Tommy was sure Burnley could go a step further and win the title. The whole team would need to stay fit, just like they had done in the Cup in 1914. They just needed a settled team, few injuries and a bit of luck. John Haworth added three new faces to the squad. Forwards Benny Cross and Walter Weaver arrived joining Alf Basnett, who came through the reserves. With Jerry Dawson ever-present in goal, and with Halley, Boyle and Watson in front of him, Burnley stood a good chance, but it wouldn't be easy.

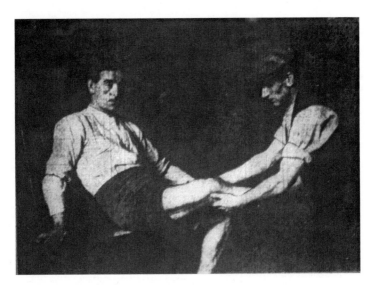

Figure 42: Tommy receives a leg massage from Charlie Bates prior to the start of the 1919-20 season.

Chapter 11: One Last Chance

O Captain! my Captain! our fearful trip is done,
The ship has weather'd every rack,
the prize we sought is won.

– Walt Whitman

In pre-season Tommy felt fit and was ready for another challenge. If he was going to win the title it had to be this year. At thirty-four, he knew he wouldn't have long left at this level. Bert Freeman, nearly a year older than Tommy, also knew it. The years were catching both of them up and after ten years together, this could be the last season they'd enjoy playing together.

Figure 43. Burnley team photograph at the start of the 1919-20 season

During the summer, improvements to Turf Moor had seen a new facility built for referees and officials under the stand and an additional entrance made where the old referees' changing room was located. An attempt to subdue the fire which had been burning in the 'Star' embankment for several years had been made over the summer with some 800,000 gallons of water used to flood the fire out. The players were once again under the training of Charlie Bates, now assisted by the former Burnley goalkeeper, big Jack Hillman. In addition, the players' wages increased. The starting salary for players was now five pounds a week rising by one pound for each year of service and the maximum salary for professionals like Tommy and Bert was raised to nine pounds a week plus 'talent money'.

At the start of the season the squad stood at twenty-nine professional players. There was good cover in all positions and the squad had eight surviving members of the 1914 Cup winning team. Full of optimism, the Burnley team began the season in good spirits but for the first three games against Bradford City at home, followed by Huddersfield Town and Bradford City away, they couldn't do anything right and lost all three games. It was Burnley's worst ever start to a season and by the second week of September they were bottom of the League.

A key factor that had affected the team's performances over the three games was the lack of a leader. In pre-season Tommy pulled a pulled calf muscle and had therefore not featured. He made his comeback in the reserves against Blackpool. After coming through that game with no problems, John Haworth brought him straight into the side for the home match against Huddersfield Town. Haworth made the tough decision to drop crowd favourite Bert Freeman in favour of newcomer Joe Anderson and bring in Bob Kelly alongside him. Burnley lined up Dawson, Smelt, Dave Taylor, Halley, Boyle, Watson, Nesbitt, Kelly, Anderson, Cross and Weaver. Burnley's first goal came after a shot from Tommy was charged down by a defender only for Bob Kelly to score from the rebound. From the kick-off, Burnley won the ball and attacked with Billy Watson. He passed to Tommy who struck the ball like a rocket from thirty yards out. The ball flew straight past Mutch in the Huddersfield goal. After the interval Burnley scored a third as Watson passed the ball to Nesbitt who had only the keeper to beat and cheekily lobbed the ball over his head on fifty-four minutes. It was all one-way traffic and Burnley should have added more goals to their tally, the game finishing Burnley three, Huddersfield Town nil. Burnley's season was finally off and running. "A Transformed Team. Burnley find the right track at last against Huddersfield. Boyle's Greatness a big factor in the victory," reported a much happier Kestrel in the *Express*.

Each week Burnley climbed another place in the table and stayed unbeaten. Against Middlesbrough in the next home game, Burnley were a goal down and came back to win two-one. In the return match at Ayresome Park, Burnley drew nil-nil. Then Chelsea came to Turf Moor and Burnley put four goals past them to go mid-table as Aston Villa led the Division on twelve points. After a three-one victory at Bradford Park Avenue, Kestrel in the *Express* wrote of Tommy's impact on the game:

> When Bradford took the lead through Hartles, Tommy Boyle rallied his forces and sparing neither energy nor verbal encouragement. Boyle rose up in strength and by sheer good captaincy and will power pulled the team together. For a long time the Burnley team failed to profit by the example he set of playing an open game.

In the Bradford Park Avenue rematch at Turf Moor, Joe Anderson scored the winner in a one-nil victory to put Burnley seventh and go seven matches unbeaten. The team next travelled to London for the match against Tottenham. Dave Taylor was injured early in the game so Tommy had to reorganise his remaining ten men. George Halley shifted to right-back and Billy Nesbitt filled in for Halley. Tottenham scored through Banks and it looked as if Burnley wouldn't get anything from the game but they clawed their way back and grabbed an equaliser through Joe Anderson. Ten-man Burnley then scored again through Anderson, with a solo run that beat two Spurs defenders before he slotted the ball past Jacques in the Tottenham goal. An amazing turn-around. After the match Tommy was written up in the celebrity column in the *Burnley News* with the subtitle "he is a typical Englishmen – he is never beaten".

Figure 44. Tommy Boyle caricature (Burnley News)

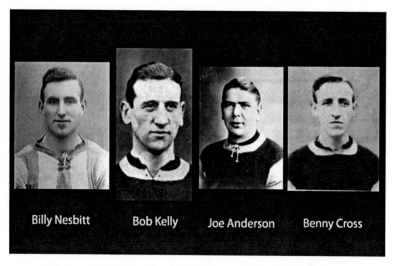

Billy Nesbitt   Bob Kelly   Joe Anderson   Benny Cross

*Figure 45. Billy Nesbitt, Joe Anderson, Bob Kelly
and Benny Cross.*

With full-back Dave Taylor injured for the Tottenham game at home, Cliff Jones came into the side. Kestrel thought that Spurs were the best side he had seen all season. Burnley won again, two-nil, with goals from Bob Kelly and Benny Cross to climb to fourth. Burnley next travelled to Newcastle United. The team was unchanged again and Tommy silenced 50,000 Geordies with a penalty on thirty-six minutes. Bob Kelly made it two-nil just before half-time with a fine volley. Newcastle pulled a goal back on seventy minutes and after that the Burnley defence was tested time and again, but the team held out for the two-one victory. It was now ten games unbeaten and Burnley were second in the table just a point away from Aston Villa at the top.

A record attendance for a League match at Turf Moor, 38,860, turned out for the Newcastle return match at Turf Moor. Burnley were unchanged for a sixth consecutive game.

Burnley found themselves a goal down after seventeen minutes as Dixon scored for the visitors, but two minutes later

Bob Kelly equalised. Ten minutes after that Burnley took the lead with a fine goal from inside-forward Benny Cross. Then three minutes after half-time Tommy started the move that settled the win. Kestrel in the *Express* said: "Boyle who had been conspicuous with his long passes out to the wings again led to Kelly beating Finlay and quickly passing the ball to Nesbitt who returned it to Kelly who was brought down in the penalty area." The referee pointed to the spot and Tommy stepped up to score his second penalty in a week against Newcastle United to make it three-one to Burnley.

A two-all draw at Boundary Park in November saw Burnley reach the top of the table, and the following week they played Oldham at home. Burnley were outstanding and four goals to the good by the interval, with two from Bob Kelly and two from Benny Cross. In the second half Wall pulled a goal back for the visitors, before Tommy scored a belter after a shot by Watson was cleared to the feet of the Burnley captain who hit it hard past Taylor in the Oldham goal. Five-one. George Halley stopped a good Oldham attack and cleared the ball to Benny Cross, who put Bob Kelly through for his hat-trick. Six-one. After the restart, Joe Anderson robbed Goodwin and put the ball through for Kelly to score his fourth goal. Seven-one: Burnley's best League performance since 1901.

The all-out attack

After a goal-less draw at Anfield, the return match with Liverpool took place on 11 December in front of 26,000 spectators at a cold Turf Moor. Burnley gained a fine one-nil victory, winning in the second half after using what Kestrel called "the value of the long pass". Kestrel also said that the goal was scored by "the whole of the Burnley front-line moving in almost military precision" – Kelly got the ball and passed it out to Nesbitt, who ran down the line like a hare and put in an excellent centre for Weaver to shoot past Scott in the Liverpool goal. Burnley had now gone sixteen games without defeat.

They had had no injury worries and the side was almost the same that had started the season in September. Could they maintain their form over the busy Christmas period and go into 1921 unbeaten?

The week before Christmas, Burnley dispatched Preston North End two-nil at Turf Moor and on Christmas Day Sheffield United arrived in town. Joe Anderson was star of the show. He scored Burnley's opening goal in the first minute; the whole forward line advanced as one. Bob Kelly fed Billy Nesbitt on the wing, and he ran and whipped in the centre for Anderson who simply passed the ball into the net with his left foot, "which brought much laughter," reported Kestrel. Tommy handled the ball twice in the Burnley box, which the referee fortunately missed, then minutes before half-time Benny Cross got on the score sheet to score Burnley's second goal with a great shot. After the interval, Joe Anderson scored his second, third and fourth goals in succession with Bob Kelly scoring the final goal. The Clarets were rampant, beating George Utley's Sheffield United with ease.

The players had Boxing Day off as it fell on a Sunday and on the Monday they travelled to Bramhall Lane, Sheffield. Tommy expected a response from George Utley's side. He told the team to remember 1914 and the game after their semi-final victory where they had been hammered five-nil. The Bramhall Lane pitch was its usual quagmire, Kestrel noting the thick mud that clung to the boots and slowed the movement of the players. In front of a crowd of sixty thousand, United's biggest of the season, the game ended in a one-all draw, Burnley coming from behind after a goal by Johnson to equalise through Bob Kelly.

Burnley in seventh heaven

On New Year's Day Burnley won three-nil at Deepdale to start the New Year celebrations with a bang, and next up was the first round of the FA Cup against Leicester City away at Filbert

Street. Leicester were mid-table in Division Two, and 29,149 turned out for the first round Cup tie. Burnley again turned on the style. Joe Anderson scored first with a header from a Billy Watson free kick. It then looked like Anderson had scored a second when the ball went in, but King, the City defender, had the final touch. Anderson then scored his second and Burnley's third before Smith pulled a goal back for Leicester just before half-time. After the interval Bob Kelly scored and then two quick goals from Anderson saw Burnley six-one up, which became seven when Benny Cross scored. Burnley slackened off toward the end as Leicester replied with goals from Roxburgh and Paterson. The final score was Leicester City three, Burnley an outstanding seven.

Anderson makes monkey

The game the whole town always looked forward to came on 15 January when Blackburn Rovers arrived at Turf Moor. Burnley had gone twenty League games unbeaten and the team was again unchanged, Burnley lining up Dawson, Smelt, Jones, Halley, Boyle, Watson, Nesbitt, Kelly, Anderson, Cross and Weaver. Ronnie Sewell played in the Rovers goal. Before the game, Joe Anderson was presented with a pet monkey as a mascot in front of the huge home crowd of 41,584 spectators, another new record attendance for the home side. On a pitch that was soft on top but frozen underneath, Burnley began well and scored through Benny Cross before Rovers equalised shortly afterwards as Smelt, making a clearance, hit one of his own players and presented the ball to Sandham to tap in. Bob Kelly gave Burnley a two-one lead just before half-time. Halfway through the second, Tommy scored Burnley's third, hitting the ball from thirty yards out with Sewell obstructed by his own defenders as the ball flew over him into the top of the net. There were "rising tempers" in the game, according to Kestrel. Walter Weaver was on the receiving end of 'ankle-taps' from Thorpe, and ended the game with badly bruised and swollen ankles. The referee was kept busy as the Burnley team recorded another fine victory over their neighbours by four goals to one.

As Burnley excelled on the football field, unemployment in the town, particularly in the mills was on the increase. The decline in orders in the cotton industry and the effects on Burnley were noted in *The Times* :

> Many of the mills are only working two days a week, the average wage being earned being £1 a week for adults. People in the area have said the situation is as bad as during the American Civil war. 70% of production was affected in Burnley.

Then the mineworkers went out on strike. Poverty was everywhere. The *Burnley Express* headlines announced "There is real distress in Burnley". Hundreds of people were short of food; the Mayor, Edwin Whitehead (Bert Freemans's father-in-law), announced, "I do wish that all those who have dinners will try to support those who have none."

Burnley's only change at Ewood Park was Eddie Mosscrop, who came in for the injured Walter Weaver on the wing. Eight minutes from the start Bob Kelly gave Burnley the lead with a header following a George Halley free-kick. Then Hodkinson equalised for Rovers with a shot into the roof of the Burnley net that gave Dawson no chance. In the second half goals from Joe Anderson and the returning Eddie Mosscrop secured the points for The Clarets, taking Burnley six points clear at the top of the League on thirty-seven points after twenty-four games.

Burnley travelled to Lytham for a week of training for their second round home Cup tie against Queens Park Rangers. Team headquarters were set up at the Granville Cafe in Clifton Street which were close to the football ground and the baths. After playing QPR in 1910, Tommy was taking the southerners seriously: they had progressed through to the qualifying stages having beaten non-league side Merthyr at Shepherds Bush in the first round.

Queens Park Rangers brought around 200 fans along in a crowd of well over 41,000. Burnley went down to ten men after thirty-five minutes when Benny Cross damaged his shoulder; he played on before having to retire, and ended up in the infirmary needing an X-ray. Billy Watson was also struggling with his shoulder and also ended the match in the infirmary. Eddie Mosscrop had an outstanding game, giving Blackman, the QPR defender, a torrid time. Joe Anderson opened the scoring with a header from a Mosscrop cross and then Rangers equalised through Smith. Bob Kelly scored two to make it three-one at half-time. In the second period Burnley scored through Anderson, a carbon copy of his first goal, and two minutes from time QPR added another though Birch to make the final score four-two to Burnley. There was talk on the terraces of Burnley doing the double after the Cup draw was made, for which Burnley faced a trip over to the east coast to face Second Division side Hull City.

The New Invincibles

Tommy was suffering pains in his back and a severe cold ruled him out of the Aston Villa match. He had done well in getting through January without being ill or injured, but the talk on the terraces was, how long would he be out? Could the team cope without the skipper? Apart from losing Tommy, Burnley were unchanged. They began well and after twenty minutes a handball in the area gave Billy Watson a penalty that he scored to put Burnley a goal up. Fourteen minutes later a one-two between Anderson and Nesbitt led to Anderson scoring with a header. For the rest of the half, Villa were on top and pulled a goal back through Humphries. The second period was dominated by Burnley, Anderson in particular. He scored again seven minutes after the interval, followed by a Dick Lindley goal two minutes later. Anderson then scored three more, his last goal an absolute gem, having dribbled through the Villa defence to slot the ball past Sam Hardy, the Villa and England keeper. Seven-one to Burnley. They were simply unstoppable. Burnley led the First Division by seven points ahead of Bolton Wanderers with a game in hand and a goal difference of plus forty. Burnley were now 'The New Invincibles', according to Kestrel in the *Express*:

> The 21 years old record of Sheffield United and the 32 year old record of Preston North End are gone. The Old Invincibles [PNE] are a memory; The Turf Moor Invincibles are a living fact.

Burnley's next opponents in the League were Derby County at Turf Moor. After the Villa game, any scoreline was possible. How many would it be - eight, nine or ten? Derby, however, were well prepared and needed the points as they were at the foot of the table. Burnley managed to win, two-one, but it came at great cost. Leading scorer Joe Anderson went off the field with a broken cheekbone. It was feared the bone had become dislodged in his left cheek and another knock could be serious. His face swelled up so much he couldn't see out of one eye. After the game George Halley developed symptoms of pneumonia, and Billy Watson and Eddie Mosscrop were also both on the sick list. The team had gone six months without serious injuries and now they had all come at once.

The Burnley team set off for Lytham on the Monday morning to prepare for their third round Cup match at Hull, and despite their injury situation the talk in the press was of Burnley progressing easily at the expense of the Second Division side.

FA Cup third round: Hull City v. Burnley, 19 February 1921

The Tigers were not having the best of seasons and were down in seventeenth place in Division Two and Burnley had never won at Anlaby Road. City had a good Cup record at home and had pulled off shocks in the past against higher opposition Chelsea (1909), Newcastle (1913) and West Bromwich Albion (1915), so a giant-killing was on the cards. Top-of-the-League Burnley made two changes, Bert Freeman coming in at centre-forward for the injured Joe Anderson and winger Walter Weaver switching to George Halley's position. Burnley lined up Dawson, Smelt, Jones, Weaver, Boyle, Watson, Nesbitt, Kelly, Bert Freeman, Cross and Mosscrop. Three to four hundred Burnley spectators made the trip over by chartered train, as Kestrel noted, "wearing hats in the club colours, and one group carried a large cardboard dummy, minus the legs which they planted on the field".

Burnley began well and for the first twenty minutes were the better side. But Hull were a tough, physical outfit and disrupted Burnley's normal passing game. Mosscrop came in for some rough treatment from Bell, the City defender, and was kicked often, "spread-eagled once and Catherine wheeled" later. Weaver received the same sort of treatment after being "laid out" by Gilhooley. A minute before half-time Cliff Jones handled the ball just outside the penalty area and from the free-kick Hull scored through Brandon. Anlaby Road erupted and City held their lead until half-time. In the second half they went two up with another goal from Brandon, an unstoppable thirty-yard strike. Then on seventy-seven minutes, Hull made the game safe as Bert gave the ball away in defence too easily to Wilson, who nipped round him and poked the ball into the net past Dawson. Top of the League Burnley had been well-and-truly outdone by the Second Division underdogs, three-nil. The team were mauled in the press for the three-nil defeat, which was seen as a massive giant-killing. The unbeaten run of matches since September had come to an abrupt end. Out of the Cup Burnley could now channel all their efforts into winning the title. Could Tommy rally his troops after such a humiliating defeat? Kestrel reported in the *Express* on his experience with a group of abusive Burnley supporters on the return train journey from Hull. Apparently, they were shouting from the carriage window, 'Does anyone want to buy the Burnley team?' Kestrel said: "There were obviously some disgruntled people after losing their unbeaten run to a Second Division side by such an unpredictable score."

Back to winning ways

On 26 February Burnley beat fifth-placed Bolton Wanderers by three goals to nil in front of Burnley's largest ever League crowd of 42,653. Joe Anderson was back and though his face was still swollen he played the full game, with Bob Kelly, Benny Cross and Billy Nesbitt scoring the goals for The Clarets.

Cliff Jones, Billy Nesbitt and Bob Kelly all received the call up for the England v. The North international trial, which took place at Turf Moor on Monday 28 February. A crowd of 35,000 turned out, but England were decisively beaten six-one with Sunderland's Charlie Buchan scoring a hat trick in the match. Afterwards, Bob Kelly received his call-up for the full England v. Scotland international that took place at Highbury on 12 March. Burnley drew at Burnden Park, one-all, with a brilliant performance from Jerry Dawson. Kestrel described Dawson's performance as "the most wonderful exhibition of goalkeeping ever seen". Tommy also came in for praise: "Boyle was a tower of strength. With all his old wiles, he tried to engineer attacks which ought to have been made better use of, but it was his captaincy which was of even greater value to his side."

Jerry Dawson was in fine form again for the next game when Arsenal visited Turf Moor. Kestrel called it "the worst game of the season", and put it down to the strain of all the matches on the players. It was a last-minute decision by John Haworth to include Tommy in the side and also Joe Anderson, who could run but not head the ball. Thirty thousand people turned out to see The Clarets win by a single goal from a Billy Watson penalty. It was a dirty game that the referee failed to get a grip of. Kestrel reported on the Arsenal tactic of punching Burnley players in the back when they had the ball, using their elbows to gain an advantage and shoving their opponents to break up the game unnecessarily.

Burnley travelled to Highbury the following week. Tommy missing the game through injury. Kestrel reported that it was more of the same dirty tactics from the Londoners. Joe Anderson was carried off after being kicked in the mouth and when he returned he made the wound worse by heading the ball and had to go off again. Baker, the Arsenal right-back, scored first and it looked like Burnley's run was about to come to an end. But a bloodied Anderson returned in the second half refreshed. Picking the ball up twenty yards out from the Arsenal goal, he beat two defenders and struck the ball past Williamson in the Arsenal goal to earn Burnley a well-deserved point.

Easter arrived, and for Burnley a gruelling four games in eight days. The schedule - Manchester United and Manchester City home and away, so it wasn't too far to travel for the supporters. City were the bigger threat; they were fifth in the League with United tenth. Manchester United arrived at Turf Moor on Good Friday, 25 March. Kestrel recorded that Burnley struggled early-on as the United goalkeeper, Mew, was in good form. Burnley managed to score in the twenty-seventh minute with a disputed goal from Benny Cross. Cross hit the ball towards Mew who was beaten, full-back Silcock was on the goal line to head the ball out, though he was clearly behind the line as he did so. The linesman flagged and Cross's goal stood. Tommy played an excellent game, "The Mastery of Boyle" ran Kestrel's headline in the *Express*. He was in raptures over the captain's performance:

> Boyle can said to be the outstanding figure on the Burnley side, dominating the game and directing its movements, and in all the

work of Burnley the mastermind of its captain was visible. With his head he did some great work. His feet were tuned to the point of long accurate passes to the wings and he bound the team into one indomitable and progressive whole.

Burnley's win took their League run to thirty games unbeaten, a new League record. No other First Division club had gone so long undefeated during a season. The day after the victory over Manchester United, Burnley travelled to meet Manchester City at Hyde Road. City had not lost at home all season and were in good form, having won their last four games on the trot. Burnley were at full strength apart from George Halley and lined up Dawson, Smelt, Jones, Basnett, Boyle, Watson, Nesbitt, Kelly, Anderson, Cross and Mosscrop. The match referee was Mr Slater of Blackburn. A concerned Kestrel in the *Express* commented on the state of the ground and the crowd problems before and during the game:

> The gate was closed well before kick-off and around the ground where the houses could be seen, people were perched on rooftops. There were fans also on the players dressing room roof and at one point a spectator nearly fell through a skylight into the changing room below. At one time the crowd swayed disconcertingly for a time, they swayed forward from the top of the embankment. Those nearer the barriers were thrust forwards and injured, more or less seriously and as the pressure increased several of them were trampled underfoot...

Another incident prior to kick-off involved a crowd stampede as fans tried to get closer to see the game. Spectators were lined all around the field, less than a yard from the touchline. From another part of the ground that was only lightly policed, "a portion of the crowd broke in", leading to more crowd congestion. If that wasn't enough, Kestrel reported that "a portion of one of the stands caught fire as the game took place"!

On a pitch with little grass on it, the home side took the lead in the first half. They scored again sixteen minutes after the restart with a goal by Barnes, which Dawson struggled to see coming toward him in the bright sun. Burnley got back into the game nine minutes later as City gave away a penalty. Tommy stepped up to take it. A chance to pull a goal back. He missed, hitting the ball wide of the post. Then, four minutes from time, the busy Barnes scored again for City with a header to put the game beyond Burnley's reach. Their unbeaten run was over. When the results came through, Liverpool, in second place, had drawn at Blackburn and were creeping up on The Clarets who were now seven points ahead of them with eight games to go.

Kelly's marvellous goal
Manchester United v. Burnley, Old Trafford, Easter Monday 1921

After defeat at Hyde Road it was important to get something from the United match. Championships are usually won by the most consistent sides, through hard graft and a little luck. None were more skilful in the art of goal scoring than Joe Anderson and Bob Kelly. In front of 30,000 at Old Trafford and with no team changes, Tommy wound up the team before they emerged onto Old Trafford pitch. He was determined that they were not going to throw it all away in the final furlong. Burnley led one-nil going into the interval. Then, halfway through the second half, Manchester United won a corner at the Stretford End. As the centre came across Tommy brought the ball under control to clear his lines and spotted Bob Kelly, who was in his own half when he collected the ball. Kelly crossed the half-way line turning and beating two static United half-backs who had pushed up to the halfway line to seek the equaliser. Kelly advanced across the field, as the United full-back, Moore, came across to meet him, he was followed by the United keeper, Mew. Seeing the gap narrowing between them and Mew a mile off his line, Kelly cut the ball back across the advancing goalkeeper and into the United net. "It was a glorious goal", described Kestrel. A third goal from Anderson, a left foot cracker, wrapped up the points for The Clarets to put them nine points clear at the top with seven games to play. The finishing line was now in sight, they needed to keep their nerve just a little bit longer.

In the return game between Burnley and Manchester City on Wednesday 6 April, Burnley gained their revenge for the defeat at Hyde Road, winning by two goals to one. They then travelled to The Hawthorns to take on reigning champions, West Bromwich Albion. Albion had struggled to find the form that saw them take the title the previous season ahead of Burnley. In a lively game, it was Albion who found their form, and with two goals from Crisp, Albion won two-nil. Tommy was wound-up. He was cautioned, Kestrel recording that, "Boyle lost his self-reliance and in the second half one of his tackles led to him receiving a little lecture from the referee."

In recognition of setting a new League record of thirty games unbeaten, the Burnley board applied to the FA for permission to reward the players financially. The club asked for a sum of twenty-five pounds per man, but the FA allowed them to grant a figure of twenty-five guineas.

The following Saturday, 16 April, 26,422 turned out to see Burnley play their home game against West Bromwich Albion. The team needed a win after the previous week's defeat at The Hawthorns. The one-all draw meant that with four games remaining, a point at Goodison Park the following week would clinch Burnley's first Football League title.

Everton v. Burnley, Goodison Park, Saturday 23 April 1921

For what was their biggest match since the 1914 Cup final, Burnley lined up: Dawson, Smelt, Jones, Basnett, Boyle,

Watson, Nesbitt, Kelly, Anderson, Cross and Mosscrop. It was a blazing hot afternoon, the sun beating down on a crowd of over 44,000 that included a large number of Burnley supporters. Kestrel noted that:

> it was a pleasure to watch the Turf Moor side when we saw them playing that scholarly scientific game into which every man fitted like a section of a jigsaw puzzle, baffling the opposition defenders and carrying out movement with a neatness and precision...

Burnley had a good opportunity to go in front on six minutes but missed the chance and then suffered a number of Everton attacks, managing to fight them off, Sam Chedgzoy going close for Everton. Midway through the first half Bob Kelly had a chance but the ball was cleared by Fern, the Everton goalkeeper. Fazackerley, Everton's centre-forward, stood alongside the Burnley defenders and ran onto a long ball, and it looked like he could have been offside. With only Dawson to beat, Fazackerley placed the ball past the advancing keeper and into the Burnley net. Despite Tommy's claim for offside, the goal stood.

The Everton cheers had hardly died down when Burnley replied. Benny Cross forced a corner, which Mosscrop took and floated the ball across. Anderson met the cross and his header downwards found Cross, who banged the ball into the Everton net to equalise. Shortly after the restart, Everton lost Crossley with a thigh injury. Then on sixty-four minutes, Burnley had the ball in the net again through Anderson, but he was ruled offside, receiving the ball from Kelly. Both the Burnley and Everton trainers spent a good deal of time on the pitch with treatment to Boyle and Smelt for Burnley and Dickie Downs, Tommy's former teammate at Barnsley.

Finally, Mr Ward of Kirkham blew his whistle to bring the game to an end and with it the signal that Burnley had won the League Championship. As he had done after the Cup final, Tommy collected the match ball. He later had it painted Claret and Blue and inscribed in gold lettering with the words;

Burnley FC Champions Division 1

T W Boyle Captain 1920–21.

The ball would sit nicely on the mantelpiece beside the 1914 Cup final ball

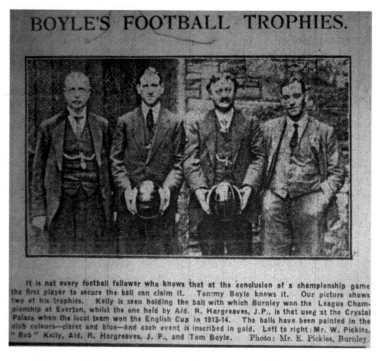

It is not every football follower who knows that at the conclusion of a championship game the first player to secure the ball can claim it. Tommy Boyle knows it. Our picture shows two of his trophies. Kelly is seen holding the ball with which Burnley won the League Championship at Everton, whilst the one held by Ald. R. Hargreaves, J.P., is that used at the Crystal Palace when the local team won the English Cup in 1913-14. The balls have been painted in the club colours—claret and blue—and each event is inscribed in gold. Left to right: Mr. W. Pickles, " Bob " Kelly, Ald. R. Hargreaves, J. P., and Tom Boyle.   Photo: Mr. E. Pickles, Burnley.

Figure 46. Tommy with the two match balls from the Cup final and the Everton away game which confirmed Burnley as League champions.

Kestrel in the *Express* commented on Tommy's contribution to the season:

[N]o man among the team can have a greater pride than Captain Tom Boyle, who has led the team to so many great victories since he took up the captaincy. To have led them first to promotion, then to the Cup and now to the Championship in the course of five League seasons is a record of which any man might well be proud.

Although the League season still hadn't finished, Tommy had promised Rev. Father McDonald, formerly of St. Mary's Church and now in Manchester, to take a team to play a charity match in Manchester. A number of Rovers players turned out to help the causes of poverty and helping 'fallen ladies of the night'. It was a busy week; and the following evening he officiated in a schoolboys' match at Turf Moor.

GRAND FOOTBALL MATCH AT TURF MOOR BURNLEY
ON TUESDAY APRIL 26th
Blackburn Grammar School v. Burnley Grammar School
Kick Off 6.30 pm
Referee: Mr T. Boyle (Capt. Burnley FC)
Linesmen: Mr. A. Basnett and Mr G. Douglas (Burnley FC)
Prices Stands 1/-, Enclosure 6d, Ground 4d.
Scholars half price.

The following night it was the East Lancashire Charity Cup final at Ewood Park.

The new League champions met their neighbours, Blackburn Rovers, for the return leg of the East Lancashire Charity Cup. Around 4,000 spectators turned out to see both sides at full-strength. The game itself was marred by a serious injury in the first half to Duckworth of Rovers, who in going in for a header with Billy Nesbitt fell badly and fractured his left forearm. Eight minutes later Burnley took the lead through Bob Kelly and then Jimmy Lindsay followed up with a second goal. The game ended with Burnley holding onto their lead and a two-nil victory. The winning team and the captain were presented with medals and the trophy.

It was announced before the home match against Everton on Saturday 30 April that Bert Freeman was to leave the club. Bert was only five months older than Tommy but had been left out of the side for most of the season as Joe Anderson had played so brilliantly. It was the parting of the ways for the pair of them who had lived and played together for nearly ten years. They'd had a good partnership, and Tommy never forgot that night in October 1914 when his roommate had saved his life. He still owed him a drink for that.

Burnley are crowned League champions

From losing their final away game on the Bank Holiday Monday, The Clarets' final game of the season took place against Sunderland at Turf Moor on Saturday 7 May 1921. After a gruelling season Burnley, Tommy and the rest of them had made it to the end. The huge silver League championship trophy awaited them in the stand at the end of the game. Burnley lined up for their final match: Moorwood, Smelt, Taylor, Basnett, Boyle, Watson, Nesbitt, Kelly, Anderson, Cross and Mosscrop. A crowd of 22,034 turned out to witness an exciting game that ended two-all. It was a low turnout compared with some of the record crowds that had filled Turf Moor during the season, but with the worsening employment situation in Burnley, it was understandable. Almost a quarter of the town were out of work as mill after mill closed through lack of business. At the end of the match the Burnley captain led his team up the steps and was presented with the trophy by Mr J. P. McKenna, President of the Football League. The final League table read:

Football League Division One 1920–1
Burnley   P42 W23 L6 D13 F79 A36 Pts 59
Man. City   P42 W24 L12 D6 F70 A50 Pts 54
Bolton Wand   P42 W19 L9 D14 F77 A53 Pts 52

Figure 47. Tommy receives the League Championship trophy at Turf Moor.

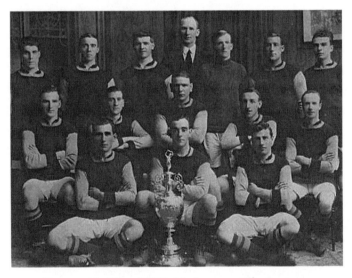

Figure 48. The 1920-21 League Champions.
Copied with permission from Burnley Central Library.

Championship medals were awarded to Jerry Dawson, Len Smelt, Cliff Jones, George Halley, Tommy Boyle, Billy Watson,

Billy Nesbitt, Bob Kelly, Joe Anderson, Benny Cross and Walter Weaver. John Haworth, as the Burnley Secretary, received a medal, as did trainer Charlie Bates. The Football League later granted Burnley permission to have three extra medals struck for Eddie Mosscrop, Dave Taylor and Alf Basnett. In presenting Tommy with the huge trophy and his medal, Mr McKenna said:

> I have the greatest pleasure in handing over this trophy and the medal you have so worthily won. It is a medal that every League captain wished to win and in my opinion there was no more worthy a winner than you.

In reply to The Football League President, Tommy said:

> I am not much of a spokesman but I am very pleased to be the captain of the Burnley team. I thought that the team had fully earned the Cup they had won this year. I am pleased to say that there is a very good feeling between the directors and the players and we are all one union at Turf Moor. I wish also to thank all the spectators for the hearty support they have given to the team this year.

The crowd covered the pitch and three cheers went up for the captain and the team. There was an honorary dinner for the team's achievement planned but this wouldn't take place until August. The club had done well through the turnstiles this year, netting some thirty-four thousand pounds in receipts from the League games and making a bumper profit of thirteen thousand pounds, a handsome figure in hard times.

Billy Watson had played in all forty-two League games, Tommy had missed only four and George Halley had played twenty-six before his injury. When the three half-backs had managed to play together, the team had lost only once. The team had gone through the whole season using only twenty-three players.

They had set a League record after going thirty games unbeaten within a season. But unlike the ceremony associated with the team's FA Cup win in 1914, there was no charabanc tour of the locality to show off their latest prize. Despite it being a much harder feat, over forty-two games, the League championship victory was a much less grand affair, played at a much lower key. There were a few photographs printed in the local newspapers and nothing like the excitement that had been generated leading up to the Cup win.

The Charity Shield

The 1921 FA Charity Shield was contested for the first time between the years FA Cup winners Tottenham Hotspur and new League champions Burnley. Prior to the game lots were drawn to decide who would host the match and Tottenham won. Tottenham, as Second Division champions the year before, had taken part in the Charity Shield the previous season, losing to West Bromwich Albion; a game that was also played at White Hart Lane. Press reports on Saturday before the match stated that neither Tommy nor Dave Taylor had signed a new contract, but both players travelled with the squad and were eligible to play in the 'charity' match. Burnley lined up: Dawson, Smelt, Taylor, Basnett, Boyle, Watson, Nesbitt, Kelly, Anderson, Cross and Mosscrop. Tottenham Hotspur lined up Hunter, Clay, MacDonald, Smith, Walters, Grimsdell, Banks, Seed, Cantrell, Bliss and Dimmock. The match was refereed by Mr Warner of Nottingham.

Monday 16 of May was a hot sunny afternoon in north London and attracted around 18,000 spectators in conditions more suited to cricket. The ground was hard and the ball "lively", said Kestrel in the *Burnley Express*. Spurs scored after twenty-five minutes with a goal from Bliss and shortly after that the same player had another shot that struck Dawson's post. Cantrell then put Tottenham two goals in front with a goal that had several Burnley players, including Tommy, questioning Mr Warner whether it was offside, but the goal stood. Tommy's remonstrations were not appreciated by the referee and he was later censured for misconduct by the FA. Burnley were not at their best said Kestrel after the long season. The Charity Shield was presented to the Tottenham captain by Major Prescott, the MP for Tottenham, and Mrs Prescott presented both teams with their medals. After the match, Mr F.J. Wall, Secretary of the FA, commented "there was no doubt that the season had to be shortened".

A new contract

By the first week of June, Dave Taylor had settled on a new contract and Tommy was the only Burnley player not to have signed a new deal. It was reported that the club were prepared to sell him if anyone came in for him at the right price. The captain was not happy with things and was making a stand for the written promise of a benefit in 1922–3 which would effectively give him a two-year contract and secure his services until he was thirty-seven. He had been granted a benefit the previous season in lieu of the five years' continuous service from when he signed in September 1911 to 1916. Despite the war years, he was still a registered Burnley player and had stuck by them throughout. Like all professionals, he had not received any payment in 1916 and his benefit was delayed until the League resumed. The League's rules were clear: "War service does not break continuous service and clubs may enter into agreements with players after three years continuous service providing a benefit after five years continuous service." The other Burnley players had backed down, but not Tommy. He was a stickler for detail and believed that he was right, the League's rules were clear. The club had not included his war service as part of continuous service. In September 1921 Tommy was due a second benefit, so what he was seeking was a delay to that and a two-year playing contract with the benefit due in the second season. As he saw it, the club could afford it based on the thirteen-thousand-pound profit they had announced, so he stuck to his guns to get the best deal he could.

There was a stand-off and relations between the captain and the Board broke down. Then after the Club's Annual General Meeting in June, it was reported that the club had had a change of heart and decided to allow service in the army to count toward benefit matches. They had no choice by League rules. The club also agreed to Tommy's request of a written guarantee of a benefit in the 1922–3 season. He'd got what he wanted and on the back of his belligerence several Burnley players benefitted from his actions. Billy Watson, Dave Taylor, Eddie Mosscrop, Cliff Jones, George Halley and Bob Kelly would now also receive benefits in lieu of their war service. At a maximum of six hundred and fifty pounds for First Division players (less tax at six shillings in the pound) the benefit was a huge sum for the club to meet. Having won his case, Tommy put pen to paper in July.

Chapter 12: Farewell Burnley

Only the truth that in life we have spoken,
only the seeds that in life we have sown.
These will pass onwards when we are forgotten,
only remembered for what we have done.

– Sams, from *'War Horse'*

Tommy was a happy man come the start of the 1921–2 season. With a contract for two more seasons assured and money in the bank, he was feeling better than ever. That summer the Boyle household was never happier, as on 10 August Annie gave birth to a baby girl at their home in Rectory Road. Tommy and Annie named her Decima Betty Boyle. The Boyles' new arrival was reported in the newspapers and a number of supporters and players from the club gave Tommy and Annie presents for the baby. The Boyles were now a family. Tommy bought the biggest pram in the shop and the proud couple were seen out in Towneley Park walking on Sunday afternoons.

Five days after baby Decima's arrival, the League champions played their first match of the new campaign in a pre-season warm-up game when Boyle's XI took on Morgan's XI at Turf Moor. Then, in the first League match, The Clarets got off to a winning start at St. Andrew's, beating Birmingham City three-two. Tommy played well, according to Kestrel: "the game produced no harder worker than Boyle who stuck the hot pace very well indeed and showed his old wiliness." After losing at Roker Park in the next game Burnley found their old form and by 22 October they had won nine out of their first eleven games to make it an excellent start and go top of the League, two points clear of Liverpool.

Halley Boyle and Watson were as solid as ever, with only two goals conceded in six matches, and the Burnley forwards in excellent form having scored eighteen goals, a second title was already being talked about. Despite the economical situation in Burnley the big crowds were returning, 31,536 having attended the Bradford game. Things were looking good.

On Wednesday 2 November a celebration evening was held to honour the captain at the Co-Operative Restaurant in Burnley. Tommy was presented with a silver porridge bowl and spoon for his baby daughter. A number of friends and admirers were present, including players and directors of the club. In replying to the speeches made, Tommy thanked his guests:

> This was the happiest function [I have] attended in my life. It was a pleasure to know that, apart from the friends I have made in the world of football during my career I have also made good friends in other walks of life. (*Burnley Express* 5 November 1921)

Then sometime during the following week Tommy was struck down by the flu outbreak that was sweeping the country. Hundreds of people were affected and many people died. It put Tommy in bed for nearly a month and Cliff Jones, Benny Cross and Dave Taylor were also out of action with it. As a consequence, Burnley dropped points in the League and slid down the table. A three-all home draw with Preston was followed by defeat at Deepdale. Billy Watson had also been out of the side, looking after his wife Lily who was unwell. The couple had also lost a child the year before. Then just a few weeks later the club received the sad news that Billy's wife had died in Southport Hospital on 15 of November. The whole team attended Lily's funeral to show their support to Billy after his sad loss.

The newspapers reported on how much Burnley were missing their key players. The defence had shipped nine goals in three games, and Sportsman in the *Burnley News* presented figures comparing the team with and without Tommy's influence:

93 Appearances: won 51, drawn 23, lost 19 with Boyle

22 Appearances: won 10, drawn 4, lost 8 without Boyle

The bad month of November continued for Burnley when the death of Director John Catlow was announced. Catlow was licensee of the Masons Arms in the town. He had joined the Burnley board in 1910 and had been one of the directors who had travelled to Platts Common to sign Tommy that Friday night in September 1911.

HARD LABOUR FOR BURNLEY SUPPORTERS

John O. (32) and Charles W. probably now regretted their violent and lawless conduct at the Bradford City ground on September 3rd. At Leeds assizes, Mr Justice Salter ordered both men to receive 20 lashes with the cat. O. to have twelve months imprisonment with hard labour, W. 9 months hard labour. The prisoners jumped the turnstile, knocked the attendant senseless with a padlock and attempted to steal admission money.
(*Burnley Express, 7 December 1921*)

Tommy recovered from flu and returned to the side for the Tottenham game at Turf Moor, which saw Burnley win and return to the top of the table, a point ahead of Liverpool as the season went into December. Five wins out of seven over the month saw the Champions running neck and neck with Liverpool going into the New Year. Burnley had now gone thirty home League matches without defeat, yet despite their excellent form in the League they dropped out of the FA Cup, losing to Huddersfield Town in the first round after a replay. They could now concentrate all their efforts on retaining the League title for another season.

A bloody affair:
Arsenal v. Burnley, 21 January 1922

The match at Highbury took place in awful conditions on a rain-sodden pitch and ended goal-less. The conditions for football were poor and the only incident of the first half happened ten minutes before half-time. Tommy collided with Graham, the Arsenal centre-half, and received a bad cut to his forehead. He played on with blood pouring down his face, using the linesman's handkerchief as a makeshift bandage and declining to leave the field for attention. At half-time he still couldn't see properly and reorganised the team, moving himself from defence to play on the right wing. In the second period Kestrel in the *Express* said he was unlucky not to have scored and would have done but for the blood running into his eyes. At the end of the game Tommy had the wound stitched by Dr Paterson, the Arsenal player who was currently out of the first team with a leg injury.

The years and the injuries were catching up with the old war horse. Now a father, with a family to consider, he needed to start thinking about the future and security for Annie and the baby. Tommy had been considering his future after the game for a number of months and, like many other Burnley players, had decided on running a pub.

A nice little place

*Figure 49. The Pedestrian Inn, Grimshaw Street, Burnley
(Picture courtesy, the Burnley Library picture archive)*

On 11 February 1922, Thomas William Boyle's name appeared as licensee above the door of The Pedestrian Inn, a small beerhouse on the corner of Grimshaw Street and Parker Lane in the town centre. The Burnley public were not short of a place to drink in the town. The Chief Constable's report for 1922 recorded some 271 licensed premises selling alcohol in Burnley including 83 pubs, 41 beerhouses, 35 wine and spirit licenses and 83 beer licenses for consumption off the premises. In addition to these there were forty-one private clubs and thirty-one licensed billiard halls where you could get a drink if you were a member. Even though there was a place to drink on nearly every street corner, since the war the trade had been restricted by the Licensing Act. Pub opening hours were limited. You could get a drink from eleven-thirty until three p.m. and then from five-thirty to ten p.m. Monday to Saturdays. On Sunday, opening hours were limited to two hours over lunchtime and three hours in the evening. The police were constantly on the lookout for any publicans who tried selling alcohol outside these times.

The Pedestrian Inn was owned by the Grimshaw family, who ran the Keirby Brewery in Burnley, and Tommy and Annie became tenants. They took over the pub from Edward Wylde, who had vacated the pub to take over at the Clifton Arms, one of a dozen licence transfers that took place that month. The Pedestrian was only licensed for the selling of beer and soft drinks, not wine or spirits. It was a small place, not much larger than a five-roomed house. Downstairs was a bar parlour with an upright piano which welcomed ladies on a Saturday night and in the front, a tap room where the regulars played dominoes. The walls were decorated with theatre and music hall posters and over the bar Tommy made a display of his trophies and the two match balls from 1914 and 1921.

A number of Tommy's teammates ran pubs in the town. Dick Lindley, Tommy's Cup final teammate, ran the Empress Hotel in Market Place, which boasted "The Finest Billiard Room in Town". Dick later took over The Queen's Hotel on the seafront at Lytham opposite where the team had trained for the Cup final. Alf Basnett took on the Bridge Inn in Bank Parade and later a pub in Gannow Lane, where he was landlord for over thirty years, well into the 1950s. Cliff Jones took over the Salford Hotel on Royle Road in 1921, which was renamed the Town Mouse in the 1970s, and Benny Cross from the Championship-winning side took on The Turf Hotel for a number of years and was still landlord in there in 1937.

The day he took over the pub Tommy was playing in the Blackburn game at Turf Moor before a huge crowd of nearly 41,000, Burnley's biggest gate of the season. Burnley lost two-one to their rivals. It marked the Clarets first home defeat in thirty-three home games, an unbeaten run that went all the way back to September 1920. In his post-match analysis, the normally pro-Claret Kestrel in the Burnley Express commented on "the decline of Burnley" and the fact that "young blood was needed". The cracks were beginning to show and it was the first time the reporter had shown any lack of faith in the team and its leader.

Burnley v Arsenal 23 March 1922

The following Saturday, 21 March, Burnley made amends by winning one-nil at Bolton with Tommy in charge. Two days later, on Monday afternoon, Arsenal were the visitors to Turf Moor for a game that was rearranged due to the FA Cup. Burnley had managed to claw their way back into title contention with the win at Burnden Park on the Saturday. They had to win this game in hand to keep the pressure on Liverpool at the top. Burnley lined up Dawson, Smelt, Astin, Halley, Boyle, Basnett, Nesbitt, Kelly, Anderson, Cross and Weaver. It was a tight encounter and Burnley managed to scrape a win, one-nil with a goal by Bob Kelly. But the main concern after the match was the injuries to two players, Billy Nesbitt and the captain, both of who limped off the field with leg injuries.

It must have been a bad injury. Tommy had never quit the field in his life. He either played on with an injury or went off for attention and came back on after repairs. The word got round in the crowd of how unlike him it was not to return. Something was definitely wrong. At the end of the game, Tommy found himself on Charlie Bates's treatment table, subjected to all his magic potions and skills, including the new-fangled deep-heat and electro-massage kit the club had bought.

Tommy was missing for three weeks and made his return in a reserve match against Stoke City at the Victoria Ground on 11 March. After an hour of the match Tommy gathered the ball, spotting an opening and started to go forward towards the centre-circle. He hadn't gone far when his left leg collapsed after he felt something snap at the back of his knee. He was carried to the side of the field in agony. The pain was nothing like he'd felt before and he screamed in pain with every movement. The Stoke doctor strapped him up and from the railway station he limped home on crutches. He called Doc Hodges out who told him the knee needed complete rest and he would need to wear a plaster cast to prevent any movement. Fortunately, the tendon wasn't broken, but his season was over.

A pain so deep

The pain in Tommy's knee paled into insignificance with events that unfolded a fortnight later. It was the day of the big match at Turf Moor: the FA Cup semi-final between Huddersfield Town and Notts County, the first time Turf Moor had hosted a match of such importance. A 50,000 crowd was expected and the town and the pubs would do a roaring trade as football supporters invaded the town. Many of the visitors would want to see Boyle's pub and enjoy a pint and a chat in his company before the match. But the doors of The Pedestrian Inn were closed that Saturday lunchtime. Tommy had sent for Doctor Holden in the middle of the night. Decima had been unwell for the past three days suffering from pneumonia. It had been a long night. Doctor Holden did all he could, but despite all his efforts, the child's heart couldn't stand the strain and the tiny bundle of joy of Tommy and Annie's life was gone.

Heartbroken, the couple were not seen for several days, the doors of the Pedestrian barred shut, a note, CLOSED FOR BEREAVEMENT, pinned to the door. The couple were devastated. They couldn't even register the baby's death, the task being left to Annie's sister. Their daughter, an only child, a loss and a grief so intense, a pain no parent should ever have to bear. It was a terrible time for Tommy and Annie. Living over a pub was the totally wrong environment for Tommy in coming to terms with Decima's death. With drink close at hand and being unable to walk properly, he was trapped inside and sought solace in beer. But despite their loss, the Boyle's were not alone in grieving for their baby daughter. The death rate among infants in Burnley was greater than one in ten. Burnley's chief medical officer's report for 1922 showed that 279 infants (children under one year old) out of 2,346 births in Burnley had died that year. A figure of more than five babies a week, dying mainly from respiratory diseases like bronchitis, pneumonia, pleurisy, and also from tuberculosis.

Decima's funeral took place the following Wednesday at Burnley Cemetery and the child's death was reported in the newspapers, albeit a brief mention in the football news column by Kestrel: "I am sorry to hear that Boyle lost his little daughter by death on Saturday (25th)."

Back on the football field, by the first week of April, Burnley's Championship hopes had faded away after they took only ten points from their last twelve games. In Tommy's absence, Dave Taylor had deputised as captain and Alf Basnett had come into Tommy's place at centre-half. The title was conceded to Liverpool when Burnley could only draw at home and then lose at Anfield. Burnley finished the season in third place. They had been League leaders at Christmas but with the loss of players for one reason or another they simply couldn't maintain their form going into the second half of the season. The defence was referred to in the *Express* by Kestrel in his end-of-season analysis on 10 May:

> The greatest regret of all has been the break-up of the grand old line of half-backs which will be remembered as long as Burnley is a club – Halley, Boyle and Watson. The departure of Boyle, the greatest captain the club has ever possessed, has been coincident with the general depreciation in the work of the team. It is much to be feared that the three will never be seen together again.

A month after Decima's funeral Tommy met with John Haworth and Harry Windle to talk about the future. They wanted him to play when he was fit but not in the first team, so as a compromise it was agreed he would play in the reserves and coach the new 'A' Team. It wasn't what he'd planned or wanted, but he was fortunate that he had a year's contract left and the club had been good enough to let him develop his skills as a coach and carry on working in the job he loved. His future was confirmed briefly in the *Daily Mirror*:

BOYLE AS COACH

Tommy Boyle has been signed on as Burnley coach, as it is very unlikely the condition of his leg will permit him to play again.

Burnley's summer tour of Italy began in the middle of May, but Tommy didn't travel with the tour party. Without their old captain, Burnley played a number of games against local Italian teams and also against Liverpool, who they beat one-nil, and gold medals were presented to the winning team.

Figure 50. Tommy enjoying himself as trainer-coach at Burnley in 1922-23.

Despite finishing the season in a respectable third place, Burnley recorded a profit of only one hundred and thirty-seven pounds on the whole season. It was an amazing turnaround on the financial success of the previous year where the club recorded a profit of thirteen thousand pounds. There had been a big drop in attendances; crowds had fallen by a third due to a combination of the team's inconsistent form and the employment situation. Although the club's assets and cash at the bank were healthy, it didn't bode well for the future as most clubs had noticed a similar decline in their incomes. Burnley's neighbours Blackburn had lost over five thousand pounds on their season.

The A-Team

Tommy had done anything but rest over the summer. He had to get out of the pub if he was to have any chance of kicking a football again. He wasn't about to quit just yet. He'd been written off before and had come back, so why not again? The pub was beginning to feel like a prison and the events of Decima's death haunted him. While Burnley were touring Italy, the plaster cast was removed from his knee and Tommy started walking with the aid of a stick. The knee gradually started to free itself. The pain had subsided and he'd managed to get some freedom back in the joint. As the days went by, daily massages, long walks and light exercise started to bring use back into his legs.

In late May he was back at Turf Moor doing some light running and skipping, with his knee strapped up. Charlie Bates looked on and scratched his head as he watched Tommy doing lap after lap around Turf Moor. Charlie told him to take it easy, to slow down; he was heavier now so must not turn as quickly or the knee might flare up again. After feeling the odd twinge here and there Tommy took notice and listened to Charlie, he was right. If he couldn't play all the time, at least his wages were assured until the end of the season and he had his coaching duties with the A Team to keep him busy. After that who knows where it may lead? Tommy would turn out with the newly formed A Team, playing in the North East Lancashire Combination against sides including Blackburn Rovers A, Rossendale United, Darwen and Clitheroe Town. He'd put on a few pounds, but despite being heavier and a bit slower he still had the eye, the technique and the skill to put the ball where he wanted it to go. He would be a useful asset as an old-head looking after youngsters less than half his age.

In the summer the football club had bought a piece of land a few miles away from Turf Moor next to Lowerhouse Mills canteen in order to support the A Team matches. Abel Hudson had set out a pitch, and the players used the Lowerhouse Mills canteen for changing in. At Turf Moor the Bee Hole end terracing had been concreted over, providing a much improved terraced standing area with crush barriers, and the opposite ends of the ground were now terraced, with the cricket field end covered.

Tommy, his knee now better, played in the Burnley Players versus Burnley Police charity cricket match, coming in as fifth man, scoring five runs and helping the Burnley team to eighty-one for five before bowling the police out for fifty-nine runs.

Burnley A v Blackburn Rovers A

The Burnley A Team season began on 23 September and Tommy played as centre-half against the Blackburn Rovers A Team at Lowerhouse Mills. Burnley lined up: Page, Hastie, Bolton, Blackadder, Boyle, Nuttall, Dobinson, Thomas, Sullivan, Greenhalgh and Hornby. A sizeable crowd turned out for the game to see the old skipper and the Lowerhouse Mills Band played for what was Tommy's first game since the Stoke reserve match back in March. An inspired Boyle's A Team hammered the Rovers As, five-one. The two Burnley Grammar schoolboys, Thomas and Sullivan up front, grabbed all five goals between them and the *Express* reporter made a note on Tommy's contribution,

> With Tommy Boyle at centre-half, the Burnley A team had little difficulty in taking the points from the Rovers A team in the first home match. Boyle was a tower of strength and his valuable instructions to the Burnley juniors gave them an advantage. Boyle turned out to test his knee which was bandaged and during the whole of the match he seemed to have no trouble with it.

He had enjoyed every minute of it. A full ninety minutes without feeling any pain and the youngsters had listened to him and learned.

As autumn turned to winter, Tommy's annual health problem, his chest, flared up again and he didn't feature for some weeks. He made his comeback against Clitheroe Town on 25 November, inspiring the juniors to a three-one victory on his old stamping ground at Turf Moor. He appeared alongside Billy Nesbitt who was making his own comeback from injury. Tommy did well, again playing the full game with no problems in his knee, and the week after John Haworth promoted him up to Burnley reserves for the match against Port Vale reserves at Turf Moor. Tommy played at full-back, not his usual berth, with Stephen Simms at centre-half, having been dropped from the first team in favour of Alf Basnett. With Billy Nesbitt on the wing, Burnley reserves won three-nil.

In the New Year, Tommy played in both the reserves and the A Team, and in the games he played in the sides rarely lost. He could still make an impression, as reported in the *Burnley Express* in late February following a four-two victory over Birmingham City reserves at Turf Moor:

Boyle's stewardship kept the men in the right positions and he tended them well to win the match. At centre-half Boyle wove a wonderful display and rendered great service to his side knitting together the defence.

He helped the A Team get to the top of the North East Lancashire League and scored his last Burnley goal at Turf Moor in a reserve team match against Stoke City on 17 March. His final game for the reserves came at Trafford Park against Manchester United reserves on 3 April, before taking his final bow in a claret and blue shirt eleven days later at Lowerhouse with the A Team.

The curtain falls

Burnley A Team v. Barnoldswick Town, Lowerhouse Mills, 14 April 1923

The A Team had already wrapped up the NEL Combination by the time their last game of the season kicked off at Lowerhouse. With no prospect of a fresh playing contract it was Tommy's final bow. He had made six appearances for the A Team over the season and after twelve years with Burnley this was it, the final curtain call. The Burnley A Team lined up: Cook, Dobinson, Shenton, Sugden, Boyle, Nuttall, Ayres, H. Heap, Sullivan, Greenhalgh and C Heap. A bumper crowd of nearly 2,000 turned out to see Tommy in his last match in the famous claret and blue shirt. The game itself mattered little as the team had won the League and it provided nothing worthy of note, the season fading out as a one-all draw.

The young lads in the dressing room after the game were enjoying their first taste of victory. Their futures in the game were ahead of them, while Tommy's were now behind him. Some of the kids playing weren't even old enough to drink and the NEL championship trophy was filled with ginger beer and passed around. Tommy wanted a proper drink. He took off his boots, knocked off the mud and shoved everything into the bottom of his kitbag. After showering alone he escaped the confinement of the dressing room and slipped into the Lowerhouse club bar for a pint. He needed time to think things through and plan his next move. Twelve years had passed by in a flash. He'd decided that running the pub was hard work and there would be no new contract at Burnley, no way back. He could have a go at coaching or, like George Halley and Bert Freeman were doing, offer his services to a club in a lower division. The knee was okay, he could still play, though as Charlie Bates had told him, not like he once had. He had his benefit money coming, but the money meant nothing. Playing meant everything. The atmosphere, the crowd, the adrenaline rush. He'd play for nothing if it meant he could pull on a shirt and a pair of boots again. He called in the newsagent's and bought a copy of *Athletics News*. On the bus into town he studied the end-of-season situations vacant. Like Bert and George, he would have to set his sights a bit lower if he was to continue playing. That's what he wanted. He didn't dare tell Annie.

For Burnley's final home League match of 1922–3 season, only 8,480 spectators turned out to watch The Clarets take on Birmingham City and lose two-nil. It was the smallest League crowd since the old Second Division days. Burnley finished the season in fifteenth place, their lowest placing since gaining promotion in 1913. The public had drifted away, unhappy with the quality of football on offer, the inconsistency, and many simply couldn't afford to attend. With the slump in the cotton industry, rising unemployment, strikes and poverty everywhere, the club reported that receipts were down by a third on the previous season and Burnley posted their biggest ever loss of six thousand pounds for the season.

Chapter 13: Back in Business

Wrexham FC invites applications from First Class Players. All positions. Apply stating position, age, height, weight and clubs last played for.

Apply to, Mr. E. Robinson, Manager, 26 Wellington Road, Wrexham.

– Athletic News, 30 April 1923

Like an ageing prize-fighter, Tommy Boyle wanted one more fight. It wasn't easy giving up the game he'd played nearly every day of his adult life. He needed football. Billy Meredith was still playing at Manchester City at forty-seven; he was ten years younger, so why not? He'd asked at Burnley, but after posting their big loss, times were hard and they couldn't afford him. He'd said his goodbyes and had been paid well with six hundred and fifty pounds in benefit money and a free transfer after twelve years of service. After scouring the situations vacant in *Athletics News* Tommy answered Ted Robinson's call at Wrexham and went down to North Wales to talk to him. After a couple of hours' discussion, Tommy put pen to paper signing a one-year contract and joined Wrexham as player-coach. He'd tell Annie later tonight.

Tommy had received offers to play for other clubs, but he settled on Wrexham as it wasn't that far to travel from Burnley and he could continue running the pub for the time being; well, Annie could continue running the pub while he was playing on Saturday afternoons. *She'll understand*, he kept telling himself.

Ted Robinson wanted a leader and was impressed with Tommy and his achievements. Robinson made him team captain, and he would take up his old berth at centre-half. Robinson also wanted results and a big name, former international like Tommy would draw in the crowds to cover his wages. Wrexham had been elected to the newly formed Third Division (North) only two seasons before in 1921 and had finished last season in tenth position. Robinson and the Wrexham board of directors were ambitious and wanted a top two placing. Their new investment, who was keen to impress, said it was achievable. He was just the man to get them promoted. But would the old-timers legs hold up?

On Saturday 18 August, Wrexham held their first pre-season trial match, The Reds v. The Whites. Around 3,000 Wrexham supporters turned out to see the club's new acquisition. The *Wrexham Advertiser* said that Boyle and Savage for The Reds were in good form, the Reds winning the trial by three goals to two and raising eighty pounds for charity from the gate receipts. Tommy came through the full ninety minutes of the trial without injury. He was ready for the start of the season, ready for the fight and ready to fire up his new team in Division Three when another engagement arrived.

Up in court

On the same day as the trial match in Wrexham, a story broke in the Burnley newspapers of an incident that had happened in The Pedestrian Inn a few weeks earlier.

TOM BOYLE SUMMONED

Alleged Sale of Drink After Permitted Hours

Thomas William Boyle had been summoned to appear [15 August] before the police court the Wednesday before on a charge of selling beer after closing time on the 30th July. He appeared along with the customer who he had allegedly sold the alcohol to who was charged with consumption after hours at The Pedestrian Inn. The case was adjourned until the following Wednesday while the prosecution and defence gathered evidence.

Tommy returned to the magistrates' court the following Wednesday. His summons had aroused a lot of interest in the town and the public gallery was full. The charge was read out by the recorder as: selling intoxicants after hours to two men who were charged separately with the consumption of the intoxicants on the premises. Tommy was charged and pleaded not guilty. The prosecution was conducted by Mr Lloyd, the Deputy Town Clerk, and Mr W Mossop appeared for the defence.

The prosecution's case rested on the police evidence. At around one a.m. in the morning of 31 July, Inspector Kilburn, on his beat, had been passing The Pedestrian Inn on the corner of Parker Lane and Red Lion Street. The main entrance of The Pedestrian Inn was on Parker Lane but there was a passageway on Red Lion Street through which one could get to the back of The Pedestrian Inn. Kilburn had heard voices coming from the passageway and had investigated, discovering that the voices were coming from The Pedestrian Inn. He noticed a window was open and the noise carried out into the yard. Kilburn entered the yard and listened at the door for a few minutes. He then left to find two other PCs (Reeves and Hirst) and the three returned to the yard and listened. The police heard corks being drawn from bottles and then heard a woman's voice say, "Whose is the lemonade?" They heard glasses being moved about and then heard the woman say, "That will be three shillings."

Shortly afterwards, Mrs Boyle, wife of the defendant, went out into the yard and saw the Inspector and the two other officers. The three officers followed Mrs Boyle into the premises and into the room called the bar parlour. In front of the three men were three bottles of Bass ale, with the corks drawn. In the glasses was an amount of pale ale. Mrs Boyle had a bottle of stout in front of her. The wife of one of the two men had the lemonade. The Inspector said he had heard voices outside. Mr Boyle said, "We have only come back from Wigan since twelve o' clock [midnight] and these are my guests." The Inspector said he didn't think all of them had come back at twelve o' clock, after which Mr Boyle said, "Well, I have." The Inspector claimed that the two men were under the influence of drink but Mr Boyle was not. He said Mr Boyle became abusive and was told to behave himself or a case of obstruction could be brought. The police's case rested on the sale of intoxicants outside hours.

Mr Mossop, for the defence, claimed that the two men and a woman were indeed Tommy's guests and that no money had changed hands. The front doors of The Pedestrian were locked and the curtains drawn. He also claimed that the window was only open eighteen inches to let some air in and the police must have climbed over a wall to unbar the gate to enter the yard.

After presenting the case for the prosecution, Mr Mossop called his witness and Tommy took the stand. He told the court that he had kept The Pedestrian Inn since February 1922, and in that time there had been no summons against him and no conviction of any sort. On 30 July he had gone to Wigan with three men to watch a bowls match. The four had returned to Burnley by taxi after midnight. It had been arranged that one of the men would stay at The Pedestrian overnight as he lived in Cliviger, some distance away, and he had asked both of the men to come back to the Inn for a nightcap. The three of them had entered by the front door and Mrs Boyle and the wife of one of the men were waiting in the bar parlour. Tommy offered his guests a drink, and Annie took the order and returned with the drinks. She never asked anyone for any payment for the drinks, and neither did Tommy, Boyle claimed.

Tommy said he heard the latch on the back door lift and Annie went out to investigate, saying "Come in" to the officers.

"We are in," replied one of the officers. Insp. Kilburn had then said, "What are these men doing here?"

Tommy said they were his guests and they had just returned from Wigan. He was asked about the three shillings and denied he had heard it mentioned. Tommy said he was "a little vexed" when he heard that three shillings had been mentioned.

Mossop asked Tommy, "Now, Boyle, I will ask you as a sportsman, did any money pass for those drinks?"

"No."

Mr Lloyd asked, "Mr Boyle, you have been appealed to as a sportsman, you are not putting on any bias today, are you?"

"No."

Replying to further questions from Mr Lloyd for the prosecution, Tommy said that when he went into the house he opened the window in the bar parlour and also the back door of the house to let air in. The back door was open when the police came in and they walked straight into the house. All the witnesses were asked whether any money was exchanged for the drinks and all denied it. Tommy had invited them in and money was not requested. Mr Mossop said the magistrates must admit to reasonable doubt that money had been exchanged for the drinks. The evidence of the police, he contended, was not as convincing on that point as the evidence of the witnesses. He did not believe the police had committed perjury; they believed they had heard something but had been mistaken. Mr Mossop summed up by saying that if there was any doubt in the minds of the magistrates, the defendant was entitled to the benefit of the doubt.

The magistrates retired and the Chairman said that after very careful consideration of all the evidence put before them they found the case proved and Boyle would be fined ten pounds and special costs. The summonses against the other men were adjourned for three weeks. The fine, ten pounds, was nothing to Tommy. He'd spend that on the horses in a week. It was the principle of the matter that offended him. He thought he was right and he was not going to leave it at that. He planned to appeal against the conviction, but before the appeal he had to captain Wrexham in their first match of the League season at the Racecourse Ground.

League Division Three (North):
Wrexham v. Ashington Town, Saturday 25 August 1923

The weather in North Wales was awful for the start of the new football season. Three days of rain had soaked the Racecourse Ground, making the pitch heavy. The rain didn't stop 6,300 hardy Wrexham spectators turning out to see their team under new leadership. Tommy, wearing the red shirt of Wrexham, took him back to his old Barnsley days. Ball tucked under his arm, he proudly led the team out and proceeded to win the toss. Wrexham would defend the Town End. Wrexham lined up: Godding, A. Jones, Pugh, Regan, Boyle, Savage, Harrison, Cotton, Jackson, J.R. Jones and Lenney. The Welshmen got stuck in right from the first whistle. They were three-nil up by half-time. By the end of the match they beat the north-easterners comfortably, four-nil. It was a great start and marked Wrexham's biggest home win in twelve months. Two days later at Walsall on Bank Holiday Monday, Wrexham fell behind to an early goal only to equalise by half-time and then score the winner in the second half to win two-one, with another two goals provided by Cotton. In the third match in a week away at Ashington Town the following Saturday, Tommy steered Wrexham to their third win in a row in front of a crowd of 5,000, Wrexham winning two-nil. Three wins out of three and Wrexham were top of the League. The football correspondent in the *Wrexham Advertiser* gave a positive review of Wrexham's first week of the season and the transformation of the team under the new captain: "For coolness, Boyle had no equal." If the court case was gnawing away at the back of Tommy's mind, it certainly wasn't showing on the field.

The Burnley newspapers confirmed on 1 September that Tommy was going to appeal against the charges to the Quarterly Sessions. He returned to court with two solicitors, Messrs Mossop and Bowling, and gave notice of his intention to appeal against the conviction. The magistrate fixed the amount of Boyle's surety at fifty pounds and the two other bondsmen at twenty-five pounds each. Tommy had raised the stakes; he would show them he was right.

A bigger crowd of 10,500 turned out at the Racecourse Ground for the mid-week home game against Walsall which ended in a nil-nil draw but for the Wrexham defence, it was another clean sheet. Wrexham's first defeat came away at Rotherham County where they lost two-one, but the result was reversed the following week to send Wrexham back to the top of the table with a one-nil win at the Racecourse, the *Wrexham Advertiser* reporter noting:

> Boyle's speed has aroused considerable adverse criticism. He did well but there were times when his colleagues had to come to his assistance through lack of speed. Although I hold no brief for Boyle, the success of the Wrexham club is due mainly to a fact generally admitted and for good football and experience of controlling and placing his team. He is in a sphere of his own and if he is replaced by a speedier substitute, I question whether the organisation of the side or the results will remain as good.

On the field it was all going very well. But after Wrexham's seventh game of the season and a goal-less draw against Wigan Borough at the Racecourse Ground on 19 September, and despite Wrexham's lofty position at the top of the table, Ted Robinson and the Wrexham board were not happy. Robinson dropped his influential captain along with Lenney to the reserves in favour of Moorwood and Williams. It's not clear why Tommy was dropped. It could have been his 'slow' performance that Robinson didn't particularly like, or perhaps the Wrexham board had got wind of Tommy's impending court case and didn't want any bad publicity rubbing off on the club. Why drop the captain when the team were top of the League? Whatever the reason, when Tommy saw the first team and reserve team sheets in the dressing room he couldn't believe it.

Wrexham's next two League matches were against Darlington Town, home and away. They lost both games and as a consequence were knocked off the top spot. Ted Robinson had put Tommy's name on the reserve team sheet for the match against Brymbo and Green United in the first round of the Welsh League Cup. Tommy didn't turn up. Nor did he for the next reserve game despite being fit. He wasn't playing in the reserves. *Bloody reserves, are they kidding?* The Wrexham management were furious and suspended him, sine die. The *Wrexham Advertiser* reported on 27 October,

> At present Boyle is at loggerheads with the Directors by whom he has been suspended. Since Boyle was dropped, nothing but failure has come the way of the Welshmen!

After seven games with Tommy in charge of matters on the field, Wrexham had been flying high at the top of the Third Division and playing well. Without him, Wrexham had slumped to mid-table and half the crowd had voted with their feet.

The Quarterly Sessions

Tommy's appeal came before the Quarterly Sessions at Burnley Magistrates' Court on 22 October 1923. Tommy's solicitor for the defence was Mr Jackson, while Mr Lustgarten presented the case for the police. The witnesses from the first court appearance – Annie, the two other men (who were to be charged separately) and the woman who were in The Pedestrian on the evening the police came in – also appeared. The public gallery was full again, consisting mainly of local people interested in the case along with a number of journalists.

The proceedings began where the first appearance in court had ended. Mr Jackson read out the grounds of the appeal. He said that his client was not guilty of the offence charged; that the conviction was not warranted by the evidence before the justices; that on the facts of the case, the conviction was illegal, unjust and bad on the face of it; and that no evidence was given that the appellant sold any intoxicating liquor to any of the men in the bar parlour that night.

Mr Lustgarten called his first witness, Inspector Kilburn. Kilburn went through his account of what occurred in the bar parlour that night from his notes. When Kilburn was asked what Tommy had said, when confronted that money had changed hands, Tommy had replied, "Nothing has been drawn here." Kilburn then said the licensee became abusive and Kilburn said he had told him he would report him for obstruction if he didn't quieten down.

Mr Jackson, for the defence, then questioned Kilburn. "Was there any attempt by my client at secrecy in regard to the money for the drinks?"

"No."

"Did you hear the jingling of any money or see any money on the table?"

"No."

"Did you hear, 'Three bottles of Bass, a bottle of stout and a lemonade, that will be three shillings, please.' "

"No."

"Thank you, Inspector."

Mr Jackson then called his witness and Tommy took the stand.

"You were captain of the Burnley Football Club and gave it up?"

"Yes."

The court recorder intervened, saying, "And took to bowling?"

Jackson asked, "There is not so much risk about bowling?"

Boyle replied, "Sometimes."

Jackson commented, "There is in this instance, I agree!"

There was laughter in the courtroom. Then Tommy was asked to give his account of the day he went to Garswood Hall in Wigan (on 30 July) to play in the bowling tournament. Three men had accompanied him and they left Wigan at around ten p.m. in a taxi. They had arrived back in Burnley around twelve-thirty. They dropped one man off at the Commercial Inn and the other two were invited in for a drink. One of the men was staying overnight; a bed had already been made up for him in The Pedestrian by Annie.

Jackson asked, "Was there any mention of three shillings?"

Boyle said, "Yes, when the Inspector came in."

"Before he came in?"

"Yes, I asked the two others for a shilling each for the taxi and said I would put three shillings to it for the taxi driver."

Jackson moved on to asking Tommy about Kilburn mentioning the three shillings in payment for the drinks. Tommy said that yes, he had got a bit excited when Kilburn said that money had changed hands for the drinks. "It would be three shillings if anyone had paid for it," Tommy had said. According to Tommy, Kilburn had then said, "How are you, Tom?" Tommy had replied, "I do not want any of that, if you have got your information you had better get off the premises."

Jackson asked, "It has been suggested you were worse for drink, what have you to say to that?"

"I was not the worse for drink," said Tommy.

"I don't suppose you had been teetotal all that day?"

"No, sir," admitted Tommy.

"Thank you, no further questions."

Lustgarten then stood up to put his questions to Tommy. "You had quite a number of drinks, I suppose one or two, or rather more than one or two?"

"About ten," replied Tommy.

"How many drinks have you to have before you are drunk?"

"I never get that far," said Tommy.

Lustgarten asked, "Do you allege that the constables are inventing this entire story?"

"They are mistaken."

"They say they overheard Mrs Boyle say, 'That will be three shillings.' Is that an invention?" probed Lustgarten.

"It must be," said Tommy.

"May it have been said?"

Tommy replied, "I should have heard it if it had been said."

"Then it is an invention?"

"Yes."

"Then they have invented all these things?"

"Yes, I suppose so."

When called to the stand, Annie and the three witnesses all corroborated Tommy's story that the drinks were ordered by the licensee, they were not charged for and there was no intention that they should be paid for.

After all the witnesses had been questioned, Mr Jackson summed up his case for the defence. He made the point to the magistrate that a licensee can have guests on his premises after hours, so long as no money changes hands. He emphasised that the time of the morning and the fact there were people on the premises would automatically indicate to the police that the law had been broken. Jackson mentioned that it was not possible to accurately fix the time the men arrived at the Pedestrian Inn. He pointed out that the three shillings were mentioned only in relation to the payment to the taxi driver and that the police could not confirm that a taxi was waiting outside the pub to take one of the men and his wife home. The court recorder pointed out to Jackson that the police had not been asked whether a taxi was waiting outside. Jackson pointed out that if the officers were at the back of The Pedestrian they would not have heard the taxi waiting out in front and its engine may have been switched off.

All that was significant was whether any money had changed hands and there was no evidence in the bar parlour to suggest it had. In conclusion, Jackson impressed upon the court that there was a possibility a mistake had been made on the night. He was satisfied that the appellant was not guilty and did not want a formal charge to drive him out of the licence trade.

In delivering his brief final address, Mr Lustgarten submitted that there was no reason whatever for believing the police officers had been mistaken in the conversations they had heard.

The magistrates then retired to consider the case. Fifteen minutes later the court recorder returned to pass judgement. Tommy was asked to stand to receive the verdict of the court. The decision of the magistrates was affirmed. The appeal had failed to satisfy the court recorder that it came within the exceptions under Section 5, Subsection C of the Licensing Act 1921. He thought the police in the case had reluctantly discharged an unpleasant duty. The result was that the appeal was dismissed and costs would follow the event.

Tommy sat down heavily. In taking the case to appeal, he had believed he would win. He thought he had friends in high places - certainly among the police. He believed he was right and wanted to clear his name over something that he had not personally done. It wasn't his voice the police had heard or thought they heard asking for three shillings, but as licensee, he carried the can, no one else. There was no money on the table that night the police walked in and no money had changed hands. But all that counted for nothing. Kilburn had spoken to him on first name terms that night. Kilburn obviously knew Tommy well, but then so did quite a number of policemen on the Burnley Force. Tommy knew the Chief Constable, Wilfred Fairclough, and had given his time freely in aid of police charities, playing in cricket and football matches nearly every year since he'd arrived at Burnley. When off-duty, a number of policemen were regular visitors to The Pedestrian. They would regularly call in for a drink and a chat. Tommy felt personally betrayed. *Sewn up like a bloody kipper.*

In addition to the original ten-pound fine, he would have to pay the costs of the first court case and the appeal court costs of around fifty pounds plus the solicitors' fees, taking the total legal bill to around a hundred pounds, a small fortune. It would have been within his means to pay, but it wasn't the money that was important to him. He had lost the case. *Lost.* 'Why would they pick on me and make me out to be a criminal?' *Who was it I've upset?* After the appeal he was inconsolable. He stormed back to The Pedestrian, slammed and locked the door.

By the time the appeal came to court Tommy's suspension at Wrexham had been in place for a month. Even in his fury he knew he needed to get back playing. But unless the Wrexham ban was lifted he couldn't play professional football - anywhere. He would have to apologise for not turning out for the reserves and face a fine. That would be it. But when he read in the papers the next morning that Ted Robinson had signed a replacement centre-half, Francis Corbett from Hednesford, his mood deepened. *They don't want me back. Well bollocks to the bloody lot of them.*

The brewery representative came round to the Pedestrian the morning after the appeal, expressing concerns over his conviction, but owing to the slump in trade they were not about to take away the tenancy from one of their most popular pubs. That wouldn't do anyone any good. They wanted Tommy and Annie to stay on and make a go of it; after all, anyone can make a mistake. *Mistake?* Tommy lost his temper and said he'd not made a mistake. He'd had enough of the pub and chucked the towel in there and then. *Sick of the pub, sick of the bloody police, and sick of bloody Burnley.* It was time to move on. He told the brewery representative they were quitting The Pedestrian by the New Year.

After the court case and Decima's death, the couple wanted a fresh start. The town was getting him down. With mills closed and looms idle and with thousands of weavers out of work, the locals were not drinking anyway and the license trade was in the doldrums. People were not attending football matches either. Only 13,000 had turned out for Burnley's home game against Newcastle on 5 December where nearly three times that figure had attended the same fixture three seasons before.

As Christmas approached, the couple served out their notice at The Pedestrian and Tommy was searching for a way back into the game. He had read about a number of players working abroad as trainers and coaches. Fred Spiksley was coaching in Mexico and a number of other players he knew seemed to be making a good living from coaching across Europe in France, Germany and Austria.

On 29 December, the license of The Pedestrian Inn was passed to Dinah Duckworth, and the Boyles were gone. Just over two years later, in March 1926, The Pedestrian Inn served its last pint as the town council compulsory purchased the pub to make way for Burnley's new Central Library. At Christmas, Tommy had received a letter from Wrexham terminating his employment forthwith. He didn't bother replying and was never mentioned again at Wrexham. Without his involvement, Wrexham slid down the table, ending the season in fifteenth position. After such a promising start with Tommy at the helm, it had gone wrong for all concerned.

A fresh start

The start of 1924 saw Tommy and Annie living in West Kirby near Liverpool. It's not clear why they chose to move there; it was said Tommy was about to start a business in Liverpool but this never materialised. Released from his contract at Wrexham, Tommy was a free agent and was actively seeking work in the game. Tommy's sister, Margaret, and her husband ran a boarding house in Blackpool and one idea was that they might go into partnership with them. The couple moved to Blackpool for the fresh air and with the intention of finding work for them both. After his experience in The Pedestrian, the boarding house idea was too tying for Tommy. He was the outdoors type, and felt cooped up if he was indoors too long. In moving to Blackpool, for Tommy there was the added attraction of the bowling competitions that took place in the town. He'd always been a keen bowler and spent time playing at the Waterloo Hotel and also at the Talbot Hotel, home to the major UK bowls tournaments. But more than anything he wanted to be back working in the job he loved, doing what he was good at.

It isn't known which club but Tommy had received an offer of a player-coach job in America, which he turned down. He was more in favour of the vacant manager's job at Aberdare Athletic, the South Wales club who were in the Third Division (South). He had seen that George Utley had taken over as manager at Sheffield Wednesday and his old team mate at Burnley, Dave Taylor had become the manager at St. Johnstone. Frank Bradshaw, the former Arsenal player, had resigned at Aberdare causing the vacancy. Tommy fancied the job and applied but was unfortunate. After the interviews were held, the job went to the former Preston player Sidney Beaumont. But Tommy's fortunes were about to change as July came around.

Von Boyle of Berlin

By the start of the 1920s, Berlin was leading a cultural revolution. Like the Belle Époque in pre-war Paris, post-war Berlin had become Europe's cultural nerve-centre. Berlin was humming and drew in all kinds of people including authors, musicians, bohemians, architects, academics and artists from all over Europe. Albert Einstein was teaching in Berlin University and had recently won the Nobel Prize for Physics. Bertolt Brecht's early plays were being shown, while in cinemas Fritz Lang was experimenting with new forms of expression through film. The city was fresh, exciting, with lots on offer to tempt the traveller. Its main squares, like the Alexander Platz, with its hotels, beer-halls and open-air cafes, were a magnet for a growing number of visitors, attracted to what the city had to offer in terms of its culture, arts and museums. At night, Berlin came alive with scores of nightclubs, jazz-kellers and cabaret clubs, places like the *Girl-Kabarett* where the twenty-year old Marlene Dietrich appeared. Josef Goebbels came to Berlin in 1926 and noted, "This city is a melting pot of everything that is evil – prostitution, drinking houses, cinemas, Marxism, Jews, strippers, negro dancing and all the offshoots of modern art." But decadence apart, Germany was developing rapidly in many other areas too, including sport.

Figure 51. Central Berlin 1924.

Football in Berlin

Before the war, sport in Germany was predominantly amateur, but this was changing as the Germans watched and learned from other nations, particularly Britain. Germany had hundreds of sporting clubs that catered for a range of activities including; athletics, hockey and tennis, and began to focus on the most popular spectator sport, football. The Germans had long admired the English professional game, its League structure and the FA Cup competition. In developing football in Germany, a number of the larger sporting clubs advertised in England for professional trainers and several old professionals who were out of work were only too ready to accept the salaries on offer. Football in Germany in the early 1920s was divided into eight regional associations, each containing their own League structure, with clubs competing for their own Regional League title. By 1923 some 313 football clubs were registered in the Berlin region, with the twenty most prominent clubs competing in the Oberliga for the Brandenburg Football Championship. This evolved into two leagues, a First Division (Staffel A) and a Second (Staffel B) each with ten teams. Below these, three feeder leagues were established, simply named A, B and C to supply the bigger clubs. A short season of eighteen matches was supplemented by a play-off competition where the winners of the seven regional championships played each other in a knock-out tournament for the overall German Football Championship.

By 1924, a number of English coaches were working in Germany offering their services. William Townley, the former Blackburn Rovers player, had coached at a handful of clubs in Germany, Curtis Booth was at Dresden coaching, Maurice Parry was at Eintracht Frankfurt and Tommy's former Burnley teammate Jimmy Bellamy, with whom he had played with between 1911 and 1913, was coaching at SC Freiburg. Jimmy Hogan, another former Burnley player, was one of the most influential English coaches working on the Continent at the time and had written widely in the English press about the development of football in Europe. Hogan had worked in the Netherlands, Austria and Hungary before the war and had made connections with several people on the European football scene. In a number of press articles re-printed in the *Burnley Express* he gave examples of where English players were employed with German clubs, saying, "Germany is the one country on the continent which really appreciates the English trainer." When Tommy read Hogan's story he was hooked. Tommy knew Hogan and Jimmy Bellamy. If they could both make a go of it, so could he. With no regular money coming in, his mind was made up. He wrote to both Hogan and Bellamy to see if they could help and whether they knew of any opportunities.

In early 1924 Otto Nerz took over as manager at the Staffel B club Tennis Club Borussia Berlin, known affectionately to its supporters as TeBe. After the war Nerz had travelled extensively throughout England, watching teams like Aston Villa, Arsenal, Newcastle and West Ham. Nerz admired the fast, physical, attacking style of the English game. He could see professional football taking off in Germany; it was growing and more than a million sports club members were paying monthly subscriptions into clubs across the country, pumping money into the game. English teams (including Barnsley and Burnley) had been coming to Germany for years and handing out hidings to German teams with little effort. That was all about to change.

Jimmy Hogan had met Otto Nerz and his fellow German coach Sepp Herberger during his time in both Austria and Germany and the three of them had often compared notes, so when Tommy's letter arrived Hogan asked Nerz if he knew of any positions available. Hogan told Nerz that he had probably seen the Burnley captain in action himself while on his travels in England and that under Boyle's captaincy, Burnley had won the English Cup in 1914 and the League title in some style only three years before in 1921. Hogan's word was good enough and Nerz wrote to Tommy offering him a position as an assistant youth trainer at TeBe. For Tommy it was a start on the football management ladder.

The club itself was based in West Berlin and began life in the early 1900s as a table-tennis club before starting a football section in 1903. Nerz wanted to take TeBe all the way to the top and compete with the biggest club in Berlin at the time, Hertha BSC. Nerz had over a hundred youngsters on his books at TeBe, all aspiring professional footballers. He couldn't possibly train all of them himself, and Tommy's help and professional input would be welcome. Nerz needed someone who could nurture up and coming talent. Nerz offered Tommy a one-year contract as a youth coach with his own small apartment in West Berlin close to the stadium.

When Tommy told Annie he was going there was a blazing row, bigger than they'd had after he'd told her about the Wrexham job. He needed the job, he told her, what else were they going to live on? Two weeks later, in the middle of August, he was on the night ferry to Ostend, en route to Berlin.

TeBe's League season began in September. The team would be up against nine other clubs all based in the Berlin region. The strongest clubs in Staffel B were Alemannia 90, Wacker 04 and Union-SCC Charlottenburg. If TeBe were to gain promotion to Staffel A, they would need to beat these bigger clubs who were more established. Tommy set to work with his young cohort. The boys all had apprenticeships so training took place in the late afternoons after they had finished work, which suited Tommy well. Nerz had an interpreter who spoke good English and Tommy learned a few words of German himself. After a few weeks into the job, he began to settle in and wrote home to tell Annie how he was getting on. Things were going well and he was looking forward to Christmas to be home for a few weeks leave.

Back home in Burnley during the last week of November, John Haworth the Burnley Secretary, made a trip to Preston in an open-topped car to the headquarters of the Lancashire FA. During the journey it started raining and by the time Haworth arrived he was soaked to the skin. The day after he was confined to bed with what Doc Hodges initially diagnosed as a case of severe bronchitis. It later turned to pneumonia, and a few days later John Haworth died at his home on 4 December 1924. He was only forty-eight years old. The Haworth family, the football club, the supporters and the whole town were devastated. The club flag was lowered as a mark of respect as Arthur Barritt, the Assistant Secretary, took over the first team affairs until a new secretary could be appointed. Tommy didn't learn of his old manager's death until he came home a week later on Christmas leave. Haworth had been the catalyst that had forged Burnley into a team. It had been his dream, his vision, his careful assembly of a team based on speed and skill that had brought the good times to Burnley. That dream was now shattered.

Christmas came and went and on 7 January 1925 the *Burnley Express* reported that:

> Tom Boyle returns to Germany this week having entered into a further 18 months contract with a Berlin Club. He was a disappointed spectator at the Burnley v. Preston match.

Things were going well at TeBe and with the offer of an extended contract; Otto Nerz was impressed with what Tommy was doing with the youngsters. Tommy would have known Burnley were on the lookout for a new manager and may have made an enquiry about the position himself. But a fortnight after he'd returned to Berlin, on 21 January, Burnley announced that Albert Pickles was to become the new Burnley Secretary and the man to carry on John Haworth's legacy. Albert Pickles was forty-eight. He was a qualified book-keeper and had been a keen amateur footballer in his day. He had been on the Burnley Board of Directors since 1918. He had no experience of playing professional football or football management, but Harry Windle wanted someone in the post he knew and could trust. The ideal candidate for the job who could have carried on John Haworth's vision was plying his trade in Berlin, passing on to scores of young Germans all he had learned from twenty years in the game.

TeBe v. The Corinthians F.C. - 13 April 1925

In March 1925 it was reported that The Corinthians, the famous amateur side founded in the nineteenth century, were on tour in Germany and were to play TeBe in April. The *Burnley Express* of 18 March 1925 reported:

> Tom Boyle said he was training a good team in Berlin and the Corinthians were going out to oppose them. He has the option of another 12 months [contract] but would rather be back in the old country.

The match took place on 13 April in West Berlin, with Otto Nerz's team taking on the Corinthians who fielded three former England internationals, Ashton, Bower and Creek. In their previous tour games Corinthians had beaten Cologne four-two and Hamburg four-one with Creek scoring a hat-trick. They were a very good tactical side, but Nerz had studied them and had seen their weaknesses. In a tight match in front of a good crowd in west Berlin, the TeBe youngsters played well and gained a creditable one-all draw. Corinthians historian Rob Cavallini said:

> In meeting a highly trained team of Berlin amateurs, the Tennis-Borussia, who had been able to give Arsenal a game in 1924, the Corinthians found themselves fully tested, and were, perhaps somewhat fortunate to secure a draw of one goal all.

Although the result was only a draw, it was the club's best ever result against an English side. Tommy had trained his young charges well.

Going home

It was clear from the *Burnley Express* report however, that after eight months in Berlin, Tommy was homesick. With only a basic understanding of the language, and few he could call friends, he longed for the comforts of home; football, bowls and English beer. Despite the offer of a twelve-month extension to his contract, showing TeBe appreciated what he was doing, Tommy decided it was time to go home. He wrote to Annie to say that he'd be home at the end of the season which finished the middle of June.

By the end of the season TeBe had done well. The team had gained a creditable second place in Staffel B behind Alemannia 90 Berlin and the two clubs were promoted to Staffel A for the first time in their history. Tommy's involvement with the youngsters had paid off for Nerz who thanked Tommy for his services. The following season, 1925–6, TeBe ended the season runners up to Hertha BSC in Staffel A and six seasons later in 1932; TeBe won its first Regional Championship.

Tommy arrived back in England on 12 June. In his last postcard he'd said to Annie that he would be arriving at Blackpool North station around teatime. As the train pulled in he looked for her on the platform. She usually came to meet him but as he collected his bags and checked the waiting rooms it was clear she wasn't on the station, so he made his own way home. When he got there the front door was locked. Fumbling for his keys, he opened the door and went inside. A pile of post greeted him on the mat and the house was cold with no fire in the grate. It wasn't like her to not to be in, but looking around it felt as if she hadn't been around for a few days at least. He spotted an envelope on the mantelpiece addressed plainly, *Tommy* and sat down and opened it. The letter told him basically that she had left him. She was alright and had gone to start a new life somewhere else. She said there was no one else involved, simply that she needed to get away and start afresh.

Since Decima's death Tommy hadn't been her around long enough to notice that she had changed. He'd been too wrapped up in other things, the court case, Wrexham and a year away in Berlin to see that it had affected her. Decima's death had hit her more than he knew and over the past year they had simply drifted apart. She'd taken her personal things, a few photographs and left everything else. He searched the house for clues to where she might have gone but found none. He asked the neighbours and at his sister's boarding house if they had seen her. He checked the pubs they went in together, but no one knew anything. No one had seen Annie for at least a fortnight. She had handed in her notice at the shop she worked at a fortnight ago and said nothing to anyone about where she was going. Tommy went over to Burnley to talk to Annie's family to ask whether they had seen or heard from her. No one knew where she might have gone. He showed them Annie's letter and they tried their best to console him, but were equally concerned. He went to the police to see whether they could do anything, but all they said was that she couldn't be classed as missing as the letter read as if she didn't want to be found.

As the weeks went by Tommy visited Platts Common to explain to the family what had happened. He spent some time with his uncle's family in Worsthorne and with his old teammates in Burnley: George Halley, Jerry Dawson and Bob Kelly. With his earnings from Germany and a bit of cash at the bank, he'd be okay financially for a while, but he needed a job and something to do to keep him out of the pub and the bookmakers. Over the summer months he spent most of his time consoling himself in Blackpool pubs, telling stories of his days in the game to anyone who wanted to listen.

When he wasn't in the pub he'd be outside playing bowls. Bowls gave him a focus and the prize money was good if you could progress far enough in the big tournaments. He had a good eye for the sport. Tommy had played bowls since his youth on the bowling green in Platts Common with his dad; he practised regularly and was good at judging line and length. Tommy had played bowls with Bob Kelly and both of them had enjoyed the sport and had won competitions in Burnley. Tommy entered the major UK bowls championship competition held at The Talbot Hotel in Blackpool and progressed through the rounds to the finals.

Burnley on the slide

In August the 1925–6 football season got underway for Burnley at Villa Park, Albert Pickles' first full season in charge. No one at Villa Park that day would have predicted the score line.

Burnley lost captain and centre-half Jack Hill with only twenty-five minutes played after a clash of heads and played the rest of the match with only ten men. By that stage Burnley were already two goals down. They had conceded the first goal after only thirty seconds through Capewell, who went on to score four more goals. With no centre-half and no skipper to steer the ship, Burnley fell apart and let two more goals in before half-time, Capewell completing his hat-trick. It got worse in the second half, with Burnley conceding six goals in a twenty-five minutes goal-frenzy. In total poor Jerry Dawson had to pull the ball out of the net ten times. It was Burnley's worst defeat since the 1917–18 wartime drubbings. The final score at Villa Park: Aston Villa ten, Burnley nil.

Meanwhile in Blackpool, the fifty-third Annual Bowls Tournament at The Talbot Hotel had been underway for a fortnight and had attracted a field of over 1,000 entrants. In the final, played in front of nearly 2,000 spectators, a tightly fought contest between Tommy Boyle of Blackpool who was up against W. Whitehead of Kearsley. The contest was close all the way through. The two had been on level terms at ten, fourteen, sixteen, seventeen and nineteen before Whitehead finally won with a nicely placed couple of woods at the end to win the match twenty-one to nineteen and with it the trophy and first prize of five hundred pounds. For Tommy in his first major bowls final the runner-up's prize of two hundred pounds was a nice consolation prize, equal to a year's wages.

Tommy and Eddie Mosscrop were Harry Windle's guests for the local derby match against Blackburn Rovers at Turf Moor on 31 October, which attracted a raucous crowd of around 27,000 spectators. Before the kick-off, one of the linesmen had not turned up so the referee asked the Burnley officials to find someone among the staff or the game couldn't begin. Tommy stepped forward and said he'd do it. The club found him some kit and he was given a rousing reception by the Burnley spectators as he stepped onto the field in his jacket, waistcoat, familiar long white shorts and some borrowed boots. He was in his element running the line. The missing linesman eventually turned up ten minutes into the game full of apologies and took over from Tommy, who had clearly enjoyed himself. He went off the field to rapturous applause from the Burnley crowd. It was about the only happy incident in the game which ended in a three-one home defeat for Burnley, leaving them rooted to the foot of the First Division. The team seemed to lack any fighting spirit. "Boyle would have bloody sorted 'em out 'ad he been in charge," the *Express* reporter overheard among the restless voices at the end of the match; "the fire seemed to have gone out in them" he wrote up in his match report.

Boyle for manager

By November Burnley were in serious trouble in the League and also at the bank. The accumulated losses of the last three seasons and the continued decline in attendances had put the club's finances well into the red. The bank was unhappy and called in the Burnley directors to discuss the financial situation. The meetings outcome meant one thing: the club had to raise capital by selling some of its assets in order to balance the books. The supporters were equally unhappy and by Christmas, Burnley were bottom of the League, having won only five games. The shaky defence having let in sixty-five goals. In an attempt to raise money, a new share issue was floated but it only raised a thousand pounds. It wasn't enough and so four players, Roberts, Basnett, Parkin and Fergus, were all placed on the transfer list.

The second half of the season would need to show a massive improvement or Burnley were staring at relegation. A campaign among some Burnley supporters began calling for a change of manager. For several weeks, anonymous letters criticising the running of the club were printed in the *Burnley Express*, showing the concerns of the supporters, (and perhaps some of the shareholders) none more so than this one:

> Repeatedly supporters and shareholders have asked the directors to appoint the club's old captain, Tom Boyle as coach and guide. Surely his judgement of a player cannot be beaten; why don't the directors appoint such a person like Boyle as their team manager? Surely the old captain could be depended upon to carry out the duties as coach and team manager. He is the one outstanding person to my mind who helped to make our club famous. (*Burnley Express*, 7 November 1925)

An opportunity for the former captain to get involved in management at Burnley arose just before Christmas when Arthur Barritt, the Assistant Secretary who had taken charge when John Haworth had died, left the club to take up a new position at Blackburn Rovers. Despite the pressure from spectators, and after the negative press articles, the Board didn't appoint Tommy. It's not known if he actually applied for the vacancy or not. Instead the club appointed Edgar England as the new Assistant Secretary who joined the club from neighbours Nelson FC. The club then denied they were about to sell their star player, England international and inside-forward Bob Kelly. Stories circulated that the club had received offers for Kelly from a number of clubs including Hull City, Arsenal and Newcastle United. The rumours were finally confirmed in early December when it was announced that Kelly had been sold to the highest bidders Sunderland, for a record fee of six thousand five hundred and fifty pounds, which cut the debt and made the bank manager happier, for the time being at least.

But in losing the services of Kelly, Burnley lost out at the turnstiles as more supporters voted with their feet and the crowd numbers fell further. At the end of January 1926, only 10,500 turned out at Turf Moor to watch First Division football as Burnley gained a point in a dull two-all draw with West Ham United. The point however was a welcome one, as it lifted Burnley off the bottom of the table for the first time in many weeks. Burnley then travelled to top of the League Arsenal, the press expecting a hammering and came away with an amazing result winning two-one and lifting The Clarets out of the bottom two. They fell back into the relegation places again; not winning for another six weeks until Bob Kelly and his new Sunderland team arrived at Turf Moor. Sunderland were soundly beaten five-two, to clock up Burnley's best result of the season with the new centre-forward, Harry Hargreaves, leading the attack.

That same week, Tommy's name was in the papers again after an incident on a train on the way to Blackburn. Tommy appeared in court on 17 March, but he wasn't in the dock this time – he appeared as a defence witness in the case of a woman at Blackburn Police Court. Tommy had been travelling on a train to Blackburn to watch the Burnley v. Rovers derby match at Ewood Park. After the train left the platform at Rishton, the woman, Minnie Hamilton, aged forty, ran after it and attempted to get on. She managed to open the carriage door but then slipped on the footboard and fell down. Tommy quickly grabbed and held on to the woman's arm and hoisted her into the carriage as another passenger pulled the communication cord and the train came to a halt. He'd saved her from falling under the wheels and probably her death. Hamilton was fined ten pounds by the court for attempting to board a moving train.

A miracle at St. Andrew's

With the busy Easter period looming and Burnley desperately needing the points to stay up, veteran goalkeeper Jerry Dawson made his 701st appearance in goal for the Newcastle United game as Burnley beat the Geordies one-nil. In the next game at Turf Moor against Manchester City, City went home with both points, winning two-one, and sent Burnley back to the bottom again. Something out of the ordinary was needed to lift Burnley. It came at St. Andrew's where bottom side Burnley faced a mid-table Birmingham who had played well at home all season. Burnley took City apart, winning seven-one with forward Louis Page famously scoring a double hat-trick with three goals in each half. It was an amazing feat by Page and a vital result as the bottom three clubs had also all won. Two more wins against Spurs at White Hart Lane and against Cardiff City at Turf Moor saved Burnley's skin by a single point on the final day of the season. It had been an awful year, marked by Burnley's rickety defence, which had let in a record 108 goals.

The following season saw a transformed Burnley team. After four games of the 1926–7 season, Burnley were top of the League and kept up their good form until Christmas before slipping down to fifth place by the end of the season. They had done much better and one of the highlights of the season was Burnley's first FA Cup tie to be broadcast live to the nation that took place on 19 February 1927. Burnley played Chelsea at Stamford Bridge and a wireless set was installed in the Turf Moor boardroom with huge speakers to relay the Radio 2LO live commentary to the crowd watching the Burnley reserves fixture. Burnley lost at Chelsea, two-one, in front of the biggest football crowd of the day, 63,328.

Hopes of a Burnley revival after finishing fifth in 1927 were dashed the following season when Burnley started badly, losing their first five games, and were rooted to the foot of the table again. The finger was again pointed at the Burnley defence. By the end of the season they had shipped ninety-eight goals and finished nineteenth in the League, again miraculously escaping relegation by a single point. The team had suffered with injuries with Jerry Dawson suffering a broken arm, the leading goal scorer Louis Page had been injured for a number of games and then the reserve keeper Sommerville had his collarbone broken. Burnley's luck had run out.

Tommy was still living in Blackpool. He was now earning a living in the building trade as a labourer and in his spare time had entered the annual bowls tournament at Blackpool's Talbot Hotel. The *Burnley News* of 26 September 1928 reported:

> Tommy Boyle the Burnley FC Ex Captain was beaten in the second round of the Talbot Bowling Tournament at Blackpool on Monday by W Fielding of Middleton who received five. Boyle who received four was beaten 21-20.

The wheels finally come off
January 1929 saw Burnley play Sheffield United at home in the FA Cup where they won two-one, then the week after they fell

to a ten-nil defeat in the League at Bramhall Lane. Two months later in March, with crowds now well below 10,000, the club put six players on the transfer list to raise funds. By the end of the 1928–9 season, Burnley again finished in nineteenth spot, a single point above the relegation places. The writing was on the wall. They couldn't carry on like this, avoiding the drop season after season. The club were locked into a downward spiral of poor form, falling gates, loss of revenue and having to sell their best players to survive. In December, as 1929 drew to a close, two more Burnley stars left. Winger Jack Bruton was sold to rivals Blackburn Rovers for six thousand pounds and a month later Joe Devine was sold to Newcastle United for five thousand pounds to balance the books.

If Burnley Football Club was suffering, the town was suffering along with it. The cotton industry had no new orders coming in and each week another mill closed. As a consequence unemployment in Burnley soared. In December 1929 nearly 6,000 people in Burnley were registered as unemployed. By May 1930 that figure had more than doubled.

14,678 UNEMPLOYED
RETURNS HIGHEST ON RECORD
The highest number of unemployed on record in Burnley stood at 14,678 as ten cotton mills were closed. The total number of unemployed made it less than one in seven working people across the town and in some wards one in five were unemployed.
(*Burnley News*, 21 May 1930)

People in some parts of town were starving. Soup kitchens were set up providing food for the poor and the Mayor appealed for those in work to feed the ones who were unemployed.

Tommy Boyle was also heading in the wrong direction. He was in and out of work, working odd jobs mainly on building sites, carrying the hod one day and working on the roads the next.

The drink had got the better of him. Without Annie or anyone to rein him in, he went into freefall: too much booze, no regular work and when he had been paid, the bookies and the brewery usually ended up taking it all off him.

1930 and as a new decade dawned, Burnley were sitting comfortably in eighth place in Division One on twenty-four points, just seven points from the top. In January the Burnley chairman Harry Windle announced his retirement and W.E. Bracewell took over two months later. A meagre January and February offered only one win and by the time Blackburn Rovers arrived at Turf Moor on 15 March Burnley had fallen to seventeenth place in the table. The three-two win over Rovers brought two valuable points to stop the rot. The week before Easter, Liverpool arrived at Turf Moor and were beaten four-one, the result putting Burnley in sixteenth position with three games of the season remaining. The teams below Burnley all had games in hand, so The Clarets had to keep winning to be sure to be safe. Two away games loomed over the Easter holiday at Everton and Middlesbrough. Burnley lost both of them and by 19 April were in serious trouble, in their familiar berth of one place above the relegation places. Could they pull off another miracle escape and stay up for the third year running? Possibly, but this year they were at the mercy of other teams losing.

One game remained against Derby County at home, a match Burnley had to win while other teams around them had to lose. It all went down to the final Saturday. The teams at the bottom had all won their games in hand, dragging Burnley into the relegation fight on the final day of the season. Burnley beat Derby convincingly, six-two, but they had to wait and see how the other teams had gone on. After the match, supporters gathered outside Turf Moor, eagerly awaiting the Manchester United v. Sheffield United result at Old Trafford. A home win for Herbert Bamlett's Manchester United would seal Burnley's survival. But when the score came it was bad news for Burnley supporters. Sheffield United had won five-one away at Old Trafford and Burnley went down to Division Two on goal average.

It was a black day. After seventeen seasons in the top flight, after all the good times they had shared in, visits to Manchester United and Blackburn would be replaced by trips to Bury and Oldham. As the reality of relegation sunk in, the players who had been involved in the club's greatest achievements were scattered across the country doing all kinds of jobs. Alf Basnett and Dave Taylor were in football management at Hereford and St. Johnstone. George Halley had taken to academia and was studying at Ruskin College in Oxford. Billy Watson was back doing his old job in Southport painting and decorating. Tommy Boyle was struggling. He'd been sacked from several jobs for bad timekeeping and for turning up drunk. At one building site he'd been told to leave after arguing with the site foreman and threatening to punch him.

The 1930–1 season for Burnley in Division Two began poorly but gradually picked up. One memorable match was against Reading where Burnley scored eight goals at Turf Moor, but only 9,889 spectators saw it. By Christmas Day, Burnley were third in the table and looked to be possible candidates for a quick return to the First Division. The second half of the season saw The Clarets only win only three games up to Easter and their continued slide down the table began. Too many games were drawn and several defeats saw Burnley hit mid-table. There were calls from some supporters to sack the directors. For the penultimate game of the season against Cardiff City at Turf Moor, only 4,200 spectators turned out. It showed the staggering decline in attendance from just a decade before when Burnley had swept all before them and crowds ten times that figure were the norm.

A troubled man

In 1931 Tommy was living in a lodging house run by Mrs Bradshaw on Peter Street in Blackpool. He was in and out of work, drinking heavily and mixing with the wrong people. He was starting to get the wrong kind of reputation in the town. In May he was in trouble with the police and spent a night in the cells. The following morning he was up in front of the magistrate on a charge of being drunk and disorderly in a public place.

EX-BURNLEY FOOTBALLER FINED
TWO MEN IN COURT AT BLACKPOOL

A street scene in Blackpool last night led to Thomas William Boyle (45) of Peter Street, being fined 20 shillings by the local magistrates today for being drunk and disorderly. A police sergeant said he saw two men commence fighting in Bank-Hey Street. They fell to the ground the other man on top of Boyle. Boyle was drunk and the other man who appeared to be the aggressor, was sober, said the sergeant.

The man struck Boyle several times and for a few minutes the highway was obstructed by a crowd of people.

BOYLE'S DENIALS

Boyle denied that he was drunk. He had treated two girls and the other man to a drink and when he left the hotel and walked up the street, the man hit Boyle and tore his pants. The other man who pleaded not guilty said that when he entered the hotel Boyle said he had drawn £50 and invited him to have a drink. Witness treated him back and when he left Boyle called him foul names. Boyle wanted to fight and said, "Come on the sands." The witness closed in with him. Inspector Elliott said Boyle had played professional football for Barnsley of which town he was a native and also for Burnley. Since he had been in Blackpool he had followed employment as a labourer.

(*West Lancashire Evening Gazette*, 22 May 1931)

Sober again but with a screaming headache and sporting a black eye, Tommy pleaded guilty in court and was fined two pounds. Then only four weeks later he was back in the same courtroom on another charge:

LONG JOY RIDE AT NIGHT
EX-INTERNATIONAL FOOTBALLER ON THE DOLE
MAN WHO SHOOK HANDS WITH THE KING
Counc. John R F Hill of Bispham summoned Thomas Boyle an ex-international footballer, of no settled address, at Blackpool Police Court today, for refusing to pay a taxi fare. The amount claimed was £4 19s.

An order for payment was made. The driver of the taxi cab said that Boyle got in with a woman and instructed him to go to Accrington. They called at two hotels in Accrington and then Boyle ordered him to go to Burnley where they again called at hotels. At Burnley he told Boyle that the amount was running up and he said: "That's all right. Who's paying?"

Later he was told that by the time he returned to Blackpool the fare would be about £5, and Boyle replied, "£5, You'll be lucky to get £1."

Subsequently the driver had to wait outside an hotel for half an hour and as Boyle did not return left him.

Boyle in evidence said he did not order the taxi and that another man did. He could not pay as he was on the dole. The Clerk asked, "Were you on the dole when the taxi was hired?" Boyle, "Yes." Clerk, "Then you were doing very well."

In answer to the Mayor who presided, the driver of the taxi said that Boyle's reference to another man was a concoction.

The Deputy Chief Constable said that Boyle was fined last month for being drunk and disorderly. He did not know what was coming over him. He seemed to be going the wrong way lately.

Turning to Boyle, the Deputy Chief Constable said, "You are an ex-international footballer Tommy?" Boyle: "Yes. I have shaken hands with the King. (*West Lancashire Evening Gazette*, 22 June 1931)

Tommy decided to plead not guilty this time. The judge wasn't listening, however, and said he was getting tired of seeing him cluttering up his courtroom. He found him guilty as charged and fined him four pounds and nineteen shillings with eight shillings and sixpence costs. It was clear from the Deputy Chief Constable's comments, "he did not know what was coming over him", that Tommy's behaviour was becoming a concern.

Four days later, on 26 June, he was back in court again. This time it was more serious. An incident had taken place two weeks earlier, on 11 June on a tram on Blackpool promenade. Allegedly, Tommy had assaulted a tram driver near the Golden Mile, after refusing to pay the appropriate tram fare.

DID NOT PAY TRAM FARE
EX-INTERNATIONAL WHO HIT CONDUCTOR

Thomas Boyle of Peter Street, Blackpool who was stated to be an ex-international footballer, was fined £2 by the local magistrates this afternoon for attempting to avoid payment of a tram fare and £2 for assaulting a tram conductor.

It was stated he was summoned on Monday for non-payment of a taxi fare and was fined last month for being drunk and disorderly.

"He seems to be going a bit queer lately," said Inspector Potter. Boyle did not appear in court.

Mr E C Lee, of the Town Clerk's department said Boyle boarded a tram in Highfield Road, South Shore and gave the conductor a penny. At Waterloo Road he was still on the tram and when told he had gone past the penny fare stage he would have to pay another penny, but he refused to give any more. He said he was about to get off the car and then he ran down the stairs and jumped off. The conductor followed him and blew his whistle for the driver to stop. The conductor again demanded the fare whereupon Boyle struck him on the cheek. A pedestrian went to the conductor's assistance and the defendant struck him also. In the scuffle the money in the conductor's bag was scattered all over the floor. The conductor said Boyle tried to strike him with a wood used for bowls and which he had since ascertained had been stolen from the Half-Way House. (*West Lancashire Evening Gazette*, 26 June 1931)

In his absence (it was not stated why he wasn't present in court) Tommy made no plea and the judge fined him four pounds with costs of one pound, two shillings and sixpence or face twenty-eight days' imprisonment. It's doubtful he could have paid all the fines which had now amassed and someone may have stepped in and helped pay these for him or the magistrates would certainly have sent him down. It is said that some of Tommy's old friends and former playing colleagues helped to pay the court costs. Someone must have stepped in to help him, as after the third court appearance things quietened down a while, certainly in Blackpool.

Back in Burnley

At some point after his last court appearance, Tommy packed up what possessions he had left in Blackpool and caught a train to Burnley. He needed money and on his arrival at Burnley Barracks station he headed for the nearest pawnbroker's. On the shop counter he deposited two leather footballs. Both were painted claret and blue and engraved in gold lettering. One was the match ball from the 1914 FA Cup final, the other from the League match at Goodison Park which confirmed that Burnley were 1920–1 League Champions. From his overcoat pocket he pulled out a handkerchief and spread its contents on the counter. A glittering array of treasures from his career: badges, football medals, athletics medals. Among them his 1910 Cup final runners-up medal, the 1921 League Championship medal and his 1914 FA Cup winner's medal, the latter solid gold. A lifetime's achievement laid out on the counter before him.

"Are you sure you want to let these go, Tommy?" asked the pawnbroker, who recognised him and what he had before him.

"Aye," Tommy nodded.

"What'll you be after?" asked the shopkeeper.

"Hundred quid," Tommy said.

"Nay, I haven't got that kind of money lad; times are hard and things aren't selling. Tell you what, I'll give you fifty quid for the lot. You can always come back and buy 'em back again next week?" The pawnbroker couldn't believe his luck. It was the greatest haul of football prizes he'd ever seen.

Tommy agreed and they shook on it. He took the fifty pounds, shoved it into his back pocket and headed for the nearest pub, The Bowling Green Tavern.

As winter approached Tommy had nowhere to stay, was on the dole and had lost everything. In 1931 Leslie Chapples was working as an apprentice in the news department of the *Burnley Express*. Leslie's father was licensee at the Bowling Green Hotel, on Clifton Street off Westgate. It was one of Tommy's old haunts where he enjoyed a drink and a game of bowls, sometimes with his old teammate Bob Kelly. In his book *My Burnley Memories,* Leslie Chapples recalls:

> Many years ago I arrived home to find a stranger seated at the tea-table and stared unbelievably when I realised that the visitor was none other than the legendary Tommy Boyle. I soon

realised that Tommy was no intellectual and his subject of conversation were very limited, delivered in a thick, gruff northern accent. Poor Tommy! He had indeed fallen on hard times since his halcyon days on the football field!

Leslie's father must have known Tommy well for him to be sat at their kitchen table. He had probably given him a meal and a bed for the night until he could sort himself out.

In late September and October 1931, Burnley had two important visitors in the form of Ghandi and Winston Churchill who were both visiting the mill towns in the North West for quite different political reasons and certainly not for the football. Burnley had managed to sell only 615 season tickets and despite being third in the Second Division on Christmas Day 1931, attendances had collapsed. After a poor Christmas period, the 23 January home game against Charlton Athletic told of Burnley's demise. Burnley lost the match –one-nil and the result placed them nineteenth in Division Two, their lowest League position for thirty years. By now average attendances at Turf Moor were around 5,000 and the club and the town were both struggling to survive in a period of severe hardship. Hunger marchers from towns across the north-west were on the verge of arriving in London to demonstrate about poverty and unemployment, one woman marcher from Burnley remarking;

> ...I have worn out two pairs of clogs on this two-hundred mile march. I have blistered and sore feet but my spirit is not broken. I am going to get to London even if I have to do the rest of the journey on my hands and knees. *(Peter Kingsford, p.129)*

In trying to help the football club out of its poor financial position, a group of Burnley supporters got together to form the Burnley Supporters' Club and a public event was held to launch the new venture. It was where Tommy Boyle made his last documented public appearance and the famous old half-back line of Halley, Boyle and Watson took their final bow.

Chapter 14: Together Again

"The golden moments in the stream of life rush past us and we see nothing but sand; the angels come to visit us, and we only know them when they are gone."

- George Eliot

Halley, Boyle and Watson:
Famous Half-Back line returns to Burnley's Assistance

The launch of the new Burnley Supporters' Club took place at the Salem School on Manchester Road in Burnley on the evening of 28 January 1932. To a packed hall and with many locked outside, his worship the Mayor (Alderman Place, JP) introduced his guests to the audience. Present on stage were the Bishop of Burnley, the Reverend E. Priestley-Swain; Mr Edward Tate, the newly elected chairman of Burnley Football Club; Mr H.B. Willan, Chairman of the newly-formed Burnley Supporters' Club Committee; Councillor F.G. Wilkins, President of the Leeds United FC Supporters' Club; and Alderman Whitehead. The majority of the audience, however, had not come to listen to them but to see their old favourites, six former players who had turned out on the evening for nothing. First up the steps and onto the stage to great applause was a smiling Jerry Dawson who hadn't changed a bit apart from his waist-line. A spectacled Eddie Mosscrop followed; who had travelled over from Southport after school had finished for the day. Next up was Alf Bassnett who was now running his own pub, The Bridge in Bank Parade, after a spell managing at Hereford United.

But the three men the audience wanted to see most of all were saved until last. The Mayor announced to tumultuous applause, with the whole audience standing and cheering, half-back legends George Halley, Tommy Boyle and Billy Watson. They climbed the steps together and stood side-by-side, hands raised in unison, smiling and waving to the audience before taking their seats. The 'holy trinity' together again for the first time in ten years. George Halley was working as a plasterer when he could get the work, after his short spell at Ruskin College in Oxford 'bettering himself'. Billy Watson had gone back to his old profession as a master painter and decorator and was just about surviving in the slump. Tommy was struggling with life itself. He looked pale and his face was gaunt as if he hadn't eaten a decent meal or had full night's sleep in a week. His clothes looked lived in, as if they were the only ones he owned.

The formal proceedings were opened by the Mayor, who gave the apologies that were received from the Everton player Dixie Dean and also from C.E. Sutcliffe, the former Burnley Director and President of the Football League. The Mayor began his address by saying how the state of the team reflected the state of trade in the town and that more investment was needed in both. The Mayor said he was a shareholder in the club (in his wife's name) and likened the current situation to a half-empty theatre, asking the audience, "Do you get the best results from the artists?" and then going on to say it was surely like that for the footballers, who could not put the same spirit into the game. He knew of two ways for the public to get involved, by taking up the one-pound share issue from the club (paid for in four, five-shilling instalments) or by joining the Supporters' Club. Burnley had a lot to thank the Football Club for. On match days, the Mayor mentioned that the tram receipts increased and the centre pubs, hostelries and caterers all benefitted. He then handed over to the Chair of the Supporters' Club, Mr H.B. Willan, who stood to applause.

Willan thanked the Mayor and outlined the mission of the Supporters' Club that had come in for some degree of criticism in the press. "All the Supporters want is to see a team that is a credit to the town again," Willan said. "I can assure you as Chairman of the Supporters' Club Committee that we have every confidence in the Burnley Football Club Board, as it is at present constituted." He went on to say that the funds raised by the SCC would be used solely for the acquisition of new players. "The money will assist the Football Club in payment or part-payment of any player transfer fee, and if later the player should be sold for profit, the figure will be refunded to the SCC." Willan hoped that within three months the SCC would have recruited 10,000 members. His intention was to form council ward committees that would raise funds locally through running events.

Councillor Wilkinson from the Leeds Supporters' Club mentioned that they had recently raised seven hundred pounds through a weekly draw and through whist drives, dances and cricket matches in the summer. This money was being used to purchase a section of the new stand.

The Mayor then introduced the first of the players who were to speak, to cheers and great applause. Eddie Mosscrop took to the podium, removing his rimless spectacles before he spoke. "As an old player," he said, "I think the twelve years I spent with this team were twelve of the happiest years of my life. I always look upon Burnley as my second home. It is always a pleasure to go through it, dirty as it is." The audience laughed.

Referring to the Mayor's point about attendances, Mosscrop said that he had learned that the gates were of 5,000 and below. "Five thousand on Turf Moor, one of the best equipped grounds in the country, seems to be a handful," he said. "There is nothing more than upsets the players than empty terraces. There is something contagious in the cheers of a crowd and people applauding you." Mosscrop talked of the cheers helping the players and the barracking that didn't help. He said he once had a bad spell at Burnley and was going down the wing and miss-kicked the ball, when one spectator commented, "Nay, lad, you 'ad better go back to school, you can't lake at football!" [Laughter] Mosscrop went on to say that a club like Burnley should not be in the Second Division. The club had known bad times before, he said, "You just need to find the right man who will turn the whole team around, and through a bit of good fortune."

Eddie Mosscrop stood down to applause from the floor and Billy Watson stepped up to speak. The Mayor introduced him as "one of the finest half-backs who ever played football". Watson received a standing ovation as he took to the podium. He began: "There are two things I really wish for. One was that I could go back twenty years and that the other players could too in helping the club in a playing sense today." He thought the only way in bringing about a revival was by bringing the right tone to the team. He said, "The greatest change in the history of the team I played in was when they got Tommy Boyle". There were calls of "Hear, hear" and Tommy shifted in his chair and nodded approvingly toward Watson in acknowledgement of the comment made by his old teammate.

Billy Watson was followed by Alderman Whitehead and then Edward Tate, Burnley's new Chairman, spoke. It was then George Halley's turn to address the audience. He rose to great cheers. "I wish I could turn back the clock about ten years," Halley began in his thick Scots accent. "The club are trying to find a remedy, but a remedy for what? They have not yet diagnosed the disease. What is the reason for the club's decline?" he asked the audience. In Halley's opinion one of the chief reasons for the decline in football was the recent changes to the offside rule. "Hear, hear," agreed the audience. "Football today is not the spectacle that it once was," said Halley. "No person is going to pay a shilling and only get sixpence in return. The supporters want something more than a spirit of enthusiasm. The club at present is not good enough." There was louder applause; Halley had touched a nerve.

Throughout the speeches, Tommy had sat quietly at the back of the stage, nodding occasionally in acknowledgement when the audience applauded. He had something in his hand and looking down at the small object in his palm, his mind wandered elsewhere, to another time and another place.

It was a warm spring day in Platts Common. Easter 1902. A huge crowd gathered to watch the athletics finals on Easter Monday. He could hear the sound of the crowd as he led at the final bend, not much further to go, their voices driving him on as he approached the finishing tape in the 440 yards final. Breaking the tape and winning with a yard to spare. That was where it all began. Thirty years ago. He could see his mother and father, Pat and Ellen, their faces bursting with pride; his brother and sisters cheering their little brother home. His gold winner's medal hanging proudly around his neck. It was the only thing of value he had left in the world. He looked down at the engraved disc in the palm of his hand and knew it would have to go or he couldn't eat tomorrow. The first thing he'd ever won. The last thing he'd ever own. *Thirty years, where the hell had it all gone*. His hand tightened shut as he put the medal back in his pocket.

George Halley had finished and sat down next to Tommy to loud applause. The audience were waiting expectantly for the next speaker, something from the man they wanted most to hear. The man who had spoken to them in the past after all the things they had won and done together. The captain, the leader of the champions, Tommy Boyle. It went quiet in the hall. Halley had spoken well and stirred the passion among them. Heads now turned toward Tommy, the audience expecting a few words from their former leader, the man who maybe could bring them success again. But their wishes were not granted.

After George Halley sat down, a few seconds later the Mayor stepped up to the podium. He didn't mention the former captain but summarised the evening, thanked everyone for coming and finished with a few words about the importance of their support for backing the football club, ending enthusiastically with, "Without you, the supporters, there is no club, YOU ARE THE CLUB!" His words echoed around the hall and a rousing standing ovation and applause followed.

The meeting broke up around half past nine and for the players there was time for a couple of drinks before last orders. The men signed autographs in the hall and then slipped out of a side door down to the Cattle Market pub for the last hour. After a few drinks their tongues loosened and the old stories came out and for an hour, it was the good old days. Then the landlord rang the bell for last orders bringing an abrupt end to the evening. After they finished their drinks and said their goodbyes, the players agreed to keep in touch and to meet up again soon and maybe go to a game. Billy Watson and Eddie Mosscrop left for Southport, Jerry Dawson caught the last bus home to Cliviger, and George Halley and Alf Bassnett went their own separate ways home after seeing Tommy off on his way.

Hands deep in pockets, Tommy set off up Manchester Road, passing the Town Hall. The road he'd walked down twenty years before when he first arrived in the town. The road he'd travelled down carrying the FA Cup in 1914. He stopped for a moment and looked up at the balcony where he'd offered the Cup to the huge, swaying crowd that sunny afternoon. *What a week that was,* he grinned to himself. The streets were empty and cold now. January was bitter and his chest was playing up again. Better get off. But it wasn't home he was going to tonight. With no home to go to, it was the gentleman's refuge in the old Cavalry Barracks and a bed for the night, the night before his forty-sixth birthday.

That evening at Salem School, it had been clear to the others that Tommy was struggling. Throughout the evening his mind had been somewhere else, the lads had clearly noticed it in the pub. Tommy stuck around Burnley for the following weeks telling his stories in the pubs and clubs to anyone who'd stand him a pint. As the advancing years had robbed him of doing the only thing he ever loved, a deep resentment of authority and anger took hold of him. After too much drink his temper got the better of him and he started causing problems for the police.

Burnley's Chief Constable, William Fairclough, spent his Sunday mornings as always, cleaning his prized possession, the black and chrome Humber Pullman that came with the job and sat proudly on his driveway. He was interrupted from his task by his wife, who told him there was a telephone call from the station. The desk sergeant told him that they had brought Tommy Boyle in on Saturday night for being drunk and disorderly and causing trouble in the Red Lion. He was in a cell sleeping it off. It was the second time in a week. Fairclough sighed and told the sergeant to release him once he'd sobered up. It couldn't go on like this. If there were any more incidents he'd have to be put away. He was becoming a liability and a danger to himself. His head wasn't right and he needed help, proper medical help. They had been friends once but that only went so far. Tommy Boyle's favours had finally run out.

Chapter 15: Whittingham

I was hungry and you gave me food,
I was thirsty and you gave me drink,
I was a stranger and you welcomed me,
I was naked and you gave me clothing,
I was sick and you took care of me.

– Matthew 25:35

What actually happened to Tommy in the weeks that followed the players' reunion on 28 January until his admission to Primrose Bank on 24 February is unclear.

In the days leading up to his admission to Primrose Bank, there was no record of Tommy causing problems in Burnley pubs in the newspapers or in the court records held on file at the Records office in Preston. And when Tommy's hospitalisation should have made front page news, there was no mention of that either. The only reliable evidence regarding Tommy's behaviour was that written on Bill Mair's Reception Order dated 29 February, written five days after his arrival at Primrose Bank which said that he had been violent towards patients and staff and had tried to escape several times. He may have become violent before that, as Leslie and Stephen Chapples suggest in their book, *Life in and Around The Weavers Triangle*. That source states that Tommy had,

> ...such a bad reputation that the police were normally called as soon as he walked on to licensed premises.

This implies that his temper had become a problem for the local police. But if he was intent on causing trouble each time he walked into a Burnley pub, he should have faced charges, particularly if he had been violent towards other people or had damaged property. Even a well-known celebrity like Tommy Boyle wouldn't have escaped the long arm of the law for long. His three run-ins with the law in Blackpool had all resulted in visits to the magistrates' courts and fines. All three incidents there had made the papers, yet in Burnley, nothing. Why would that be? It was unusual that there was no further mention of Tommy in the sports pages after the Salem School event. To fill space, sports journalists like Brunbank, Kestrel and Sportsman in the local Burnley papers often gave one or two lines on former players, keeping readers updated on what they were doing now, particularly if they had been ill, been hospitalised or had died. Yet after January 1932, nothing else was ever printed about Tommy Boyle. It was strange. Someone with such a high public profile as Tommy Boyle had suddenly ceased to exist. No mention was made of his whereabouts and no letters of enquiry from fans were published in the press. Nothing was reported about how he was, or where he'd gone. It was as if a veil of silence had descended over the town. It is likely that the police did bring Tommy into the Infirmary, as Chapter One outlines. The police were often called on to provide that service.

REMOVAL TO ASYLUM

When Wilfred E. of Nelson was brought before the Burnley Magistrates last Monday week on two charges of breaking and entering, stealing an overcoat and a pair of boots, the Chief Constable intimated that he thought the man was mentally unbalanced and asked that he might be remanded to Preston for a week in order that he might be kept under medical observation. On Monday when the case was called, the Chief Constable stated that he had received a communication from the Home Office stating that the man had been removed to an asylum.
(Burnley News, 2 Feb 1921)

In protecting the public, Chief Constable William Fairclough had the power to act in having Tommy admitted 'for observation' under the 1930 Mental Health Act, particularly if he was unwell, homeless and violent. Even today, the police have powers under section 136 of the 1983 Mental Health Act to "remove a person to a place of safety". But was Tommy's behaviour so bad it warranted commitment to a mental hospital – for the rest of his life?

Burnley Football Club made no official comment about Tommy yet must have discovered through its Board members, some of whom served on various town committees, including Primrose Bank's Board of Guardians, what had happened to their former captain and employee and where he'd gone. But even if the club did know what had happened to him, it was unlikely they would have announced that the club's most famous player had been taken into a mental hospital. Being admitted to such places was not talked about. The new terminology of 'mental patients' and 'mental hospitals' put forward by the 1930 Mental Health Act was far from being adopted by society. In conversation, people still spoke of 'idiots, lunatics and asylums' and viewed what went on inside mental hospitals with fear and distaste. To make matters worse, the press would often describe mental patients as '*dangerous*', as the 'Captured at Padiham' example from the *Burnley Express* in 1932 shows. From the football club's position, it would have been better if the supporters remembered their former captain as he was in his heyday, a hero, and so nothing was said about his whereabouts as a mark of respect to both Tommy and his family. But they all knew where he'd gone.

CAPTURED AT PADIHAM
DANGEROUS LUNATIC APPREHENDED
WITHOUT STRUGGLE

The intensive search for the dangerous lunatic who escaped from the Menston Asylum near Otley last Sunday ended at Padiham yesterday afternoon when the man was apprehended by a constable and taken to Padiham Police Station. The lunatic's asylum attire led to his detection. Since his disappearance last Sunday, police and motor patrols throughout Yorkshire and Lancashire had been on the look out for him in several towns and on the moors without success.

(Burnley Express and Advertiser, 23 March 1932)

Whittingham Mental Hospital

Dr Jason Gemmel was the Chief Medical Officer who presided over Whittingham Mental Hospital, which by 1932 had become the largest mental hospital in England. Gemmel had spoken on the telephone with Bill Mair, who had filled him in on his new patient who was now on his way over in an ambulance.

Figure 52. Whittingham Mental Hospital, the former Lancashire County Lunatic Asylum.
(Picture courtesy of Ken Ashton)

The journey to Whittingham from Burnley took just under an hour. The ambulance travelled via the quiet back roads of the Ribble Valley, avoiding the towns and arriving at Whittingham mid-afternoon. In the rear of the ambulance, Tommy was accompanied by two Primrose Bank white-coats. The ambulance turned into Whittingham's main gate from which led a long, mile-long, tree-lined driveway. On one side through the trees stood a cricket pavilion and next to it, a football pitch. On the other, broad lawns led to other hospital buildings and wards, and in the distance a train with three carriages was pulling out of Whittingham railway station. Straight ahead, at the end of the driveway, was the main hospital building at Whittingham, St. Luke's. The ambulance drew to a halt in front of the administration block. A three-storey, pillar-fronted red-brick building with Georgian windows, the frontage of St. Luke's ran for hundreds of yards to the left and right from the central admission and reception block. From above, St Luke's was shaped like a giant outspread hand, its patient wards stretching out like long fingers, two long male wards to the left and two female to the right.

On arrival Tommy and the two white-coats were brought into reception by a porter and offered a cup of tea. The patient's file, fastened with string around the middle like a legal document, was brought up to Gemmel's office by one of the staff. Gemmel untied it to find the medical certificate just completed by Bill Mair, which gave the account of what had gone on at Primrose Bank and any important points that had been noted by the staff there. Five days wasn't a long time to have assessed a patient fully, but that's all Gemmel had to go on. To have sent him here after only five days told Gemmel that Primrose Bank couldn't handle him and this was probably going to be a long stay patient. Gemmel read through Bill Mair's report,

Certificate of the Medical Practitioner – Lunacy Act 1890

In the matter of Thomas Boyle of the male mental wards, Primrose Bank Institution in the County Borough of Burnley. Ex-Footballer of unsound mind.

I the undersigned, William Alexander Mair. Do hereby certify as follows:-

I am a person registered under the Medical Act 1858 and I am in the actual practice of the medical profession. On the 29th

Day of February 1932 at the Male Medical wards, Primrose Bank Institution in the County Borough of Burnley I personally examined the said Thomas Boyle and came to the conclusion that he is a person of unsound mind and a proper person to be taken charge of and detained under care and treatment.

I formed this conclusion on the following grounds, viz.:-

He has delusions he owns twenty seven race horses, sending them over to Germany to race. Won a trophy in Germany that took two men to carry. Has been striking the other patients, also the staff, secreting himself in the building.

Mr Kirby, Superintendent of the male mental ward Primrose Bank Institution says he is very restless and violent at times, threatening and striking staff, refuses food, is lost to his surroundings, is always trying to escape through the windows.

The said, Thomas Boyle appeared to me to be in a fit condition of bodily health to be removed to a Mental Hospital or Licensed House. I give this certificate, having first read the section of the 1890 Lunacy Act of Parliament.

Signed: Dr. William Alexander Mair, Chief Medical Officer, 29th February 1932.

As Bill Mair was responsible for the whole of Primrose Bank, he would only have managed to visit the mental patients once or twice a month, while he would attend the sick patients in the hospital on a daily basis. Mair would have seen Tommy on his admission and at the end of his stay to complete his report. As a consequence he would have relied heavily on the supervisor of the male mental ward, Robert Kirby, to provide him with information on Tommy's progress.

Gemmel opened the Whittingham admissions register and entered the following details.

General Reference Number: 24281
Date of Admission: 29 February 1932
Date of Reception Order: 29 February 1932
Name: Thomas Boyle aged 43
Classification: Private, Male, Rate Aided
Mode of admission;   Direct/Rate Aided
Observations: RC (Roman Catholic)

(HRW 7/29 Civil Register of Certified Patients, Whittingham)

In addition to the Reception Order on Gemmel's desk, the file contained the patient's medical record, details of what medication staff at Primrose Bank had administered and any side effects, records of any mechanical restraints that had been used, police notes, any court appearances and his war record. As Gemmel read down the pages, an old envelope fell out of the file onto the carpet. It was in quite poor condition and looked like it had lived in its owner's pocket for a long time. Gemmel carefully opened it. It contained a number of yellowed newspaper clippings, postcards and photographs, their corners creased and curled. He opened each clipping carefully and read the articles. The clippings dated as far back as 1902 and were as recent as 1928. These were mainly reports from football games in the national and local papers, a clipping from *Berliner MorgenPost*, an athletics event held somewhere and the death certificate of a child. There were several faded black-and-white photographs of a man at his peak of fitness. One item in particular caught his attention. It was a postcard of King George presenting the English Cup to a football team. He turned the card over and read the back, postmarked London 28 April 1914, addressed to; Platts Common, Barnsley South Yorkshire. The message read, *Dear Sis, sorry you couldn't make it, here's a photo of our great day for your collection, meeting the King was such an honour. I'll see you all soon. Yours, Tommy.*

He read again the conclusion Mair had written on the patient's state of mind. "27 racehorses, sent over to Germany"; what on earth could he have meant? "Won a trophy in Germany that took two people to carry." This man had obviously travelled widely in his time. But what could he have possibly meant here?

Gemmel made notes, put all the clippings back in their original envelope and closed the file. The comment on the Reception Order that gave him the most cause for concern was the mention of violent behaviour. Like all mental hospitals, Whittingham had all the facilities necessary for controlling patients. Behind its leafy exterior, hidden inside Whittingham's walls were its padded cells, its harnesses, straitjackets, waist belts and electric shock facilities and all manner of instruments staff could call upon if required to restrain patients. The hospital had its own dispensary where various medicines, drugs and chemical concoctions were made up to subdue patients who needed calming: opiates, morphine, cannabis, hyocine, chloral hydrate and potassium bromide. And for the more extreme cases, when all the treatments had been tried and had failed, Whittingham had its own operating theatres.

In his notes, Gemmel began writing a list containing all the information he needed to give the staff on the ward about their new patient including his expected behaviour, medical condition, blood group and drugs to be administered.

Life at Whittingham

The first asylum at Whittingham, designed to accommodate 1,000 patients, opened on a sixty-acre site in Grimsargh near Preston in 1873. By the time Tommy arrived the patient population had grown to 3,000 and the site, now the size of a village, spread over 150 acres. The hospital buildings at Whittingham included St. Luke's, the biggest block, the annexes of St. Margaret's and St. John's and a newly built block, Cameron House. The hospital had a staff of around 450. Its medical facilities also offered specialised treatment for infectious diseases and the hospital had also pioneered the use of electroencephalograms with mental patients.

Whittingham had its own branch-line and railway station for transporting supplies, staff and visitors to and from Preston, a few miles away. There was a gas works, two churches (Anglican and Catholic), a post office, a bakery, a laundry, a butcher's and farms for the patients to work on. Ken Ashton, editor of the Whittingham website 'The Asylum', says that the institution was run along military lines,

> The structure and hierarchy were of a military nature and the rules and regulations, for both staff and patients were very clear and forthright.

Monday to Friday, the day's routine at Whittingham would have been exactly the same. Woken between six and half-six, the patients would be dressed, washed and breakfasted. By eight, patients would be at work either indoors in the laundry, upholstery shop or printing shop, or outdoors working on the farms and vegetable gardens. Break times would be fixed. Lunch, followed by more work and then home for supper. The patients would be washed and in bed by nine p.m. At weekends there would be visiting times though patients only received visitors around once a month, and only if they had behaved. On Sunday morning there would be church service and more visiting time in the afternoon. On Saturday afternoons Whittingham offered a number of sports. The institution was famed for its women's hockey team and also its cricket and bowls teams, that took part in the Preston District Leagues. According to Ken Ashton, there was at least one football team at Whittingham.

> Patients would have been encouraged to participate in the hospital team(s). There would however have been no mention of a patient's previous occupation [as a professional footballer]

as this may have caused him difficulty with the other patients. *(Ken Ashton)*

A collection of silverware won at Whittingham by the various sports teams was on display in a trophy cabinet in the St. John's building corridor.

The male and female wings in St. Luke's were divided into twenty smaller dormitories, ten male, ten female, each dorm containing twenty-five iron-framed beds, packed so close together the patients could almost touch each other. The dorms were staffed day and night by two attendants. Downstairs, the male wing had a full-sized billiards table and in the day room, set out with easy chairs and there was a piano. For the men, the hospital band was a popular pastime as was painting, and at the weekends amateur dramatics or ballroom dancing took place where the gentlemen patients could meet the ladies. Whittingham even worked its own brewery and the patients were allowed a glass of home-brewed beer or cider every day.

Whittingham drew its patient population mainly from the county of Lancashire, which in 1932 included the catchment areas of Manchester and Liverpool. All manner of people were brought in, from those suffering from mild cases of depression, to drug addicts, criminals, multiple disorder sufferers, schizophrenics and psychotics. According to Michelle Higgs, "Anyone found being unable to manage their own affairs independently could be deemed mentally ill and looked after in an asylum." *(Life in the Victorian Asylum)*

In *Lunatics of the Great War*, Peter Barham describes several cases of former soldiers admitted into Whittingham. Ex-servicemen made up almost a third of the patient population there, suffering from what today would be called post-traumatic stress disorder:

Franklin H, gentleman and ex-mill manager who had served from November 1914 to Dec 1917 was brought to the Asylum on 19th July 1919 after being examined by a JP and two doctors at Clitheroe Police Station. Somewhat wild and excitable appearance, extremely talkative, restless with intervals of nervous exhaustion. Cause – "war service". A witness had mentioned his erratic behaviour "rushing up to his front garden at 10.30 pm and shouting at the top of his voice people's names and using very bad language". His wife confided to the doctor that his language and personal behaviour were most disgusting and immoral.

In a hospital on the scale of Whittingham, new patients would have arrived almost every day. Induction included registration and allocation to a dorm, followed by a body inspection before a full medical assessment with a doctor. Michelle Higgs says, "On arrival at the mental hospital, patients were stripped, bathed and washed to check for swellings on the body, rashes, or lice. The hair was cut close and combed and the patient clothed in the regulation asylum dress." The dress code at Whittingham for male patients was a choice of either a khaki or blue serge suit, cut in the lounge style, along with soft shirts, collars and ties.

After trying several times to escape from Primrose Bank, it's likely Tommy would have tried escaping from Whittingham in the early days following his arrival. New patients were kept under close observation for seventy-two-hours and, if required, were dosed with mild sedatives to calm them down and help them settle into the institution. For more serious infringements of the rules, patients might be given a dose of croton oil, a milky looking substance that brought on terrible stomach aches. The staff found that once patients knew the routine, their behaviour improved and they would begin to work with the system rather than against it. Dale Wasserman, who wrote the screenplay to Ken Kesey's *One Flew Over the Cuckoo's Nest*, agrees. Wasserman spent time in an asylum as part of his research and had intended staying for three weeks but ended up staying only ten days:

Not because it was scary or uncomfortable but because of the opposite. It's extremely comfortable. If you hand over your will and your volition to an institution, life becomes very simple and the temptation to just keep on living it in just that way is very strong.

Tommy would probably have found that an outdoor life, with three square meals a day and things to interest him like bowls, football and a glass of beer each day could be quite comfortable. Unlike at Primrose Bank, at Whittingham he would be able to get outside and breathe the fresh air and walk around the extensive grounds, and he had more people around him who could help him when he needed it.

Yet despite this picture of a quiet lifestyle tucked away in a corner of Lancashire's leafy countryside, things were not all they should have been at Whittingham. The hospital was subjected to regular inspections by the Ministry of Pensions and records available at the National Archive at Kew for the period 1920–8 show a far from satisfactory situation there:

> A sharing of towels and toothbrushes, privacy and dignity issues reported. When the Board reported that only a few patients had nightshirts, the Lancashire Committee failed to grasp that a nightshirt was a "distinctive garment". The Board remonstrated over the toilets which were without doors, or had half doors so that gave no privacy.

> Hardly any drinking mugs supplied to patients at dinner. Scarcely any overcoats for male patients. None of the inmates were shaved, there were no nail brushes and it was unusual to catch sight of a toothbrush. No dental services on site though this was being addressed by the Lancashire committee.

> A Mr P. who had been an asylum inmate during this period described how, despite frequent epidemics of gastroenteritis

there was only one toilet in a ward for 45 people. "You can understand the position if a dozen men were rushing at the same time."

Though some roller towels were provided, patients get up in the middle of the night and use them for purposes for which they are not meant. Toilet paper is used by patients for writing purposes. No privacy. Inmates made to strip in the open dormitory on a cold bleak day. All the windows were thrown open and they had to wait in turn for a bath.

(PRO MH 95/3 Board of Control, Whittingham Mental Hospital 1920–8: National Archives, Kew) also in *Lunatics of the Great War, Peter Barham.*

By the time Tommy arrived at Whittingham in February 1932, it is hoped that these matters had been resolved and the living standards on the wards had improved. There were further issues raised at the hospital that eventually became public in the mid-1960s, as will be seen, but it is hoped that the intervening years at Whittingham when Tommy was a patient there were better times for the 3,000 patient population living there.

Tommy spent almost eight years in Whittingham. During those years he never set foot beyond its perimeter. Over those eight years his health steadily deteriorated and in the end his body succumbed to the debilitating disease that finally took his life.

2 January 1940

The cold spell that had set in over the Christmas period worsened as the New Year began. As people returned to work the day after the New Years Day holiday, a blanket of snow covered much of England. Later that month the whole country froze when an ice-storm arrived. It became so cold that the Thames iced over and small birds froze to the branches of trees. The winter had even delayed Hitler's expansion plans. The morning newspapers told stories of the war from across Europe. Soldiers of the British Expeditionary Force were on standby, ready to leave for France to give Jerry what for again. The only direct engagement for the British with the enemy was at sea with the sinking of allied shipping by German U-boats. That morning's *Daily Mirror* held a full page advert from the Ministry of Food reminding householders to sign up for meat rationing. With League football cancelled the previous August because of the war, Burnley and Barnsley had played each other in friendlies over the Christmas period with Burnley losing both games. On New Year's Day Barnsley had thrashed their rivals Sheffield Wednesday five-nil at Oakwell.

It was pitch black at Whittingham as another working day was about to begin. At first light the grounds surrounding St. Luke's were covered in a thick white frost, while the coloured Christmas tree lights still glowed brightly outside the main entrance. Male nurse John Blackburn had risen in the nurse's block at five-fifteen am and had just entered the male wing at St. Luke's to begin his six until two o'clock shift. Blackburn hung up his coat in the ward office and began his rounds of the first dormitory on the male wing, gently shaking each patient awake to get him up for washing, dressing and breakfast. Blackburn had got a third of the way round the dorm when he shook Tommy's shoulder. He got no response. Checking further, he found the patient to be stone cold.

Blackburn shouted for assistance and the bed was screened off. One attendant ran down to The Lawns, the superintendent's house located at the back of St. Luke's, to bring the doctor. Assistant Medical Officer, Dr Helen S. Murray and her superior, Dr R. Gordon McLaren, in charge of the male wing, arrived not long after. McLaren checked for vital signs but it was clearly too late. Thomas William Boyle, patient number 24281, was dead. The two doctors agreed that the patient had passed away quietly in the night and there were no untoward circumstances regarding the cause of death. Steps were taken to contact Tommy's next of kin to inform the family and to arrange for a formal identification of the body as a post-mortem would be necessary.

John Boyle was at work in Barnsley when the police called to see him and inform him of the sad news that his brother had passed away. John travelled over to Preston to make all the necessary arrangements. The post-mortem was carried out the same day, the single cause of death given by Dr Gordon-McLaren as 'General Paralysis of the Insane'. GPI accounted for the deaths of up to twenty per cent of patients in mental institutions that occurred through tertiary syphilis, which penicillin and other treatments has now been almost eradicated. In the early part of the twentieth century the disease led to a slow and painful death that could take anywhere between three to five years to take hold. Tommy's death was registered by the hospital and his profession stated as, "professional footballer, of no fixed abode."

Tommy had been in Whittingham nearly eight years, and there could have been other factors that had contributed to his demise, including hereditary factors of which McLaren would not have known about when carrying out his post-mortem. In 1936, Tommy's youngest sister Catherine had died of uraemia (kidney failure) and manic depressive insanity. Catherine was exactly the same age as Tommy when she died, fifty-three. Another question arises with the date of Tommy's death. Tommy's mother Ellen died on New Year's Day 1910, almost thirty years to the day Tommy died. Was there any connection with the thirtieth anniversary of his mothers passing?

Other factors that were later identified as being contributory factors in affecting the mental health of patients included; stress from war service, alcohol abuse, diet, poverty and stress from personal tragedies such as a mother, wife or child's death.

Any or several of these could have played a part in Tommy's worsening state of mind from the late 1920s to when he was eventually admitted to Primrose Bank in 1932.

Another important point that could have been a contributory factor to Tommy's deterioration was his occupation. Until the mid 1970s the ball used in football matches was made of stitched leather panels with an internal rubber bladder. When dry, the balls should have weighed between thirteen and sixteen ounces, but on a rainy day they soaked up water like a sponge. In winter, on a snow-covered pitch, the ball could freeze and increase in weight by another twenty-five to thirty per cent. It was like heading a lump of ice. In a contact sport like football where players take repeated blows to the front of the head and greater strain on the neck, several players had died from head injuries or had suffered mental illnesses, ending their days in hospitals or institutions. Tony Mason researched the cases of:

Ted Brayshaw of Sheffield Wednesday and England died, aged only 45, in Wadsley Bridge Asylum in 1908, suffering from chronic melancholia and tuberculosis. The later stages of his life marked by "poverty, misery and despair".

Charlie Roberts the Manchester United and England player and former secretary of the players union died aged 56 in Manchester Royal Infirmary in1939 following an operation on his skull after suffering "dizzy spells", which may have been brought about due to the heading of heavy footballs." (Association Football and English Society 1863-1915)

In more recent times, Jeff Astle, the West Bromwich Albion and England international centre-forward who passed away in 2002 at the age of fifty-nine, died of what was recorded by the coroner as "death by industrial injury". In addition to the regular head contact with the ball were the large number of blows Tommy received to his head throughout his career from elbows, boots and fist-fights, both on and off the field. The playing injuries were more prominent after the war as the story has shown. The game Tommy loved playing may have been a major contributor to the steady decline on his health and may well have been one of the causes that brought him in to Primrose Bank in the first place.

At rest in Hoyland

A week after his death, Tommy's body was brought back to Yorkshire by the family and he was buried in the family grave along with his mother and father in St. Helen's churchyard in Hoyland. The church grave register and cashbook state that for opening the family grave, the cost was one pound, of which the gravedigger was paid ten shillings and the priest the same amount for their services. Tommy's funeral took place on Friday 5 January 1940 at the same church he was christened at fifty-three years before. The *Barnsley Chronicle* reported that it was a quiet family affair conducted by Rev Fr. Reynolds from High Green.

Tommy's obituary was published in the *Burnley Express and News* on 6 January 1940 and a week later on the 13 January in the *Barnsley Chronicle*. Neither Barnsley nor Burnley football clubs knew anything about Tommy's death on 2 January until after the funeral had taken place and after his death had been reported in the papers. When some Burnley supporters learned of Tommy's death in the press they wrote to the *Burnley Express*, expressing their condolences, and a week later a reply was printed which said:

> There has been much speculation among older supporters of the Burnley Football Club as to the club's failure to have their flag flying at half-mast in memory of the old Turf Moor idol, Tommy Boyle. The club were never officially notified of Boyle's death, and, further, during the week in which Boyle died, Secretary A. Boland was off duty through illness. The funeral of Boyle had taken place before news of his death reached Burnley. (*Burnley Express*, 17 January 1940)

Chapter 16: Epilogue

For when the one great scorer comes
To write against your name,
He marks – not that you won or lost-
But how you played the game.

– Grantland Rice, *Alumnus Football*

Tommy Boyle was a hero to many and the hopes and joys he brought to the supporters of Burnley Football Club is worthy of a memory and a page in football history. He was influential in transforming the fortunes of an ordinary mill town club that had lived for decades in the shadow of its neighbours, Blackburn Rovers and Preston North End. Boyle put Burnley on the football map. He galvanised the team on the field and led them from the mediocrity of the Second Division to be among the best in the land.

When you trace Burnley's fortunes from the day he arrived in September 1911 until the early 1930s, there are parallels between the football club's rise and fall with Tommy's own personal journey. After Burnley's relegation in 1930, it took a generation and another world war before Burnley returned to the First Division with the emergence of Cliff Britton's Burnley team in 1947. With a resurrected Burnley, the big crowds returned again to Turf Moor to watch a new generation of heroes like Harry Potts and Alan Brown, who would go on themselves to manage and have a massive impact on the football club. In 1960, Burnley with Jimmy Adamson as captain won the League Championship for a second time. Two years later in 1962, Adamson came close to equalling Boyle's record of having captained Burnley to win the Cup and League, but sadly Burnley lost at Wembley to Spurs, three-one. And so to date, no other captain at Turf Moor has managed to equal or surpass what captain Tommy Boyle achieved in terms of silverware. His record reigns supreme.

April 2010

One of the first steps in helping to piece together the scattered fragments of Tommy's life seventy years after he passed away was to find when he had died and where he was buried. I contacted Dave Coefield at St. Helen's Church, who found the family grave from the original documents held at Sheffield City archives. Dave got a copy of the graveyard plan and put a marker on the spot where it was located in a corner of the churchyard and sent me a photograph. There was no headstone, the grave having been grassed over as the years progressed. I contacted the Burnley Football Club historian Ray Simpson and met with Ray to discuss the book project and showed him the photograph that Dave had sent me. Ray contacted historian David Wood at Barnsley Football Club and they both approached their chairmen to see what could be done jointly to commemorate Tommy's contribution to the game at both clubs.

Together, the two clubs generously funded the Boyle family headstone and a service of commemoration was held on Sunday 11 April 2010, led by Father Davies of St Helen's Church. It was a proud and fitting tribute to Tommy and to the Boyle family. Several of Pat and Ellen Boyle's descendents were present at the event. It was good to meet them, and they all had their own stories to tell of 'Uncle Tommy'. Together we managed to piece together the Boyle family tree, and trace the Boyles all the way back to Collon in the south of Ireland. It was quite rewarding for me to have been able to put family members in touch with other Boyles around the world living in Canada, France and America. The family still proudly hold in their possession Tommy's 1913 England cap, two of his Football League representative caps and his Charity Shield medal from 1921. These items are securely stored in a bank vault and are only brought out for special occasions.

Figure 53. Three of Tommy's caps including his 1913 full international cap and his 1921 Charity Shield medal. (Picture courtesy of the Boyle family)

Figure 54. Paul Fletcher of Burnley Football Club lays his Burnley scarf on the Tommy Boyle and family memorial headstone that was unveiled at St. Helens Churchyard in April 2010.

The 1914 Cup final match ball that Tommy displayed behind the bar in The Pedestrian was found in a loft in a house in Burnley in 1947 on the eve of Burnley's second FA Cup final appearance against Charlton Athletic at Wembley. It would be reassuring for the family to know where Tommy's other medals and trophies are held, particularly his FA Cup and League Championship medals. Someone must have them and for the family it would be reassuring to know that these are in safe hands somewhere.

In concluding the story, I wanted to find out what happened to the some of the characters that were a big part of Tommy's life and what became of them when their football days were over. I managed to trace a few of them through a number of sources on the internet, from local newspapers and death certificates. Most of all I wanted to find out what happened to Tommy's wife, Annie and to find out where she went after the couple separated.

Outside of football, few places remain of the Tommy Boyle years. The Pedestrian Inn was pulled down in 1928 and the site is occupied by Burnley Central Library. The Crystal Palace burned down in 1936 and in Platts Common, the Hoyland Silkstone colliery closed in 1970. After re-development the only building left in the village from Tommy's days is the Royal Oak pub on Barnsley Road which is still serving beer and now has its own Facebook page.

Looking back it must have been quite something to see Tommy Boyle in action all those years ago. The boy from Platts Common, the midfield dynamo commanding his forces, 'Boyle's Brigade' from the half-way line. The claret-and-blue shirt tucked into those long white shorts, pulled up nearly under his armpits. In the thick of it. Bloodied, muddied and bruised, with his fists clenched, barking out his instructions in that broad Barnsley accent, "Billy, Mossy, Teddy, c'maaan, get forward!"

*Figure 55. Coach Boyle in characteristic pose
at Burnley in 1923.*

What happened to...?

John Haworth

John Haworth came from a football family. A photograph of his uncle George, 'Jud' Howarth, and his England international cap are on display in the National Football Museum collection. The 1911 Census shows that when he was appointed manager, John Haworth lived only a stone's throw from Turf Moor at 11 Mizpah Street, before he moved later to 25 Haven Street. John Haworth was quite young for a League manager, only thirty-four when he signed Tommy from Barnsley in 1911. The 1911 Census gives his occupation as "Company Secretary Burnley Football Club." John married Gertrude in 1907 and in January 1911 the couple had a son, John Walter Haworth, who is shown as three months old on the 1911 Census.

John Haworth had the ability to recognise talent and nurture it as he did with youngsters like Bob Kelly, Billy Pickering and Billy

Nesbitt. He knew how to build a balanced team based on a strong back line, fast wing play and aerial power. In many of the match reports of the day, Haworth's name is rarely mentioned. His name is usually only given in regard to staffing issues and player signings, and very little is mentioned of his input into team tactics or the way the game was played on the pitch. I think he deserves more credit than he was given by the newspapers of the time. He was a major influence on building two teams, pre-1914 and post-1919, winning promotion, the FA Cup, three FA Cup semi-final appearances and a League Championship.

Howarth's death at only forty-eight in 1924 was a major tragedy for the club. Five seasons later Burnley were relegated. On the day of his funeral, thousands lined the route to pay their respects, all the way from Turf Moor to Haworth's home town of Accrington. Football clubs from across England and Scotland sent representatives to the funeral to commemorate his impact on the game spanning over thirty years in football management.

After his death, John Haworth left estate valued at four hundred and eighty-three pounds, ten shillings and eleven pence, hardly a fortune when you consider his achievement in securing the two biggest prizes in English football.

Harry Windle

Harry Windle completed twenty-seven years of service with Burnley FC and was a major influence during the club's most successful period. Harry lived at 259 Brunshaw Road, just around the corner from John Haworth and a stone throw away from Turf Moor. He worked for Altham's Tea Merchants (now Altham's Travel Ltd.) for nearly forty years, starting at sixteen. Being a football club chairman in those days was not a full-time job.

In 1901 at the age of twenty-four, he led a supporters' fundraising campaign to sponsor the purchase of a player with a shilling subscription and managed to raise fifty pounds for the club's funds. In 1903 Windle was asked by the directors to chair a committee to look at fundraising and four years later, in July 1907, he joined the board as full Director. After becoming Vice Chairman a year later in 1908, on the 11 June 1909 he was elected Chairman.

Windle's decision in appointing John Haworth as the new Secretary following the tragic death of Spen Whittaker in 1910 was the best decision he ever made. Windle oversaw the rebirth of Burnley as a football club and he backed his project with hard cash. He spent the club's money wisely and with Haworth bought good players and developed the stadium, increasing its capacity from 20,000 to 60,000. His time, devotion and investment paid off, with massive attendances and top division football after promotion in 1913. In addition to promotion, Cup and League success during Windle's tenure, twenty-nine international caps were awarded to players serving at the club.

Harry Windle resigned as chairman before a meeting of shareholders in January 1930 three-months prior to the team's relegation that year. He was replaced by W.E. Bracewell. Windle continued on the Burnley board and later became chairman of the Lancashire Football Association.

Harry Windle died in July 1938 in Bournemouth following a heart attack while on holiday with his wife Amelia and his family. He was sixty-one years old and is buried in Burnley Cemetery. Of Tommy Boyle, in an interview he gave in 1929, Windle said that he considered him to be the greatest player to don the Burnley jersey during his connection with the club.

Lady Ottoline and Philip Morrell

After Phillip's disclosure of his infidelities to Ottoline in the spring of 1917, the couple moved out of Bedford Square and lived for most of the war at Garsington Manor in the South

Oxfordshire countryside. They spent much of the time bringing up daughter Julian and providing shelter to a number of conscientious objectors among Bloomsbury's poets, artists and literati. Throughout Ottoline's life she had many admirers, including Liberal Prime Minister Herbert Asquith, and it was thought Philip got his first break into politics because of her association with Asquith. After the war, the Morrells returned to Bloomsbury to live in Gower Street, adjacent to their old home in Bedford Square, and a Blue Plaque marks the location of the house today. Lady Ottoline Morrell was Burnley's first celebrity fan and self-proclaimed 'team mascot' during the 1914 Cup campaign. She passed away in 1935. Philip Morrell, the former Member of Parliament for Burnley, died eight years later in 1943.

The two other Tommy Boyles

Different sources, mainly those on the Internet, refer to Tommy Boyle as Thomas Wilkinson Boyle. They have Tommy Boyle playing for Barnsley, Burnley, Wrexham and also Sheffield United, Northampton Town and Manchester United. Hopefully, the following paragraphs will clear up any confusion.

Peter Boyle played professional football for Sheffield United. He was in United's FA Cup winning sides of 1899 and 1902 and their losing side of 1901. Peter Boyle married Annie Hand and the 1901 census shows them living in the parish of Eccleshall in Sheffield. Peter's profession is stated as "Professional Footballer," and his place of birth as Carlingford, County Louth in Ireland. Their son, *Thomas Boyle,* is shown as one month old on the 1901 Census (taken in April). The birth reference is given as Boyle, Thomas, born Eccleshall Bierlow (a district in Sheffield) Vol 9c, Page 447. Thomas's birth certificate shows he was born on 27 February 1901 at 19 Alderson Place, Eccleshall Bierlow, Sheffield. He bears no middle name. One internet source states that this Thomas Boyle was born in 1897 and Sunderland was his place of birth, which is incorrect.

Familysearch.org shows Peter and Annie Boyle's (née Hand) family in detail. The Boyles had three other children, Julia (b.1905), Margaret (b.1915) and Peter junior (b.1919). Thomas Boyle followed in his father's footsteps and became a professional footballer. He won an FA Cup winner's medal with Sheffield United in the 1925 Cup final against Cardiff City. Thomas Boyle played centre-forward for Sheffield United, and later went on to play for Northampton Town and Manchester United. Peter and Thomas Boyle are a unique partnership in football as a father and son who both won FA Cup winners' medals with the same club, Sheffield United. Thomas Boyle died on 9 January 1972 in Torquay and is buried in Derby. Collon and Carlingford are not that far apart in County Louth in Ireland. It could possibly be that Peter Boyle of Carlingford is a distant relative of Tommy's father, Patrick Boyle of Collon, and that football runs in the Boyle family, but more research is needed to be certain.

Thomas Wilkinson Boyle is another name sometimes confused with Thomas William Boyle. Various websites – Wikipedia, Burnley FC, Manchester United and other sources – refer to a Thomas Wilkinson Boyle being one of their former players. It was certainly thought for quite some time in Burnley that Tommy's middle name was Wilkinson. Barnsley sources had it correct as Thomas William and Tommy's birth and marriage certificates, military records and death certificate all confirm this. I carried out a search of the national birth registers from 1885–1900 and found that a Thomas Wilkinson Boyle was born in Accrington, Haslingden near Blackburn in the first quarter of 1889. Thomas Wilkinson Boyle's birth certificate states he was born on 3 February 1889 at 88 Burnley Road, Accrington, Lancashire. His mother, Mary Boyle, was a domestic servant. Mary registered the child's birth and no father's name is given. Familysearch.org states that the boy was christened on 27 March 1889 at St. John the Evangelist church in Accrington. Thomas Wilkinson Boyle died at number

1 Sidney Street, Accrington aged sixteen months on 16 June 1890 after contracting meningitis nine days previously. His mother registered the infant's death on the same day.

Whittingham Mental Hospital

Twenty-five years after Tommy's death, in the mid-1960s, complaints of cruelty towards patients in Whittingham were brought before the Hospital Management Committee by a group of student nurses, mainly concerning the female wards. No action was taken until a new psychologist took up post at the hospital in 1968. A full enquiry was held into the original complaints and allegations of neglect and patient cruelty. The case made the national press with headlines that included "*Whittingham Inquiry in Public*", "*Big Probe into Allegation of Cruelty*" and finally, "*Horror Hospital Guilty*". For details of the inquiry, which are harrowing to read, please see Ken Ashton's website, The Asylum, or go to this link: http://www.whittinghamhospital.co.uk/The_Inquiry.html.

Further information about Tommy's time spent in Primrose Bank and Whittingham hospitals is held on file at the Lancashire Records Office in Preston, but these files are closed under the hundred years rule and won't be released to the public until the year 2032. Only then will we learn more of his experiences there.

Whittingham continued to accommodate mentally ill patients until the 1990s when finally its doors closed. The site is currently fenced off and in a state of decay as the remarkable images on Ken Ashton's website, "*Asylum*" show. The former hospital is awaiting planning permission to convert the land into a 650-home housing development.

Jerry Dawson

Goalkeeper Jeremiah 'Jerry' Dawson was born on 18 March 1888 in Cliviger near Burnley. He was the son of the local village blacksmith, Thomas Dawson, and his wife Elizabeth, who lived at number 63 Clifton Terrace, Cliviger. The 1911 Census states that Jerry was then twenty-three, single and a professional footballer with Burnley Football Club. He played with only one club, Burnley, from 1907 until 1929, and witnessed the rise and fall of the team under three managers. Jerry Dawson's record stands as the longest serving player for Burnley spanning three decades. He made over 700 appearances in a Burnley jersey and twice wore the three lions for England between 1921 and 1922. Jerry never married and never left the Burnley area. He was well known in Burnley and was a regular visitor to Turf Moor. Jerry lived a long life and died aged eight-two at 'Cliftonville' in Cliviger on 8 August 1970.

Eddie Mosscrop

Edwin 'Eddie' Mosscrop was born in Bucklow, Yorkshire on 16 June 1889. His parents moved to Southport shortly after his birth. A committed teacher for over forty years, and with a dry sense of humour, the red-haired Mosscrop managed a professional football career with his regular day job as a schoolteacher. Known as 'Mossy' to his teammates and Mr Mosscrop to his pupils, he was good friends with Billy Watson who lived nearby in Southport. Intelligent and of slight build, Mosscrop wore spectacles. On one occasion he didn't convince the Sunderland gatekeeper that he was a footballer who wouldn't let Eddie in the ground to play. Eddie lived and taught in Southport all his life, and after retiring from professional football he played cricket. He retired aged sixty from his post as headmaster at Bury Road School in Southport in 1949. Eddie Mosscrop died in a Southport nursing home on 14 March 1980 at the age of ninety.

George Halley

George Halley was born in Cronberry, a small village south of Glasgow, on 29 October 1887. At the outbreak of war, Halley was one of the first Burnley players to enlist. Joining the Royal Engineers in 1914, he travelled widely to India, South Africa and Mesopotamia. George lived at 12 Haven Street, next door to Joe Anderson (number ten) and in the same street as Teddy Hodgson, and later John Haworth, yards away from Turf Moor. After the war, Halley didn't return to Turf Moor until late 1919 when he picked up his football boots and carried on playing where he left off five years earlier. After helping Burnley win the League Championship, Halley left Burnley in November 1922 for Southend United and played later in non-League football with Bacup Borough. After his football career ended, in 1930 Halley took up study at Ruskin College in Oxford and later worked as a plasterer. George Halley died in Victoria Hospital in Burnley on 18 December 1941. He was fifty-four years old.

William Watson

Billy Watson, like Eddie Mosscrop, came from Southport. He was born in nearby Birkdale on 11 September 1890. After a seventeen-year career at Burnley, which included three England appearances ended in 1925, he went on to play for Accrington Stanley and the season after that, Blackburn Rovers. After his playing career ended Billy picked up his job as a master painter and decorator again. He died aged sixty-four in Southport on 1 September 1955.

William Nesbitt

Billy was born on 22 November 1891 at number 25 Carrfield, in Todmorden. John Haworth first saw him playing for local junior side, Portsmouth Rovers. In 1911 Haworth managed to get the nineteen-year-old released from his apprenticeship and he made his first team debut at Bradford in February 1912, replacing Eddie Mosscrop, who could not always play due to his teaching commitments. Despite Billy being acutely deaf all his life, his partnership with George Halley and Bob Kelly on the right flank was remarkable in the way they communicated using either shirt-pulling, hand signals or lip-reading. Nesbitt drove referees wild as he could not hear the whistle when straying offside. Injured in the 1921–2 season, the same time as Tommy, he later recovered his fitness, but following a dispute with Burnley over a second benefit match he moved on and joined Bristol City. He later moved to London and joined Clapton Orient. When his football days were over, Billy opened a tobacconist and sweet shop in Paddington in London. Billy eventually returned to his native Todmorden and, like his teammate Billy Watson, took up work as a painter and decorator. Billy Nesbitt died in hospital in Halifax on 11 January 1972 aged eighty.

Bertram Clewley Freeman

Bertram Clewley Freeman was born on 13 October 1885 in Grosvenor Road, Handsworth, Staffordshire, to parents Thomas Holt and Sarah Jane Freeman (née Clewley). Bert's father, Thomas Holt Freeman, was a jeweller and worked in Birmingham. In the 1911 Census, the twenty-five-year-old Everton centre-forward was living at 53 Orton Street, Walton, Liverpool. Bert and Tommy lived in shared accommodation for three years and Bert saved Tommy's life from being gassed to death on the evening of Bert's twenty-ninth birthday in October 1914. In 1919, Bert married the Burnley director and future Mayor Edwin Whitehead's daughter, Margaret Elizabeth. After his career at Burnley ended in April 1921, Bert signed for Wigan Borough, scoring thirteen goals in twenty-five appearances. The Freemans later moved to Birmingham and Bert continued playing football at Kettering Town and later at Kidderminster Harriers. In 1924 he set up a cutlery business in Birmingham and was later employed as a lift operator. He died on 11 August 1955 at his home in Birmingham at the age of sixty-nine.

Decima Betty Boyle

Tommy and Annie's only child, Decima Betty Boyle, died on Saturday 25 March 1922 of pneumonia at the age of only seven months. Her funeral took place four days later at Burnley Cemetery. Decima Betty Boyle is buried in grave number A8252 next to where Annie's parents, William and Hannah, and four of the Varley children, Frederick, Florence, Willie and Mary, are all buried.

Annie Elizabeth Boyle (née Varley)

According to several sources, Tommy and Annie parted their ways at some point between moving to Blackpool in the first half of 1923 and Tommy's return from Berlin in June 1925. I believe this event was later rather than earlier from conversations with family members. I contacted the HMCS, the Principal Registry of the Family division, based in Holborn in London to check two things: firstly, whether Tommy had left a will, to see whether Annie could be traced; and if the couple had divorced, to see whether Annie had ever remarried. Both replies drew a blank. There was no record of a last will of testament for Tommy or of a divorce taking place over a ten-year period between, 1925–35.

Tracing Annie proved most difficult and resulted in a number of false searches for Annie Boyles and Annie Varleys of similar ages over a range of possible dates of death that appeared in Leicester, Islington and Keighley. But after several false leads I came across a death entry for an Annie Elizabeth Boyle who died in Cardiff in 1971. I sent for a copy of the death certificate and it confirmed that it was the correct Annie, as it states that Annie was the widow of Thomas William Boyle, professional footballer. Annie died on 5 August 1971 at Quarry Hill House, a nursing home in St. Mellons, Cardiff. She was eighty years old. Annie had kept her married name and had never remarried.

My task was almost over. Knowing the year Annie died, I contacted Burnley Cemetery to see whether she had possibly been brought back to Burnley to be closer to the Varley family home and to be with Decima. Burnley Cemetery staff said she wasn't buried with them, so I contacted Cardiff Bereavement Services. They confirmed that Annie was buried in an unpurchased grave in Cathay's Cemetery, on Fairoak Road in Cardiff. Annie's funeral took place on 9 August 1971 at eleven-twenty a.m. It is not known who was present at the funeral. Cathay's Cemetery is the oldest in Cardiff and Annie is buried in grave twenty-seven in section EL.

The End.

Appendix

Bibliography

Ali, Jonathan, (2007) <u>Our Boys: The Great War in a Lancashire Village</u>, Landy Publishing, Blackpool

Aspin, Chris (1988) <u>Surprising Lancashire</u>, Helmshore Local History Society, ISBN 0 906881 056

Atherton, Martin, Russell, David and Turner Graham (2000) <u>Deaf United: A History of Football in the British Deaf Community</u>, Douglas Mclean Publications, Gloucester.

Atterbury, Paul and Cooper, Suzanne (2001) <u>Victorians At Home and Abroad</u>, V and A Publications, London

Barham, Peter (2004) <u>Forgotten Lunatics of The Great War</u>, Yale University Press, London

Beckett, Ian F W and Corvi, Steven J. (1988) <u>Haig's Generals</u>, Pen and Sword Books, Barnsley

Beck Peter J. (1999) <u>Scoring for Britain: International Football and International Politics 1900-39</u>, Frank Cass Publications, London

Beckford, Harry (1985) <u>Ottoline: The First Football Hooligan?</u>, Retrospect Vol 5 1985 the Journal of the Burnley Historical Society, Burnley Central Library.

Bennett, W. (1951) <u>The History of Burnley From 1850: Volume Four</u>, Lancashire County Council, Printed by Turner and Earnshaw

Benson, John (1989) <u>The Working Class in Britain</u>, Longman, London

Bevan, Ian, Hibberd Stuart and Gilbert Michael (1999) <u>To The Palace for the Cup – an Affectionate History Of Football At the Crystal Palace</u>, Replay Publishing, Beckenham, Kent

Blank, Stuart C. (2007) <u>Researching British Military History on the Internet</u>, Alwyn Enterprises, Paignton, Devon.

Bloom, Philip, (2009) <u>The Vertigo Years: Change and Culture in the West 1900-14</u>, Phoenix Press, London

Bolton, Ken and Frost, Roger, (2002) Burnley – A Photographic History of Your Town, Black Horse Books, Salisbury

Bourke, Joanna (1994) Working Class Cultures in Britain 1890-1960, Gender, Class and Ethnicity, Routledge, London

Brittain, Vera, (1978) Testament Of Youth, Virago Press, London

Brown, Tony (1999) The Football League Match by Match - 1920-21, published by the author 1999, 4 Adrian Close, Nottingham

Budd, Graham, (2000) Soccer Memorabilia: A Collectors Guide, Philip Wilson Publishers, London

Burnley Express (1919) Greater Burnley and the Great War – Roll of Honour 1914-19 published by the Burnley Express and lists the names of those who died from the greater Burnley area, their rank, home address and when they died. Burnley Reference Library Ref G192.

Buschmann, Jurgen, Lennartz, Karl and Steinkemper Hans (2003) Sepp Herberger and Otto Nerz: Die Chefdenker und ihre Theorien, (The Chief Thinkers and their theories) Agon Sportverlag, Frankfurt ISBN 3-89784-195-9

Butler, Byron (1998) The Official History of the FA Cup (updated ed.) Headline Publishing

Cecil, Robert, (1969) Life in Edwardian England, BT Batsford Publishers, London

Chapples, Leslie (1992) My Burnley Memories, published by the Burnley and District Historical Society, edited by Margaret Jones and Roger Frost, Burnley Library.

Chapples, Leslie (1986) The Taverns in the Town: A Walk Around the Pubs of Burnley of the 1920-30s, published by the Burnley and District Historical Society, Hudson History, Settle.

Chapples, Leslie and Steven (2009) Life in and Around The Weavers Triangle 2nd ed. Green Arrow Publishing, Stacksteads

Chapman, Paul (2001) Cameos of the Western Front: In the Shadow of Hell – Ypres Sector 1914-1918, Pen and Sword Books, Barnsley

Child, Stephen Martin, (2006) From Saint Peter's To Saint Marks: A History of the Anglican Churches in Burnley, published by the Burnley and District Historical Society.

Clarke, Dale (2004) <u>British Artillery 1914-19 Field Army Artillery</u>, New Vanguard (94), Osprey Publishing

Clarke, Dale (2005) <u>British Artillery 1914-19 Heavy Artillery</u>, New Vanguard (105), Osprey Publishing

Clay, Catrine (2006) <u>King, Kaiser, Tsar: Three Royal Cousins who led the World To War</u>, John Murray, London

Cooksey, John, (1986) <u>The Barnsley Pals: The 13th and 14th Battalions York and Lancaster Regiment, Wharncliffe Woodmore for The Barnsley Chronicle, Barnsley, South Yorkshire</u>

Downham, John (2000) <u>The East Lancashire Regiment 1855-1958,</u> compiled by J. Downham on behalf of the Queens Lancashire Regiment, Tempus Publishing

Dennis, Brian, Daykin, John and Hyde Derek (n.d.) <u>Barnsley Football Club: The Official History 1887-1998,</u> Yore Publications ISBN 1-874427-879

Doyle, Peter (2008) <u>Tommy's War: British Military memorabilia 1914-1918</u>, The Crow wood Press, Wiltshire

Diggle, G.E. (1975) <u>Blighty: A Portrait of Civilian life in Britain During the First World War</u>, Melksham

Dyer, Geoff (1994) <u>The Missing of The Somme,</u> Orion Books, London

Elliot, Brian (2001) <u>Pits and Pitmen of Barnsley</u>, Wharncliffe Books, Barnsley

Elliot, Brian (2009) <u>Yorkshire Miners</u>, The History Press, Stroud, Gloucestershire

Faithfull, Pamela (2002) <u>Basic Facts about Lunatics in England and Wales for Family Historians</u>, Federation of Family History Societies, Bury, UK

Faulkes, Sebastian, (1993) <u>Birdsong</u>, Vintage Books, London

Firth, Grenville (1980) <u>The Reds: A Pictorial History of Barnsley FC</u>, ISBN 0 7158 07552 E P publishing

Firth, Grenville (2009) <u>Barnsley Football Clubs Greatest Games 1890-2008,</u> Wharncliffe Books, Barnsley.

Firth, Grenville, (1978) <u>Oakwell – The Official History of Barnsley Football Club</u>, Valley Printers, Sheffield

Fishwick, N, (1989) <u>English Football and Society 1910-1950,</u> Manchester University Press, Manchester

Floyd, Thomas, (2007) <u>From Messines to Third Ypres: A Personal Account By A 2/5th Lancashire Fusilier</u>, Leanor Press.

Fort, Keith (1988) <u>Burnley Since 1900</u>, Archive Publications in association with the Lancashire Evening Telegraph

Fox, Norman (2003) <u>Prophet or Traitor: The Jimmy Hogan Story</u>, The Parr's Wood Press, Manchester.

Gartside, Patricia, L. and Jackson, Bruce (2002) <u>Model Guide to Lancashire Mental Hospital Records,</u> pub by the University of Salford and Lancashire County Council.

Gaythorne-Hardy, Robert (1963) <u>Ottoline: The Early Memoirs of Lady Ottoline Morrell</u>, Faber and Faber, London

Hall, Brian (1977) <u>Burnley – A Short History</u>, published by the Burnley and District Historical Society

Hannavy, John, (2009) <u>The Victorians and Edwardians at Play</u>, Shire, Library Books

Harding, John (2009) <u>Behind the Glory: 100 Years of the PFA</u>, Breedon Books, Derby

Harris, Clive and Whippy, Julian, (n.d.) <u>The Greater Game: Sporting Icons who fell in the Great War,</u> Pen and Sword books

Haworth, Don, (1986) <u>Figures in a Bygone Landscape: A Lancashire Childhood</u>, Methuen, London

Higgs, Michelle (2009) <u>Life in the Victorian Hospital</u>, The History Press, Gloucester

Holland, Peter (2008) <u>Swifter than the Arrow - Wilf Bartrop, Football and War</u>, Matador

Holmes, Richard, (2004) <u>Tommy: The British Soldier on The Western Front 1914-18,</u> Harper Perennial, London

Holmes, Richard, (1999) <u>The Western Front</u>, BBC Worldwide, London

Honigstein, Raphael, (2009) <u>Englischer Fussball: A German's View of Our Beautiful Game</u>, Yellow Jersey Press, London

Hopkin, Roger (2009) <u>Hopkin's History of the Football League Volume 1, 1888-1946,</u> Desert Island Books

Horsfall, Jack (1986) <u>The Long March: The Story Of The Devils Own B/210 Burnley Battery, Royal Field Artillery 1914-19</u>, published by Lancashire Library

Howse, Geoffrey, (2002) <u>Around Hoyland – People and Places,</u> Sutton Publishing, Gloucester

Hudson, John (2008) <u>Victorian and Edwardian Lancashire,</u> Amberley Publishing, Glos.

Humphries, Stephen (1981) <u>Hooligans or Rebels: An Oral History of Working Class Childhood and Youth 1889-1939,</u> Blackwell, Oxford

Hutchinson, John, (1982) <u>The Football Industry: The Early Years of the Professional Game,</u> Richard Drew Publishing.

Hynes, Samuel (1998) <u>A Soldiers Tale,</u> Penguin Books, London

Inglis, Simon (1987) <u>The Football Grounds of Great Britain,</u> Willow books, Collins, London

Inglis, Simon (1988) <u>League Football and The Men Who Made It,</u> Willow Books, Collins, London

Jones, Melvyn (n.d) <u>Elsecar 1901: Old Ordnance Survey Maps,</u> The Godfrey Edition, Alan Godfrey Maps, Consett.

Kelly, Stephen E (1988) <u>Back Page Football,</u> Macdonald and Co., Queen Anne Press, London

Kelly, Stephen (1998) <u>Illustrated History of Liverpool FC 1892-1998,</u> Hamlyn Press

Kingsford, Peter (1990) <u>The Hunger Marchers in Britain 1920-40,</u> Longman, London

Kreiger, Eric, (1983) <u>Good Old Soccer: The Golden Age of Football Picture Postcards,</u> Longman, London

Laffin, John, (1988) <u>British Butchers and Bunglers of World War One,</u> Alan Sutton Publishing, Gloucester

Lamont, D. C. (1931 and 1932) <u>County Borough of Burnley - Annual Reports of the Heads of Department: Report on the Public Health and Sanitary Administrations.</u> – Copy available in Burnley Central Library

Lanfanchi, Pierre, Eisenberg Christiane, Mason, Tony and Wahl, Alfred (2004) <u>100 years of Football: The FIFA Centennial Book,</u> Weidenfeld and Nicholson, London

Lee, Christopher (1999) <u>This Sceptred Isle – Twentieth Century,</u> BBC Books, London

Lee, Edward and Phil Whalley (2002) <u>The Pride and the Glory – Official 120- Year History of Burnley Football Club,</u>

Lee, Edward and Simpson, Ray (1991) Burnley – A Complete Record 1882 – 1991, Breedon Books Publishing Company, Derby

Lloyd, Guy and Holt, Nick, (2005) FA Cup: The Complete Story, Aurum Press

Lord, Bob (1963) My Fight For Football, Stanley Paul Ltd., London

Lowe, John (1985) Burnley, published by Philimore Press, Chichester

Lupson, Peter (2006) Thank God For Football, Azure Books, London

Macdonald, Lyn (1988) 1914-1918 Voices and Images of the Great War, Penguin, London

Macdonald, Lyn (1980) The Roses of No Man's Land, Penguin Books, London

Macdonald, Lyn (1978) They Called It Passchendale, Macmillan, London

Makepeace, Chris, (2007) A Century of Burnley: Events, People and Places Over the 20th Century, Sutton Publishing

Marshall, S.L.A. (2001) World War 1 Mariner Books

Mason, Tony, (1980) Association Football and English Society 1863-1915, Harvester Press

May, Trevor (2006) The Victorian Schoolroom, Shire Publications Ltd, Bucks.

May, Trevor (1987) An Economic and Social History of Britain 1760-1970, Longman, London

Metcalf, Mark and Wood David, (2010) Lifting The Cup: The Story of Battling Barnsley, Wharncliffe Books, Barnsley

Midwinter, Eric (2007) Parish to Planet: How Football Came to Rule The World, Know the Score Books, Warwickshire

Myers, Simon, (2008) Football, The Early Years, Fine Print Books, Stockport

Myerson, George, (n.d.) Fighting for Football: From Woolwich Arsenal to the Western Front, The story of Football's first rebel – Tim Coleman

Nadin, Jack (2007) Images of England: Burnley Inns and Taverns, Tempus Publishing, Gloucester

Nadin, Jack, (2002) Burnley's Industrial Heritage – The Cotton Mills,

Orwell, George (1937) The Road To Wigan Pier, Penguin Books, London

Passingham, Ian (1998) <u>Pillars of Fire: The Battle of Messines Ridge</u>, June 1917, Sutton Publishing, Stroud, Gloucester

Potts, Maggie and Fido, Rebecca (1991) <u>A Fit Person to be Removed: Personal Accounts of Life in a Mental Deficiency Institution</u>, Northcote House Publishers, Plymouth

Rauaud, Jean and Ralph Mannheim (1992) <u>Fields of Glory</u>, Arcade Publishing, London

Rawson, Andrew (2006) <u>British Army Handbook 1914 – 1918</u>, Sutton Publishing, Gloucester

Richard, Marianne (2000) <u>A Straightforward Guide to Understanding Mental Illness</u>, Straightforward Books, London

Riddoch, Andrew and Kemp John (2008) <u>When the Whistle Blows: The Story of The Footballers' Battalion in the Great War</u>, Haynes Publishing

Riophe, Katie, (2007) <u>Uncommon Arrangements: Seven Portraits of Married Life in London Literary circles 1910-39</u>, Chapter 6 - P179-213, Virago Press, London

Rippon, Anton (2005) <u>Gasmasks for Goalposts: Football in Britain During the Second World War</u>, Sutton Publishing, Stroud, Gloucester.

Rutherford, Sarah, (2008) <u>The Victorian Asylum</u>, Shire Library Publishers.

Sacks, Janet (2010) <u>Victorian Childhood</u>, Shire Library Publishers

Sanders, Richard (2009) <u>Beastly Fury: The Strange Birth of British Football</u>, Bantam Press, London

Seddon, Peter (2010) <u>Destroying Angel – Steve Bloomer, England's first football hero 2nd ed. Breedon Books, Derby.</u>

Seymour, Miranda (1998) 2nd Ed. <u>Ottoline Morrell: Life on a Grand Scale,</u> Sceptre

Simpson, Ray, (1999<u>) Images of Sport – Burnley Football Club 1882 – 1968</u>

Simpson, Ray, (2007) <u>The Claret Chronicles: the Definitive History of Burnley Football Club 1882-2007</u>, published by Burnley Football Club

Simpson, Ron, (1977) <u>World War One Poetry</u>, Letts Educational, London

Small, Gordon (2007) <u>The Lancashire Cup – A Complete Record,</u> Soccerdata Ltd.

Stuttard, J. (1984) <u>History of St. James' Lane Head Church of England Primary School Burnley 150th</u> Anniversary Edition, <u>Published by Burnley Library</u>

Taylor, David JA and Briggs, Elizabeth M (2001) <u>The Diaries of Sam: A Young Man in Late Victorian Burnley,</u> Published by Hudson History, Proctor House, Settle ISBN 1 903783054

Taylor, Matthew (2008) <u>The Association Game: A History of British Football</u>, Pearson Longman, London

Tibballs, Geoff, (2008<u>) Footballs Greatest Characters: Amazing Stories of Hard Men, Hell Raisers and Crowd Pleasers</u>, JR Books, London

Tomlinson, Alan and Christopher Young, (2006) <u>German Football: History, Culture, Society,</u> Routledge, London

Tonks, David (2003) <u>My Ancestor was a Coalminer</u>, Society of Genealogists, London

Tootle, Harry (1998) <u>The Moorfield Pit Disaster</u>, Landy Publishing, Blackpool

Turner, William(2000) <u>The Accrington Pals</u>, Lancashire County Books, Preston

Whelan, Peter (1982) <u>The Accrington Pals</u>, Methuen Drama Modern Classics, London

Wiseman, David (1974) <u>Up the Clarets</u> (Robert Hale Press)

Wiseman, David (2006) <u>A Case of Vintage Claret</u>, Hudson and Pearson Ltd., Burnley

Wiseman, David, (1975) <u>Vintage Claret – A Pictorial History of Burnley Football club</u>, Hendon Publishing Co. Ltd., Nelson

Wood, Gloria and Thompson, Paul (1993) <u>The Nineties: Personal Recollections of the 20th Century, BBC Books, London</u>

Newspapers

Barnsley Chronicle 1900 – 1940 on microfilm available in Barnsley Library, Shambles Street, Barnsley S70 2JF. 1900-1905 also available at the British Library, Colindale.

British Newspapers 1600-1900 – Gale, online under Library license

Burnley Express and Advertiser – from 1906 to 1924 archived on microfilm and can be accessed at Reference Section, Burnley Library, Grimshaw Street, Burnley BB11 2BD

Burnley News 1900 to 1933 (microfilm set located in Burnley reference library)

The Times Archive (Online)

The Daily Mirror (Online)

The 19th Century Newspaper Collection 1850-1900 (Online)

The Guardian and Observer Online (formerly the Manchester Guardian)

The Athletics News available at Manchester City Library, St. Peters Square and at the British Library at Colindale, North London

The Wrexham Advertiser 1923 – 24 hard copies accessed at Colindale, North London./

The Southport Advertiser - archive material from Formby Public Library

German Newspapers - Berliner Morgenpost, Berliner Tageblatt, Der Tag, Der Welt Spiegel (Available on microfilm at the British Library, Colindale)

Der Kicker, German Football magazine (online)

Sports Journals

Programme Monthly http://www.pmfc.co.uk/

Soccer History http://www.soccer-history.co.uk/about-soccer-history.asp

Sport In History http://www.sporthistinfo.co.uk

When Saturday Comes http://www.wsc.co.uk/

Visual resources covering Burnley Football Club

British Pathe www.britishpathe.com

Have an excellent clip of the 1914 Cup final squad relaxing in 'mufti.' Also a clip of 1926 showing the team training at Turf Moor with excellent views of the ground. Also a clip of Tottenham v Burnley from WHL which looks like Dawson in goal, circa 1921.

They have a clip of the annual bowls tournament at the Talbot Hotel, Blackpool showing the huge crowds drawn http://www.britishpathe.com/record.php?id=19620

Several old clips of Burnley are available from the **British Film Institute.** http://www.bfi.org.uk/nationalarchive/

The North-West Film Archive have a number of clips about Burnley from the 1920s onwards. The archive is based at Chorlton Street, Manchester and has viewing facilities for members of the public. (Bookable in advance) contact Manchester Metropolitan University for details. http://www.nwfa.mmu.ac.uk/

See also **Movietone News** www.movietone.com

ITN Source also has footage of Burnley at www.itnsource.com

Micron Video (2001) – "Rhapsody in Claret and Blue: The Official History of Burnley Football Club" features the birth of Burnley FC along with footage of the 1914 Cup Final and the 1921 League Championship.

Thomas William Boyle: Honours

Junior Football – Double Honours
1904-05 at Hoyland Star. Won the Barnsley Junior Division 1 Championship. Also the Barnsley Junior Cup, defeating Higham 2-1 in the final played at Dillington Park.

Semi-professional football
1905-06 at Elsecar Athletic. Won the Barnsley Minor Cup, defeating Rockingham Colliery in the final 2 – 0 played at Hoyland Town's ground.

Barnsley FC Appearances

First professional match, Barnsley Reserves vs Lincoln City Reserves, at Oakwell, 6th October 1906
First full League appearance, vs Chelsea at Stamford Bridge, 24th November 1906
Final appearance, vs Hull City at Oakwell, 23 September 1911

Barnsley statistics
League - 156, FA Cup - 18, Total played: = 174.
Goals, League - 17, FA Cup - 2,

Burnley FC Appearances

First League appearance, vs Barnsley at Oakwell, September 30th 1911
Last League appearance, vs Arsenal at Turf Moor, February 20th 1922
Last Reserve appearance, vs Manchester United Reserves at Trafford Park, April 3rd 1923
Last 'A' Team appearance, vs Barnoldswick Town at Lowerhouse, 14 April 1923

Burnley statistics
League - 211, FA Cup - 28, Lancashire Cup - 9, East Lancashire Cup - 6, Wartime matches - 70, other matches, tours, charity games, friendlies - 6. Total played = 330
Goals,
League -36, FA Cup - 8, Lancashire Cup - 2, East Lancashire Charity Cup - 1,
Wartime League - 12.

Wrexham FC Appearances

First League appearance vs Ashington at the Racecourse Ground, 25th August 1923
Last League appearance vs Wigan Borough at the Racecourse Ground, 19th September 1923

Wrexham statistics
League - 7, FA Cup - 0, other matches (Pre-season) - 2. Total played = 9 Goals, = 0

Germany
Youth Team Trainer/Coach for Tennis Borrussia Berlin September 1924 - June 1925

FA Cup achievements
1907 FA Cup quarter finalist with Barnsley FC
1910 FA Cup finalist with Barnsley FC, the final held at the Crystal Palace
1913 FA Cup semi-finalist with Burnley FC
1914 FA Cup winner with Burnley FC, the final held at the Crystal Palace

FA Charity Shield
1921 Burnley lost 2-0 to Spurs. The match held at White Hart Lane.

League Honours
1912-13 Second Division Runner up with Burnley FC
1919-20 First Division Runner up with Burnley FC
1920-21 First Division Championship winner with Burnley FC

England
One Full International Cap vs Ireland held at Windsor Park Belfast in the British Home Championships February 15th 1913, England Losing 2-1.

Football League and other Representative Matches

English League v Scottish League February 17th 1912
North v England, January 20th 1913 held at Hyde Road Manchester
Inter-League, Football League v Scottish League March 1st 1913
English League v Scottish League 1913
England v The North, at Roker Park, Sunderland, January 21st 1914
English League v Scottish League, Burnley March 21st 1914
English Military International v Scottish Military March 13th 1916
Scottish League v English League 9th April 1919 held at Ibrox Stadium

European Tours
European tour with Barnsley Summer 1910
European tour with Burnley Summer 1914

European Competitions
The Dubonnet Cup Final 1910 (Played in Paris)
Barnsley v Swindon (1-2)

The Budapest Cup 1914 (Played in Hungary)
Burnley v Celtic (1-1)

Comparing the performances of Burnley's two League Championship winning sides

1920-21

Burnley won the 1920-21 League Championship three games before the end of the season after losing their first three games.

Burnley's 30 game unbeaten run in a 42 match season set the standard for others to meet for years to come. The record was passed 83 years later by Arsene Wenger's Arsenal in a team which included; Bergkamp, Henry and Vieira and who remained undefeated for all 38 games of the 2003-4 Premiership season. Like Arsenal, a big factor in Burnley's success was that the side remained unchanged for many of the games through lack of injuries and only 23 players were used throughout the whole season. Burnley topped the table from November 1920 and stayed there until they were crowned Champions in May 1921.

Statistics: Played 42, Won 23, Drawn 13 and Lost six.
Unbeaten in thirty League matches
Goals scored = 79, Goals Against = 36.
Goal difference + 43, goal average = 2.19.

1959-60

Burnley won the 1959-60 League Championship on the final game of the season against Manchester City at Maine Road, taking the title by a single point. It was the first time Burnley had hit top spot all season.

Statistics: Played 42, Won 24, Drawn seven and Lost eleven.
Goals Scored = 85, Goals Against = 61.
Goal difference + 24, goal average = 1.39.

Lightning Source UK Ltd.
Milton Keynes UK
UKOW051502111111

181890UK00001B/136/P